Thomas M. Coffey was born and brought up in the United States and served as a pilot in the Pacific during World War II. After his discharge he spent two years at National University in Dublin, studying Irish literature and drama, and on his return home he worked as a reporter, feature writer, and movie and drama critic as well as writing and producing for television. He went to Ireland in 1966 to research *Agony at Easter*. In the following years he went to Japan to research his second book, about Japan's experiences in World War II, and he is currently at work on a third book.

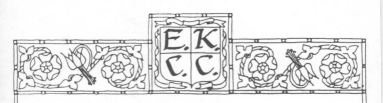

Thomas M. Coffey

AGONY AT EASTER

The 1916 Irish Uprising

PENGUIN BOOKS

Penguin Books Ltd, Harmondsworth, Middlesex, England
Penguin Books Inc., 7110 Ambassador Road, Baltimore, Maryland 21207, U.S.A.
Penguin Books Australia Ltd, Ringwood, Victoria Australia

—

First published in the U.S.A. by The Macmillan Company 1969
Published in Great Britain by George G. Harrap & Co., Ltd 1970
Published in Pelican Books 1971

—

Copyright © Thomas M. Coffey, 1969

—

Printed in the United States of America by
Kingsport Press Inc., Kingsport, Tennessee
Set in Monotype Janson

Contents

Sources
and Acknowledgments

Agony at Easter tells the story of the 1916 Irish rebellion (which launched the world's first successful revolution in the twentieth century) with rigid, hour-by-hour adherence to the facts. Presented from a viewpoint in and around Dublin's General Post Office, the center of battle, the book is a story rather than a historical document. But it is a story without fiction. Substantiation is available for every incident and every exchange of dialogue. The events and conversations are related exactly the way careful research indicates they happened. The precise wording of quotations has been used wherever it could be established, and even when the precise words were unascertainable, the sense and tone of each conversation was preserved.

Thanks to several memoirs only recently made available, *Agony at Easter* is based on a greater fund of information than previous works about the rebellion. The important sources for the factual material in the book follow:

The eyewitness accounts, personal recollections, or thoughtful observations of the following people:

Ernest Blyth; Maurice Brennan; Seamus Brennan; Ignatius Callender (*Dublin Brigade Review*, 1939); Mrs. Tom Clarke; J. H. Cox (*Irish Independent*, April 30–May 7, 1916); Joseph Cripps; Louise Gavan Duffy (in an article by Sheila Walsh, *Irish Press*, March 23, 1966); Brian Farrell; Desmond Fitzgerald; Senator Garret Fitzgerald; Sean Fitzgibbon (*Irish Times*, April 18–23, 1949); Harry Fitzsimmons; Douglas Gageby; Sean Gallogly; Julia Grenan (*Catholic Bulletin*,

June 1917); John Higgins (*Gaelic American*, July 29, 1926); Bulmer Hobson; Richard Humphreys (*Irish Press*, April 29, 1966); M. J. Lennon (*Banba*, May 1922); Sean MacEntee; Father Francis X. Martin; Professor Roger McHugh; Lil McKane; Liam McNeive; Brigid Kelly Molloy; Paddy Murphy; Ernest Nunan; John O'Connor; Sean T. O'Kelly (*Irish Press*, beginning July 3, 1961); John O'Leary; Aodhgan O'Rahilly; Desmond O'Reilly; Charles Saurin (*An t-Oglac*, March 13, 1926); M. J. Staines and M. W. O'Reilly (*An t-Oglac*, January 23, 1926); Charles Steinmayer (*An t-Oglac*, February 27, 1926); Michael Smith; Cormac Turner; W. J. Brennan Whitmore (*An t-Oglac*, January 16, 30; February 6, 1926).

BOOKS:

Bourke, Marcus, *The O'Rahilly*, Dublin, 1967.

Caulfield, Max, *The Easter Rebellion*, New York, 1963.

Chart, D. A., *Dublin* (Medieval Town Series), London, 1907.

Clarke, Tom, *Glimpses of an Irish Felon's Prison Life*, Introduction by P. S. O'Hegarty, Dublin, 1922.

Colum, Padraic, Maurice Joy, Seamus O'Brien, *et al.*, *The Irish Rebellion of 1916 and Its Martyrs*, New York, 1916.

Connolly, James, *Labour and Easter Week 1916*, Dublin, 1949.

———, *Labour in Irish History*, Dublin, 1956.

———, *Socialism and Nationalism*, Dublin, 1948.

Devoy, John, *Recollections of an Irish Rebel*, New York, 1929.

Figgis, Darrell, *Recollections of the Irish War*, London, 1927.

Fox, R. M., *Green Banners*.

———, *The History of the Irish Citizen Army*, Dublin, 1943.

Heuston, John M., O.P., *Headquarters Battalion*, Dublin, 1966.

Hobson, Bulmer, *Short History of the Irish Volunteers*, Dublin, 1918.

Holt, Edgar, *Protest in Arms*, London, 1960.

Howard, L. G. Redmond, *Six Days of the Irish Republic*, London, 1916.

Irish Times Sinn Fein Rebellion Handbook, Dublin, 1917.

Le Roux, L. N., *Life of Pearse*, Dublin, 1932.

———, *Tom Clarke and the Irish Freedom Movement*, Dublin, 1936.

Lynch, D., and F. O'Donoghue, *The IRB and the 1916 Insurrection*, Cork, 1957.

MacEntee, Sean, *Episode at Easter*, Dublin, 1966.

———, and Seamus Ryan, *Easter Fires*, Dublin, 1935.

McArdle, Dorothy, *The Irish Republic*, Dublin, 1937.

McCay, Hedley, *Padraic Pearse*, Cork, 1966.

McHugh, Roger, *Dublin, 1916*, New York, 1966.

McKenna, Stephen (pseud. Martin Daly), *Journals and Letters*, London, 1936.

———, *Memories of the Dead*, Dublin, 1916.

Memoirs of Desmond Fitzgerald (unpublished manuscript; through

the courtesy of Desmond Fitzgerald, Jr.).
Milroy, Sean, *Memories of Mountjoy*, Dublin, 1917.
O'Brien, Nora Connolly, *Portrait of a Rebel Father*, Dublin, 1936.
O'Broin, Leon, *Dublin Castle and the 1916 Rising*, Dublin, 1966.
O'Casey, Sean, *Drums Under the Windows*, New York, 1947.
————, *The Plough and the Stars*, London, 1926.
————, *Story of the Irish Citizen Army*, Dublin, 1919.
O'Connor, Frank, *The Big Fellow*, Springfield, Illinois, 1966.
O'Hegarty, P. S., *The Victory of Sinn Fein*, Dublin, 1924.
Pearse, M. B., *Home Life of Padraic Pearse*, Dublin, 1934.
Pearse, Padraic, *Plays, Stories and Poems*, Dublin, 1966.
————, *Political Writings and Speeches*, Dublin, 1966.
Phillips, W. A., *The Revolution in Ireland*, London, 1926.
Ryan, Desmond, *James Connolly*, London, 1924.
————, *The 1916 Poets*, Dublin, 1963.
————, *The Rising*, Dublin, 1949.
————, *The Story of a Success*, Dublin, 1917.
Sellwood, A. V., *The Red-Gold Flame*, London, 1966.
Shannon, Martin, *Sixteen Roads to Golgatha*, Dublin, 1966.
Stephens, James, *The Insurrection in Dublin*, New York, 1916.
The 1916 Song Book, Dublin, 1966.
Wells, W. B., and N. Marlowe, *History of the Irish Rebellion of 1916*,
    Dublin, 1916.

PUBLICATIONS:

Catholic Bulletin, July 1916.
"A Record of the Irish Rebellion," *Irish Life*, 1916.
Freeman's Journal, April 24, 1916.
Irish Independent, April 26–29, May 1–4, 1916.
Irish Independent, April 11, 1966.
RTV Guide, Dublin, April 8, 1966.
Irish Times, April 7, 1966.
Martin, F. X., O.S.A., *Eoin MacNeill on the 1916 Rising*, Irish His-
    torical Studies, Dublin, 1961.
————, *The Irish Volunteers, 1913–15*, Dublin, 1963.
————, *Leaders and Men of the Easter Rising*, Ithaca, N.Y., 1967.

Also helpful as sources of information:

Dublin Weather Bureau
Irish Department of Defense
Irish Department of Public Works
National Library of Ireland
National Museum of Ireland
Library, National University
British Museum, London
Telefis Eireann (the Irish Television Network)

AGONY
AT EASTER

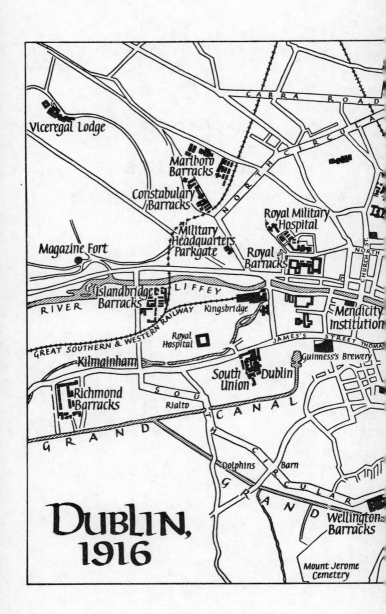

Viceregal Lodge

Marlboro Barracks

Constabulary Barracks

Magazine Fort

Military Headquarters Parkgate

CABRA ROAD

NORTH CIRCULAR

Royal Military Hospital

Royal Barracks

NORTH CHURCH ST.

Islandbridge Barracks

RIVER LIFFEY

Kingsbridge

GREAT SOUTHERN & WESTERN RAILWAY

Royal Hospital

JAMES'S STREET THOMAS

Mendicity Institution

Kilmainham

SOUTH

South Dublin Union

Guinness's Brewery

Richmond Barracks

Rialto

CANAL

GRAND

Dolphins Barn

GRAND CIRCULAR

Wellington Barracks

Mount Jerome Cemetery

DUBLIN, 1916

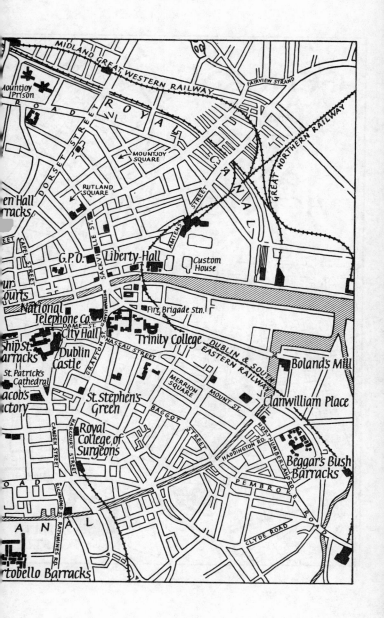

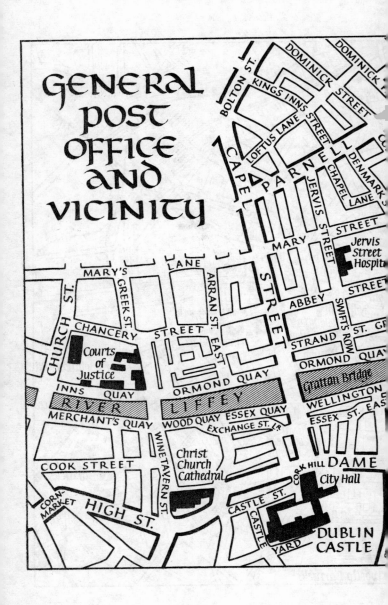

GENERAL
POST
OFFICE
AND
VICINITY

DOMINICK ST.
DOMINICK STREET
DOMINICK
BOLTON ST.
KINGS INNS STREET
LOFTUS LANE
CAPEL
PARNELL
DENMARK
CHAPEL LANE
JERVIS STREET
STREET
Jervis Street Hospital
MARY
STREET
ABBEY
SWIFT'S ROW
STREET
ST. GR
STRAND
ORMOND QUAY
MARY'S
LANE
GREEK ST.
ARRAN ST. EAST
STREET
CHURCH ST.
CHANCERY
STREET
Courts of Justice
Grattan Bridge
INNS QUAY
ORMOND QUAY
WELLINGTON
RIVER
LIFFEY
MERCHANT'S QUAY
WOOD QUAY ESSEX QUAY
EXCHANGE ST. Lr.
ESSEX ST. EAS
COOK STREET
WINETAVERN ST.
Christ Church Cathedral
CORK HILL
DAME
City Hall
CORN-MARKET
HIGH ST.
CASTLE ST.
CASTLE
CASTLE YARD
DUBLIN CASTLE

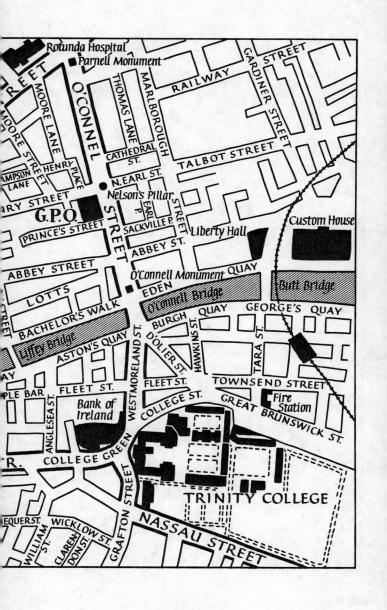

I. *Monday, April 24*

WARM sunshine was not the only unusual element in the air of Dublin, Ireland, on Easter Monday, 1916. After a fairly normal spring fortnight during which it had rained thirteen of fourteen days, this day had come up brilliant with only a few white puffs of cloud crossing the sky and the temperature what a Dubliner might call "close"—in the sixties. But a Dubliner as sensitive to his city's pulse as to its weather could feel something even stranger in the air as noon approached. A brooding curiosity hung over the holiday crowds on O'Connell Street (then Sackville Street) in the center of the city, due perhaps to all the rumors of revolution that had circulated for the past week. The possibility of a rebellion had abated now, thanks to a published statement by the man most likely to lead it, Professor Eoin Mac-Neill, president of the Irish Volunteers, the country's largest armed nationalist organization. Yet a Dubliner could still be aroused by the chance of an uprising, not because he favored it, but mostly because the thought of excitement stirred him pleasantly after the prospect of excitement had passed. It is normal enough for an Irishman, accustomed to more talk than action, to wish something dangerous would have happened, once he suspects it won't happen.

Dublin was not a city where things often happened. Its charm lay in the unique wit of its people, the casual way of life it offered, the beauty of its seaside setting astride the River Liffey, the stateliness of its public buildings and Georgian houses, and the spaciousness of its general plan. O'Connell Street, the main north-south thoroughfare, was 150 feet wide, thanks to the foresight of the city's Wide Streets Commission in the 1790s, and O'Connell Bridge, which approached it from the south, had the distinction of being wider from railing to railing than from riverbank to riverbank. Some wag had said of it that it was the only bridge in the world even wider than it was wide.

At the lower end of O'Connell Street, looking down upon the bridge, was a forty-foot monument to Daniel O'Connell, a statesman whom the Irish called "The Liberator" because he had led the ultimately successful struggle for Catholic emancipation in the early nineteenth century. At the upper end of the half-mile-long street stood a slightly less imposing monument to Charles Stewart Parnell, another statesman, who, in the latter part of the nineteenth century, was close to winning home rule for Ireland when he fell victim to a scandal for which some Irishmen haven't yet forgiven him. He was exposed in a divorce action as the lover of a married woman, Mrs. Kitty O'Shea. About halfway between these two monuments, and dominating both of them from a height of 120 feet, was Nelson's Pillar, a fluted Doric column on which stood a statue to England's great naval hero Viscount Horatio Nelson.

Between Henry and Prince's Streets, on the west side of O'Connell Street, was Dublin's General Post Office, a deceptively large, rectangular, three-story structure of classical design surrounded so closely by other buildings that it was difficult to appreciate either its magnitude or its beauty. Built in 1815, it had just been completely refurbished in recognition of its century of use. Its front portico, which covered the O'Connell Street sidewalk, was supported by eight Ionic columns, and on top of it stood statues of three figures—Hibernia, Mercury and Fidelity—

whose presence together was one of Dublin's minor mysteries.

Though there were still a few large private homes on Upper O'Connell Street, the two-block section from the General Post Office south to O'Connell Bridge was now entirely commercial, housing some of the city's finest shops and hotels. If there was such a thing as a center of Dublin, it was here. Upriver from the bridge, west along the quays, were the Four Courts building, the huge Guinness brewery, Kingsbridge railway station, and finally, Phoenix Park, one of Europe's most beautiful. Just a few blocks south of the bridge were Trinity College, the Bank of Ireland (which had been the House of Parliament during the period in the eighteenth century when Ireland had its own parliament), and Dublin Castle, which had long been the seat of British government in Ireland. Downriver from the bridge, eastward along the quays, were the Custom House and Dublin harbor, beyond which, across the Irish Sea, lay ever-present England, which had held dominion over Ireland since 1169, when a deposed Irish king, Dermot MacMurrough, invited an English army to come and help him regain his crown.

During the seven and a half intervening centuries, Ireland had made an exhausting number of attempts to throw off English rule and had a long list of martyrs to show for it—men like Theobald Wolf Tone, Lord Edward Fitzgerald, and Robert Emmet—but it still had not achieved independence. By 1916, due to certain concessions England had made over the years, and due also to the prosperity that resulted from England's participation in the European war, it was doubtful that a majority of Irishmen even wanted independence.

When Easter Sunday came and went without the Volunteer maneuver that was rumored to have been planned as an actual rebellion, most people in Dublin relaxed to some degree. But there was still a mood of uncertainty in the air that Easter Monday morning, and it was not caused just by the surprisingly warm and sunny weather, though there was that, too. The Irish, suspicious of blessings, refuse to take even sunshine at its face value. They say if it's sunny in the morning, beware. It means a stormy afternoon.

Actually, the storm came at noon Easter Monday, but not from the sky. It marched up O'Connell Street in the form of a ragtag company that could boast, as it reached the General Post Office, not more than forty men, two trucks, one closed cab, two motor-cycles, and a green Ford touring car. Though some of the men wore dark green or gray-green uniforms, one would have to look closely to notice it, so overloaded were they with a variety of impedimenta—rifles and shotguns (at least one or two each), sledge hammers, picks, pikes (in the best old Irish tradition), haversacks, ropes, shovels, crowbars, hammers, grenades, and first-aid kits, the latter deemed especially important because there were no doctors in this army and because the grenades were homemade, the rifles hair-triggered. The men without uniforms —and they were a majority—wore either their Sunday suits or their work clothes, crossed with bandolier straps, plus yellow armlets on their left sleeves. The two trucks, the cab, and the Ford that brought up the rear were as burdened as the men, with more guns and ammunition, Mausers that had been smuggled into Ireland two years before, Sniders, Lee Martins, Lee Enfields, shot-guns, miniature rifles, explosives, and crude bombs made, with hopeful Irish ingenuity, from tin cans and lengths of piping. Ragged children from the Dublin slums tagged along behind and at the sides of the staggering column, inflicting their high-pitched comments and questions upon the men.

"Where yiz marching this time?" one of them asked, and a youth on the outside rank shrugged to indicate he didn't know, which was undoubtedly true. He was one of fifty-six young Irishmen from England who had come to Dublin and joined the revolutionary movement because they would rather fight for Ireland than be conscripted and forced to fight in France for the British. After three months of Spartan training on an estate in the suburb of Kimmage, they had been routed out of their makeshift bunks by their commanding officer this morning and herded onto a Dublin-bound tram. "Fifty-seven tuppenny fares," the officer said to the conductor, handing him nine shillings and sixpence, "and don't stop until we reach O'Connell Bridge." Since the gun of one of the men happened to be pointing at the driver, the tram moved along rapidly despite complaints from other passengers. One commodious middle-aged lady was especially upset because she was being jostled and butted by the rifle of a man who was trying to sit down beside her without removing any of his equipment. "I demand you put these men off the tram," she said to the conductor. "Perhaps you wouldn't mind doing that for me, ma'am," he said. When they alighted at O'Connell Bridge and marched to the muster at a trade union building called Liberty Hall, a few blocks down the quay, the fifty-six men didn't yet know where they were going. And now, many of those who were in the company moving up O'Connell Street (more than half had been deployed elsewhere) still believed they were on a routine maneuver. So did the grinning British officers who stood in front of the Metropole Hotel watching them pass. One of the officers said to another, "Will these bloody fools never tire of marching up and down the streets?"

It was an understandable question. For more than two years the two groups represented by these marching men—the Irish Volunteers and the Irish Citizen Army—had been drilling openly and threatening revolution against the Crown without ever firing a shot. It was difficult to take them seriously.

At the head of the column approaching the General Post Office were three men in green officers' uniforms complete with Sam Browne belts and ceremonial swords. All three were commandant generals, having achieved that rank at a secret meeting the previous day.

In the center, striding belligerently, was Commandant General James Connolly, a stocky, bandy-legged man with a square, open face and a shaggy mustache. Though he now found himself in charge of the Dublin operations of the "first Army of the Irish Republic," he was a labor leader by profession. He was a dedicated Marxist as well as nationalist by persuasion. His vision of this revolution encompassed much more than Ireland's emancipation from England. He was a man of whom it might be said he was born in the wrong country and one year ahead of his time.

To Connolly's left was Commandant General Joseph Mary Plunkett, a poet, a military strategist, distantly related to Blessed

Oliver Plunkett, and son of Papal Count George Noble Plunkett. Joseph Plunkett was thin to the point of emaciation, with a slender, pale face, a sloping nose, rimless glasses, and a surgical bandage on his throat. His step was uncertain, and he looked as if he were sick unto death. An invalid since childhood, he was, in fact, dying of tuberculosis. Yet he had planned to marry, the previous day, a lovely girl named Grace Gifford, who had cut herself off from her Protestant family by her engagement to him and conversion to Catholicism. The marriage plans had been postponed because of the press of revolutionary events. And this morning, though he had needed help to get out of bed, he had arrived in time for the muster at Liberty Hall and unsheathed his saber with a flourish when he took his position at the front of the column.

To Connolly's right marched Commandant General Patrick Pearse, like Plunkett a poet, though more mystical and messianic; also a playwright, a lawyer, an educator (founder of two highly regarded schools), and the most effective Irish orator of his day. Though he left the field leadership of the troops and the front-and-center position on the march to Dublin commander Connolly, he was himself commander in chief of the "Army of the Irish Republic" and, although it had not yet been announced, already "the first president of the Irish Republic," having been duly elected the previous day by the other six members of the provisional Republican government. Two of these members were Connolly and Plunkett. The others were Thomas Clarke, Sean MacDermott, (neither of whom had taken military titles), Thomas MacDonagh, and Eamonn Ceannt. The latter two at this moment were commanding units of the Republican army elsewhere in Dublin. Pearse was a medium-size man with a solid stride. His face was handsome despite a cast in his right eye, but more than handsome, it was gravely serious. He had suffered, during the Liberty Hall muster, what to a less serious man might have been a deep embarrassment. Just as he was about to take his place at the front of the column, one of his four sisters had run up to him, grabbed his sleeve, and pleaded, "Come home, Patrick. Forget all this foolishness." He seemed not to notice her, as if, since he could not conceive of her doing such a thing to him, she were therefore not doing it. Connolly, embarrassed for him, had called the men to attention and quickly marched them off.

Walking along the sidewalk slightly behind the slow-moving troops were Clarke and MacDermott. Though Clarke was a man in late middle age, small and thin, with deep-set eyes, which for fifteen years had stared at the dark gray walls of British prison cells, he walked rigidly erect and helped support the younger MacDermott, who, crippled by polio, walked laboriously with a cane.

Driving the Ford at the rear of the column was a man named Michael O'Rahilly but called The O'Rahilly, a sandy-haired, handlebar-mustached, laughing man, whom none of the others had expected to show up today. On Holy Saturday night, he had driven this same car through several Irish counties, telling people they should not, under any circumstances, take part in the event that was now in progress. Then he had hurried back to Dublin, and here he was, taking a most active part in it himself. No one yet knew what to make of that.

As the overburdened accumulation of troops neared the General Post Office, passengers on the upper decks of trams looked down curiously and people on the sidewalks stared in wonder. Many of them had heard the rumors of a rising, but what was this? It looked more like an evacuation. A few people cheered derisively. When the column reached the Post Office, Commandant General Connolly suddenly ordered his men to halt, and after the clopping, clanging execution of this unexpected command, he paused to glance at the building in front of which they stood. A few passers-by and idlers looked on indifferently. The Angelus was ringing in the nearby Marlborough Street church. It was almost precisely noon.

Connolly took a deep breath and, with strident passion, shouted, "Left turn. The GPO—Charge!"

Although some command must have been expected, this one seemed to take the company by surprise. For a few seconds most of the men looked puzzled.

A subordinate officer shouted, "Take the Post Office!"

Sudden cries of exaltation came from these amateur troops who had waited so long for action. As quickly as they realized they had reached the moment toward which all their training had been directed, they broke ranks and began a clattering, pell-mell race for the doors of the huge stone Palladian structure. Several arrived at the main entrance simultaneously, creating dangerous entanglements as their rifles, pikes, bayonets, and equipment clashed, but within two or three minutes all were inside, including a detachment of twelve who had taken the easy way around the corner and into the Henry Street entrance.

Business had been brisk in the Post Office up to that moment. Lines of customers at the great counter and the postal employees behind it were paralyzed in place as they first heard, then saw this motley aggregation spilling in upon them. Rifles in nervous hands inadvertently announced their arrival with blasts at the ceiling. Connolly, entering the building with Pearse and Plunkett, gazed at the bemused crowd and shouted, "Everybody out!"

One of the first to move was a British army lieutenant who had been at the counter sending a telegram to his wife in London. He was prodded into motion by an Irish pike at his rear. A moment later, as people began to comprehend the situation, they launched a stampede out of the building even more precipitate than the rebel stampede into it. Postal clerks leaped the counter, hatless and coatless, to rush for the door ahead of their customers. Rebel troops, trying to assume their new dignity as occupying forces, found themselves for a minute at the mercy of the shoving, jostling crowd. Tempers shortened, Irish invective filled the air, and another gun went off, hastening the exodus. One lady, unperturbed by the commotion, still wanted a stamp and kept insisting on it until the clerk to whom she was insisting climbed over the counter past her and disappeared. The congestion at the main door was intensified by a man bent on getting into the building. He prevailed miraculously against the outgoing tide only to find himself confronted by a young insurgent soldier, pale and nervous, with a revolver in hand.

The man said, "What's up?"

The youth said, "Hands up, or I'll blow your heart out," and the man turned, with hands in the air, to follow the crowd into the street.

The British lieutenant was one of two men not allowed to leave. A young pair of aides to Commandant General Plunkett (who was now so weak from the exertion of marching six blocks he had to lean against the counter to keep from falling) rescued the lieutenant from the influence of the sharp pike behind him and informed him he was the first prisoner of the Irish Republic. One of his captors was a compellingly firm and purposeful young man named Michael Collins for whose apprehension the British government would one day offer a £10,000 reward, and who was killed from ambush in West Cork during the Irish civil war in 1922. After subjecting the prisoner to a search for firearms, Collins and his partner took him to a nearby phone booth, trussed him with the telephone cord, and left him to watch in presumed safety the progress of the revolution. Collins then turned his attention to the other man who had been detained in the Post Office, a Dublin policeman, who, as Collins advanced, gun in hand, pleaded not to be shot.

"We don't shoot prisoners," Collins said and ordered two soldiers to take the man away.

Commandant General Connolly now launched the tactical phase of securing the building.

"Smash the windows," he shouted, "and barricade the doors."

The men, who had begun to wander curiously but aimlessly through the main floor, now rushed at the big windows with sudden purpose and even delight. Axes, hammers, rifle butts, every heavy instrument at hand went up against the glass, creating, outside, a shower of shards that erupted simultaneously on all sides. People on O'Connell Street at the front, on Henry Street to the north, and on Prince's Street to the south, most of whom had watched first with indifference or derision, then with surprise as the rebels rushed inside and the routed customers rushed out, gaped now in consternation at the glass falling around them.

A woman from the slums—a "shawlie," so called because of the black shawl wrapped tightly around her—cried out, "Glory be to God, would you look at them smashin' all the lovely windows!"

Some of the rebel soldiers could be seen from outside now, standing at the windows they had broken, still swinging their weapons at the jagged glass fragments lodged in the sashes. One of them heard the woman's exclamation and laughed. Questions drifted in from outside, but the men were too busy to answer.

Inside, one of the men had run, white-faced, from the window he was attacking to the counter, where some of the leaders of the uprising had gathered. Blood was spurting from a deep, glass-inflicted cut in his wrist. Someone stepped forward to calm him and bandage him.

About a dozen Post Office officials who had apparently been in their offices in the bowels of the building when the uproar began emerged now, most of them with their hands up, and made their way nervously toward the front door, where Connolly had posted guards. Though the men were not detained, one of the guards lightly invited them to stay.

"With us here to protect you," he said, "this is the safest place in Dublin."

If some of the postal officials smiled, it was not because they believed him but because they could now see their way out of the pandemonium that had inexplicably violated the peace and order of their existence.

Aside from the tactical commander, Connolly, who was moving with purpose around the vast, high-ceilinged main room, issuing orders and encouraging the troops, none of the six rebel leaders present in the GPO had much to do during the first minutes of the uprising they had worked so passionately, and in some instances so deviously, to launch. The middle-aged Tom Clarke and the polio-stricken Sean MacDermott, neither of whom considered himself a soldier, looked more like excited spectators than participants. Clarke picked up a canteen from a box on the long counter and idly handed it to a recruit named John O'Connor, a second-generation Irish Londoner with a cockney accent so pronounced his comrades called him "Bli-mey." The young, inexperienced, dry-throated O'Connor's first distracted reaction to the "gift" was that the organizers of this undertaking must have been remarkable to have anticipated how thirsty the men would get, going into action. He was brought back to reality when it dawned on him that the canteen was actually a homemade bomb. He put it back where Clarke had found it and went to a window just north of the main door overlooking O'Connell Street. As he climbed onto a long counter under the window, a shotgun went off accidentally, the shot just missing his head as it tore into the arm of a man a few feet away. There was no doctor among the rebels and no infirmary had yet been established, so the wounded man's companions did the best they could for him with the contents of their first-aid kits.

Clarke and MacDermott stood together near the long counter, talking to each other, watching with approval but uncertainty the wild disorder around them, turning with concern whenever guns went off accidentally in the nervous hands of these inexperienced men and boys whose futures they had done so much to decide. Clarke, now fifty-nine years old, looked even older because of his frail frame, his drooping mustache, and the deep lines in his face. One of the last surviving members of the Fenian movement, which had sparked most of the rebellious Irish activity in the latter half of the nineteenth century, he had waited thirty-three years for this day. In 1883 he had received a life sentence in England for a revolutionary bomb plot, and he had served fifteen years, much of it in solitary confinement, before his release. Though he was quick to correct any impression that his part in the uprising was motivated by revenge against the British for imprisoning him, he was, nevertheless, filled with a deep satisfaction that these younger men around him, whom he had imbued with the Fenian spirit of rebellion, were finally making the defiant gesture he knew would deliver Ireland from British domination.

MacDermott, a singularly handsome man despite his infirmity, was only three years old when Clarke began serving his long prison term. Next to the youngest of eight children of an impoverished family in County Leitrim, he started as a barman, gardener, and tram conductor in Belfast; he became an organizer of the secret and revolutionary Irish Republican Brotherhood and, after coming to Dublin in 1908, developed an unshakable friendship with Clarke, first as a protégé, then as a colleague. There were those who said Clarke used him, but in recent years MacDermott's influence had become so strong in the nationalist movement that some people had begun to accuse him of using Clarke. On one occasion when this possibility was suggested to Clarke he had said merely, "If so, he's doing it for the good of Ireland." Together they had arranged, three days earlier, the kidnapping of a former comrade named Bulmer Hobson—also, they believed, for the good of Ireland. Hobson had discovered in advance what was to happen here today and had tried to stop it; he was now lodged under armed guard in a house in North Dublin. Many unpleasant things had to be done before an undertaking like this could come to fruition. But wasn't anything worth doing for a cause so great? MacDermott had said a few days before, "If we can hold Dublin a week, we'll save the soul of Ireland."

Joseph Mary Plunkett, having leaned against the main counter long enough to regain his equilibrium, was impatient now to get on with the work he had assigned himself. It was he who had evolved, with some help from Connolly, the military plans for the rebellion. Ignoring the commotion around him, he called for one of his two aides, W. J. Brennan Whitmore, to bring his maps and spread them out on a raised table toward the rear of the central room. Bending over the maps, pale and wasted, with the heavy surgical bandage on his throat, Plunkett looked like a man pointing out possible routes for his own funeral cortege. Yet he showed an astonishing flow of nervous vitality now despite the physically weakened condition in which he had begun the day and entered the Post Office. Just three weeks earlier he had undergone throat surgery for glandular tuberculosis, hence the bandage. And this morning he had been able to dress himself only with the help of his two aides, Whitmore and Collins. Although he was aware that even under peaceful circumstances he had little time to live, he seemed to feel more alive than ever in the realization that he had lived long enough to see Ireland strike a blow, that here in the very center of Dublin he could look around at a piece of Ireland, an important Irish landmark that, for the moment at least, was not part of England.

When he raised his hand to point at places on the maps, Plunkett showed off a shining filigree bangle (a gift from his fiancée, Grace Gifford) on his wrist and two huge antique rings. He took great pains to explain to Brennan Whitmore the military situation at the moment throughout Dublin—or at least the military situation as he hoped it to be. At best, it was not the way he had planned it. As chief military strategist for the plotters of the rebellion, Plunkett had anticipated that more than 9,000 men in all parts of Ireland would take arms against the British. But due to a deep division between activists and moderates within the leadership of the Irish Volunteers, only about 700 men, almost all of them in Dublin, had answered the call. It was amazing, in fact, that even 700 men had come out, because the call, originally issued for Easter Sunday, had been publicly countermanded Easter Saturday by Eoin MacNeill, the president of the Volunteers, who had been understandably angered by the almost incredible fact that the entire insurrection was planned without his knowledge. He and other moderates like The O'Rahilly who did not think an armed revolt at this time offered the best hope of achieving Irish independence had been told that the Easter Sunday, all-Ireland muster was to be nothing but a massive maneuver. When they found out that an uprising was intended, MacNeill, at the prompting of O'Rahilly, countermanded the muster order, thus robbing the insurgents of most of their potential strength.

With their ranks woefully depleted, the rebel commanders had sent undersized contingents to take several strong locations in the city: Boland's bakery to the east, St. Stephen's Green and Jacob's biscuit factory to the south, the Four Courts, the Mendicity Institution and the South Dublin Union to the west, and Gilbey's distillery to the north. Plunkett had been most influential in choosing these outposts. As soon as a communications system could be set up, he would be hearing from all of them. Meanwhile, he had no reason to suppose anything had gone amiss in the plans to seize them. The British military had obviously been taken by surprise. Proof of that was the ease with which the Irish took the Post Office, in the shadow of the Metropole Hotel, where many British officers had rooms. Some of them—those who had stood on the sidewalk and laughed at the approaching troops of the first Irish Republic—must be staring agape now at the siege preparations inside the Post Office. But they were not an immediate threat. Like almost everyone else in Dublin, the British forces were enjoying the last day of the Easter holiday. It would be easier at this moment to round up a fighting unit at the Fairyhouse race course than downtown or even at the barracks in Phoenix Park.

Patrick Pearse, less conspicuous than either Plunkett or Connolly, walked past the table on which Plunkett had spread his maps, glanced at them, moved on to this then that part of the building, observing the busy confusion but seldom speaking. Pale and unsmiling even in this hour of fulfillment of a boyhood pledge (he had once knelt on a prie-dieu with his little brother Willie and sworn someday to free Ireland or die fighting), his face showed no expression to suggest the determination or dynamism of leadership. It was his voice more than any other, however, that stirred the rank and file of the Irish Volunteers. His words, at the funeral the previous year of Fenian revolutionary hero O'Donovan Rossa, had visibly rekindled the Fenian spirit of rebellion in the thousands of young Irishmen who had come to Glasnevin Cemetery to hear him. At the slow, tantalizing pace he maintained to avoid stammering, he had said:

> Life springs from death, and from the graves of patriot men and women spring living nations. The Defenders of this Realm have worked well in secret and in the open. They think that they have pacified Ireland. They think that they have purchased half of us and intimidated the other half. They think that they have foreseen everything, think that they have provided against everything; but the fools, the fools, the fools! they have left us our Fenian dead, and while Ireland holds these graves, Ireland unfree shall never be at peace.

Yet of the thousands who had heard Pearse and cheered him at Glasnevin the year before, only 700 had turned out this morning to prove their cheers. Today, where were all those rebellious young Irishmen with their rekindled Fenian spirit? At the seashore? At the Fairyhouse races? Walking in the sun with their rosy-cheeked girls? It was a dreadful disappointment that so few had turned out, but one could scarcely blame those who remained at home. The countermand order—nothing else—had kept them there. And for that he could blame O'Rahilly as much as Eoin MacNeill, who had issued it. Without O'Rahilly standing behind him, MacNeill, however angry he might have been at his betrayal by the activist faction, would never have gone so far. Yet it was not easy for Pearse to blame O'Rahilly for anything, for O'Rahilly, too, had been completely cut out of the rebellion plans. In Pearse's view, he should have embraced the plans anyway if he espoused the cause of Irish freedom. He should not have fostered the countermand and traveled the countryside propagating it. But Pearse had to admire him when, after failing to stop the uprising, he had bravely stepped forward to join it.

O'Rahilly had been excluded from the rebellion plans because he was not a member of the secret Irish Republican Brotherhood, to which all the conspirators within the Volunteers owed their primary allegiance. The single purpose of the IRB was rebellion. A nineteenth-century Fenian organization, it had been kept alive by Tom Clarke, who had drawn into it a new generation of leaders—men like MacDermott, Plunkett, and Pearse. The IRB had encouraged the founding of the Irish Volunteers in 1913 because it needed a broad-based, popular front for its activities. From the beginning, IRB people had infiltrated the Volunteer leadership and, because they were united and dedicated, had dominated the larger organization, which had a membership of almost 10,000. The IRB leaders had supported the election of the highly respected Professor MacNeill as Volunteer president because they were certain they could manage him in a crisis. On Easter Saturday, when he countermanded their all-Ireland "maneuver," they found out they had miscalculated both his capacity for anger and O'Rahilly's influence over him.

Within the Volunteer leadership the moderate faction of MacNeill, Hobson, and O'Rahilly envisioned the use of the organization as a military pressure group, the existence of which would finally, though perhaps not until the end of the war against Germany, induce England to relinquish Ireland. The IRB faction saw the Volunteers as a determined fighting force that would eventually prevail, even in the event of defeat, because of the virtue of its cause. Their doctrine, as developed and enunciated by Pearse, was that the victory need not be as important as the fight itself, that Ireland had always struck against England at the wrong moment or too late, that bloodshed was a cleansing and sanctifying thing, and that a nation that regarded bloodshed as the final horror had lost its manhood.

Pearse, as Director of Organization, had secretly committed the Volunteers to the Easter Sunday date for the rebellion for three main reasons. First, the IRB faction had settled on that date with Connolly; second, a shipload of German arms (20,000 rifles, several machine guns, and a million rounds of ammunition), procured by Sir Roger Casement, was due to be landed Easter weekend in Tralee, on the southwest coast of Ireland; and third, the revolutionary leaders being well known to the British authorities, there were rumors that they would all be arrested simultaneously at any moment and once more Ireland would have waited too long to strike. If all these arrangements were made with guile and carefully kept from even such high officers of the Volunteers as MacNeill, O'Rahilly, and Hobson, it was because they simply could not be told. A whole set of carefully laid plans was undone when, on the night of Holy Thursday, Hobson was able to confirm his suspicions that the "Easter maneuver" was intended to be in fact a rebellion.

Within a few minutes after the invasion of the Post Office, the ground floor was beginning to look like the Donnybrook Fair after a bunch of the boys have chosen sides. The whole interior had been ripped up and rearranged, hardly anything remaining in its original place except the main counter and a scaffold near the front that had been erected for painting. Everything with weight or volume had been pushed against the now glass-free window casements as buffers against the British bullets expected shortly. Tables, chairs, mailbags, desks, books, office supplies, ledgers, pads of postal blanks, correspondence files, and old Post Office records—all things that might conceivably slow up a bullet— were stacked below and around the windows, behind which the men, full of thoughts about the coming battle, peered out at the curious, unarmed people on the streets and aimed their rifles at them experimentally, from testing angles, as if they were aiming at British soldiers storming the building. Often the men would laugh, even at the most inane remarks ("Me old lady should see me now"), but the sound of their laughter had developed a high, harsh ring, and their smiles, instead of spreading over their dirty faces, were tight circles around their mouths.

The only woman among the men in the Post Office during these first moments of the uprising was an austere lady of indeterminate age named Winifred Carney. She was Connolly's secretary and was so devoted to him she wouldn't even let him fight a revolution without her. While he moved around the building, supervising its fortification, she set herself up at the main counter, in front of a huge Webley typewriter, and was already typing orders he had given her.

Behind her, in the center of the room, a detail of men piled up the weapons and material brought by the two trucks, the cab, and O'Rahilly's touring car, which had entered the covered courtyard of the Post Office through the Prince's Street gate and were now being unloaded.

As The O'Rahilly himself came in from the courtyard, his hearty voice preceding him, everyone became quickly aware of his presence and work stopped momentarily. Many of the men resented him. They knew the part he had played in keeping down their numbers. Yet they also admired him for his totally unexpected courage in taking his place here beside them, and when he smiled, with his wide mustache spreading across his face like plumage and his eyes announcing fellowship in all directions, there was a murmur of satisfaction at the sight of him. He studied the premises with evident curiosity. When he saw Pearse, his smile faded. The two men looked at each other from a distance. Pearse waited as O'Rahilly walked toward him.

There may have been some who expected a bitter confrontation; if so, they were disappointed. No sign of rancor appeared between O'Rahilly and Pearse as they came face to face; but neither did any sign of warmth. For O'Rahilly this was unusual.

While Pearse was so shy and self-contained (except in front of an audience) many people thought him morose, O'Rahilly was ordinarily so high-spirited it took special circumstances to delete open friendliness from his expression. Simply by keeping a straight face he conveyed to Pearse his feelings. It would be difficult to say which of the two men felt he had more reason to complain against the other. While Pearse and his associates had mistreated O'Rahilly by withholding their plans from him, he, on the other hand, had seriously compromised what they considered Ireland's one great chance for freedom by preventing so many men from taking part in it. If he actually believed the present enterprise to be futile, why was he throwing himself into it so recklessly? When he arrived at Liberty Hall for the muster, he had explained his presence to one man with the remark "I helped wind this clock. I've come to hear it ring."

But to Pearse he had said, "It's madness, yet it's glorious madness and I want to be in on it."

The message was too clear for Pearse to miss. What O'Rahilly had implied, both by word and by deed, was that he would willingly sacrifice himself in this insanely hopeless venture but that he refused (unlike Pearse, Clarke, MacDermott, Connolly, and Plunkett) to lead other men to slaughter. Though O'Rahilly could hardly have intended it to be so, his very presence here today was an accusation against the other leaders. A man with the moral sensitivity of Pearse could not ignore such implications. He was fortified, however, by what he deemed more telling factors. He was a commander in chief leading an armed force, admittedly an outnumbered one, into battle. In any battle, men must die. He had long since acknowledged that men would die under his command, as thousands had died before them, in the struggle for Irish independence. With a martyr's zeal he had accepted the likelihood of his own death. The question then was not if men would die but if they would die with sufficient justification, and on that score he harbored no doubts. Perhaps many of the men who had come out today—some under the impression they were taking part in a simple route march—did not share so intensely Pearse's zeal for the cause and his willingness to die for it. He had to

assume, though, that they did. Otherwise, why had they joined
an organization like the Volunteers? Inclined by nature to believe
that anyone on his side agreed with him completely (despite
evidence to the contrary from men like O'Rahilly), Pearse had,
without hesitation, committed his troops to the likelihood of death
as completely as he had committed himself. Yet he felt the staggering weight of the responsibility, and the example of O'Rahilly
made it infinitely more difficult to bear. He looked into O'Rahilly's unsmiling eyes and waited for him to speak.

The last time Pearse and The O'Rahilly had come face to face
was Good Friday night after Bulmer Hobson's disappearance.
O'Rahilly had burst into Pearse's study, a revolver in his hand
and fire in his eyes. "Whoever kidnaps me," he announced, "will
have to be a quicker shot."

Though Pearse had obviously not managed to reassure him, he
had at least calmed him so that, after making his protest, O'Rahilly had left quietly. Pearse might have wished now that he had
arranged to have him captured and incarcerated like Hobson,
because it was the following day, Easter Saturday, that O'Rahilly
had encouraged MacNeill to issue the countermand and then
helped spread it the length and breadth of Ireland.

If O'Rahilly was tempted to mention that last confrontation
with Pearse as they faced each other now in the Post Office, he
decided against it. Glancing toward the stairway on the Henry
Street side of the building, he said, abruptly, "What about the
upper floors? Have we cleared everyone out up there?"

Pearse looked startled, as if he had expected to be addressed on
some other subject. Had anyone investigated the upper floors? If
not it was about time. He couldn't help welcoming the idea,
because it distracted both O'Rahilly and himself from more painful matters.

"The telegraph room is upstairs," O'Rahilly reminded him.
Pearse called over a quartermaster department Volunteer named
Michael Staines and told him to take a party of six or seven men,
clear the upper floors, and put them in a state of defense.

Staines and a hastily gathered squad, all carrying revolvers or
automatics, carefully ascended the wide staircase leading to the

telegraph office. The click of descending footsteps stopped them
momentarily until the accompanying nervous giggles assured
them they were about to meet only a group of female employees
fleeing the building. When the girls came into sight, most of
them seemed more hostile than they were frightened by the guns
upraised toward them. Only one girl was friendly. Recognizing
the well-armed Staines, she said, "Hello, Michael. That's the stuff
to give them." Neither she nor any of the others indicated the
possibility that Staines and his men might run into danger ahead.

With the girls descending behind them, Staines and his men
proceeded cautiously up to the landing opposite the telegraph
office. Suddenly there was a sound from their rear, and whirling
around, they found themselves covered by seven rifles in the
hands of British soldiers. One of the Irishmen, either thinking
quickly or reacting nervously, fired a pistol shot at the cluster of
neat, clean British khakis. The sergeant at the head of the party
slumped and fell, but to the amazement of the Irish, no British
guns answered the shot that hit him. When Staines called upon
the British troops to put up their hands, they did so, and when he
demanded their guns and ammunition, he found out why. They
eagerly handed over their guns because—of ammunition they had
none. They were the Post Office guard detail. What need would
they have for bullets?

As the helpless British soldiers surrendered and their empty
rifles were passed down the stairs to the main floor, Staines went
to the aid of their wounded sergeant, who was regaining consciousness. He had sustained only a grazing forehead wound.
Two men were told off to take him to Jervis Street Hospital, a
few blocks away, but when they tried to help him to his feet, he
wanted none of it.

"I dinna leave my post till I'm relieved," he said, proving himself as Scottish as he was steadfast. His captors knew better than
he what he needed at the moment, so off he went to Jervis Street,
in spite of himself, under the care of two Irish Volunteers.

When Staines entered the telegraph office, he found that the
lady in charge, also Scottish, shared the sergeant's attitude about
leaving her post. Staines gave her sufficient reasons why it was

unsafe to stay. A revolution was in progress. She was aware of that. Perhaps it explained why she wanted to stay. Left alone for a few minutes, she might easily warn the British military of the situation in the GPO.

Could she send out some death announcements that were due to go on the wire?

No. One of the Volunteers who knew telegraphy would take care of that.

She stayed on for an uncomfortable length of time, always watched but never ordered to leave. A well-bred Irishman doesn't like to order a lady about. Finally, perhaps because she realized the futility of trying to outwait them, she said, "Good day," and left.

While the two upper floors were being secured and the windows smashed and loopholed, Clarke, MacDermott, and Pearse, with a happy little elf of a man named Sean T. O'Kelly following behind, ascended the stairs to inspect the layout. (O'Kelly, an amiable errand runner, had attached himself as an aide to "the first president of the Irish Republic." Ironically, O'Kelly himself was later to become the actual president of the Irish Republic.) MacDermott and Clarke selected a large second-floor head-quarters room, where they sat with Pearse and spoke briefly about the captured British guards, the problems of fortifying the building, the kind of attack to expect from the British, and when to expect it. Time was all-important. The rebels at this moment might find it easy to handle an unarmed squad of Post Office guards, but they weren't yet in shape to defend the Post Office against a significant British force. All three men knew that. They didn't have to say much about it. Clarke and MacDermott had, in fact, very little to say to Pearse. Their admiration of him was qualified, though it was they who had brought him into the Irish Republican Brotherhood. Three years earlier, when the organization needed a strong speaker to represent its ideas, MacDermott had suggested him.

"But will he speak to our views?" Clarke wondered.

"Tell him what to say," MacDermott had said, "and he'll say it."

In the intervening time, Pearse had become the principal spokesman for the IRB and the outstanding speaker in Ireland, but Clarke now thought him vain, perhaps because he was Anglo-Irish, his father being English. Clarke was aware of a certain feeling of superiority among the Anglo-Irish. MacDermott often said Pearse received credit that Clarke deserved, because it was Clarke who had kept the nineteenth-century Irish spirit of rebellion alive and it was Clarke who had passed it on to men like Pearse, Plunkett, MacDonagh, Caennt, and MacDermott himself. But whenever MacDermott talked this way, Clarke would say, "What does it matter who gets the credit as long as the work is done?" Sometimes MacDermott, a practical man, tended to deride Pearse's brooding mysticism. "P. O. P.," he would call him, for Poor Old Pearse. Yet after the great success of Pearse's oration at the graveside of O'Donovan Rossa, MacDermott was the first to realize how important Pearse's personality might be to the movement and how difficult it might become to manage him. Pearse was not MacDermott's candidate for the presidency of the new republic. Nevertheless, he had sided with Pearse against Clarke just the previous day. When the conspirators learned, Easter Sunday morning, of MacNeill's order countermanding their advertised "maneuver," Clarke had insisted that the rebellion begin immediately, as planned, despite the countermand. Pearse, with everyone else including MacDermott in concurrence, insisted that they wait one day, using the time to send out their own messengers and countermand the countermand. Pearse prevailed. When Clarke arrived home tired and dejected Easter Sunday night, he had said to his wife, "It was the only time I've known Sean MacDermott to disagree with me."

Pearse did not remain long with Clarke and MacDermott in the office they had chosen for themselves. Restless and curious, he returned downstairs with O'Kelly again at his heels.

On the main floor, Pearse encountered Connolly, hurrying from post to post, exhorting the men in an intense, deliberate voice to hasten their work. The British might attack at any time. Simply by approaching a group of men, Connolly accelerated them. As one of his associates said of him, he had the knack of making a friendly request sound like an order. A surprising number of the younger lads in the Post Office, even at this crucial moment, needed the incentive he brought. They were willing enough to fight and die for Ireland, but apparently it had not occurred to them that it would involve this much work. No Irishman is so unromantic as to suppose he might serve his country best, at her most critical hour, by pushing furniture around and carrying bags of sand.

When Connolly saw Pearse, who was looking grave and concerned, he smiled ebulliently as if to say, well, you see, it's not so bad after all. At least we've survived the first fifteen minutes.

Connolly might easily have believed that except for his impatience they would not have been there that day, preparing for battle. He had long chided the Volunteer leaders for dragging their feet. At a public meeting where Pearse had remarked that Ireland, in the past, had always struck too late, Connolly had arisen to ask, "Are we going to strike too late again this time?" (If it seems odd that such matters would be discussed at public meetings, one must remember this was Ireland, where even the British officials could not believe half of what they saw. Groups like the Volunteers and Connolly's Citizen Army had held their armed maneuvers and their mock battles right on the streets, in plain sight. They were a source of amusement to the British officers who watched.) Connolly had once told his son he thought the Volunteers might be willing to fight only if they had steam-heated trenches. And in January 1916, just three months earlier, he had become so exasperated at what he considered the indecision of the Volunteers that he had threatened, in his union publication *The Irish Worker*, to lead his 200-man Citizen Army into battle against the might of Great Britain, alone and unaided, the following day. This threat, coming from a man like Connolly, was not too outlandish to be ignored by the Irish Republican Brotherhood faction within the Volunteer leadership—the faction that was already hard at work moving the Volunteers toward rebellion. Led by Pearse, they had sent three armed men to escort Connolly, willing or not, to a meeting that lasted three days and three nights. When that long meeting ended, it was impossible to say who had prevailed. Pearse, Clarke, and Mac-Dermott had talked Connolly out of a premature uprising, but Connolly had committed them to the Easter date. It may have been, however, that Pearse had already chosen Easter as the ideal time for an uprising. There was in his thought a mystical quality that would make the date seem fitting.

Pearse and Connolly stopped to exchange a few words as O'Kelly drifted off toward the center of the room—words about the condition of the building, the morale of the men, the need for more junior officers with a smattering of military knowledge . . . details of the moment . . . no momentous words. Connolly's mind was occupied with the preparation for the British attack. And the matters that had to be racing through the stately, labyrinthine mind of Pearse were hardly the kind he could discuss with Connolly or anyone else. Were they striking out prematurely against the imposing force of the British military? Had he and Mac-Dermott and Clarke and MacDonagh and Plunkett allowed Connolly to stampede them? No. On that score there could be no doubt. Easter was the ideal time. If the shipload of German guns had arrived . . . If MacNeill and his friends had been contained . . . But it was too late for such considerations. Pearse could wish more men had turned out at the same time he brooded about his heavy life-and-death responsibility for those who had turned out. He could feel also the difference between all the moments in the past when he had thought or spoken or written about giving his life for Ireland and this present moment, when he was faced with the absolute likelihood that he would soon have to do so. In a play he had written called *The Singer*—a foreboding play about the course of his and Ireland's destiny—he had made the protagonist say to the girl he loved: "Once I wanted life. You and I to be together in one place always; that is what I wanted. But now I see that we shall be together for a little time only; that I have to do a hard, sweet thing, and that I must do it alone." Even surrounded by followers whom he had influenced to fight and die for the cause he loved, Pearse was inescapably alone.

As they finished their short conversation, Connolly looked beyond Pearse toward little Sean T. O'Kelly, who was standing idly behind Winifred Carney in the center of the room.

"Are you busy, Sean?"

"Not at all." It would have been difficult for O'Kelly to pretend otherwise.

"Go back to Liberty Hall, then. There's a package of flags I want you to bring me."

O'Kelly knew which flags he meant. Was it possible that they had set out to proclaim a new republic and had forgotten to bring along the bright, beautiful new ensigns that would bear witness to its birth? O'Kelly hurried the few blocks to Liberty Hall, found the flags in a brown paper parcel, where Connolly said they would be, and brought them back to him. It was now about twenty-five minutes after noon—time for the proclamation ceremony to begin. Connolly gave two flags to a Volunteer officer with instructions to raise them in place of the British flags on the roof, at opposite sides of the building.

The Post Office secured and an uneasy order established inside, Pearse and Connolly emerged from the front door preceded by a company of men carrying printed broadsides. In the street about 400 people stood talking to each other in dazed wonder as they awaited the next slapstick scene in this knockabout comedy that had just opened. A curious murmur arose when Pearse and Connolly appeared, then a few sportingly hostile remarks.

"Takin' over the city, are ye? Well, yer not takin' me over."

"Bloody little they'll take over when the military arrives."

There were no cheers. Most of the people present could not even identify these insane Sinn Feiners in their silly generals' uniforms, complete with rattling sabers, who thought they could lead a pack of rabble into the General Post Office and settle down as if they owned the place. (In the minds of most Dubliners, the Volunteers, the Citizen Army, and the only vaguely known Irish Republican Brotherhood were all lumped together as Sinn Feiners—a reference to a less militant nationalist group that had a more militant reputation.) These boyos could have their fun for an hour or so. As soon as the troops showed up, they would all disappear fast enough. Breaking the windows like that, pushing respectable citizens around, they could be had up for defacing public property, creating a nuisance, disturbing the peace, and a fine selection of other charges.

Near Nelson's Pillar, in the center of O'Connell Street, just fifty feet from the Henry Street corner of the Post Office, a policeman, with his hands behind his back, stood watching the course of events. Another policeman came up to him and asked him what was happening.

The first policeman said, "The Sinn Feiners have collared the Post Office."

The second policeman, glancing at the armed men around Pearse and Connolly, said, "Bejabers, that's queer work," and sauntered on his way.

Someone spoke a few words to Connolly, and he strode out away from the building to where he could look up toward the roof. There, on poles at opposite corners, protecting the Grecian statues of Hibernia, Mercury, and Fidelity and rising above the hated, weather-beaten Royal Arms of England that had been set into the centered tympanum, were the two new flags of Ireland, waving proudly in a brisk breeze. To the left, at the Prince's Street corner, was a banner with a golden harp in the center of a green field, across which, in Gaelic lettering, gold and white, were the words "IRISH REPUBLIC." To the right, at the Henry Street corner, was the tricolor that is even today the official flag of the Irish Republic—the green of the South and the orange of Ulster, with a pure white stripe between. Connolly beamed with pride and turned to his secretary, Miss Carney, who had followed him.

"Isn't it grand?" he said, then hurried back to stand beside Pearse in front of the building.

Pearse, after looking around solemnly and perhaps sadly at the unenthusiastic gathering, raised his voice and began reading the careful, eloquent words he had written (see page 27), with some help from his associates, for this long-envisioned moment.

Pearse was pale and stony as he read his stirring document to the indifferent crowd. Poet Stephen McKenna, an old friend of his who was in the crowd, noticed that his magnetism had left him in the face of the chilling response. There were a few, thin, perfunctory cheers. There was no hostility toward his words, but no enthusiasm either. These people were quite unprepared to see

POBLACHT NA H EIREANN.

THE PROVISIONAL GOVERNMENT

OF THE

IRISH REPUBLIC

TO THE PEOPLE OF IRELAND.

IRISHMEN AND IRISHWOMEN: In the name of God and of the dead generations from which she receives her old tradition of nationhood, Ireland, through us, summons her children to her flag and strikes for her freedom.

Having organised and trained her manhood through her secret revolutionary organisation, the Irish Republican Brotherhood, and through her open military organisations, the Irish Volunteers and the Irish Citizen Army, having patiently perfected her discipline, having resolutely waited for the right moment to reveal itself, she now seizes that moment, and, supported by her exiled children in America and by gallant allies in Europe, but relying in the first on her own strength, she strikes in full confidence of victory.

We declare the right of the people of Ireland to the ownership of Ireland, and to the unfettered control of Irish destinies, to be sovereign and indefeasible. The long usurpation of that right by a foreign people and government has not extinguished the right, nor can it ever be extinguished except by the destruction of the Irish people. In every generation the Irish people have asserted their right to national freedom and sovereignty: six times during the past three hundred years they have asserted it in arms. Standing on that fundamental right and again asserting it in arms in the face of the world, we hereby proclaim the Irish Republic as a Sovereign Independent State, and we pledge our lives and the lives of our comrades-in-arms to the cause of its freedom, of its welfare, and of its exaltation among the nations.

The Irish Republic is entitled to, and hereby claims, the allegiance of every Irishman and Irishwoman. The Republic guarantees religious and civil liberty, equal rights and equal opportunities to all its citizens, and declares its resolve to pursue the happiness and prosperity of the whole nation and of all its parts, cherishing all the children of the nation equally, and oblivious of the differences carefully fostered by an alien government, which have divided a minority from the majority in the past.

Until our arms have brought the opportune moment for the establishment of a permanent National Government, representative of the whole people of Ireland and elected by the suffrages of all her men and women, the Provisional Government, hereby constituted, will administer the civil and military affairs of the Republic in trust for the people.

We place the cause of the Irish Republic under the protection of the Most High God, Whose blessing we invoke upon our arms, and we pray that no one who serves that cause will dishonour it by cowardice, inhumanity, or rapine. In this supreme hour the Irish nation must, by its valour and discipline and by the readiness of its children to sacrifice themselves for the common good, prove itself worthy of the august destiny to which it is called.

Signed on Behalf of the Provisional Government,

THOMAS J. CLARKE,
SEAN Mac DIARMADA,   THOMAS MacDONAGH,
P. H. PEARSE,   EAMONN CEANNT,
JAMES CONNOLLY.   JOSEPH PLUNKETT.

in his uniformed figure a significant person. This dismal reception was not what he had envisioned.

Connolly was undaunted. Turning to his comrade in arms, he shook his hand and said, "Thanks be to God, Pearse, that we've lived to see this day."

Pearse managed a smile. Insurgent troops began posting, on the columns in front of the building, and on every nearby wall, proclamation broadsides that had been printed on the squeaky old press at Liberty Hall. One copy, each corner held down by a stone, was placed hopefully in front of Nelson's Pillar, but only a few people bothered to step up and look at it. Slowly the crowd drifted away as it became apparent there would be no more speeches. Pearse and Connolly, followed by their men, returned inside the Post Office.

A young bride, watching from a window of the Imperial Hotel, across the street, felt woefully let down as she saw the inauspicious ceremony fizzle to an end. She was Mrs. Thomas Dillon, Geraldine Plunkett until the day before. She had three brothers in that pitiful little collection of irregulars that was daring to challenge the might of the British Empire. For the oldest, Joseph, she had once kept house. Had the uprising not intervened, he would have been married by her side to her friend, Grace Gifford, the previous day.

On the march from Liberty Hall, Connolly had detached small contingents along the way to occupy various buildings between the Post Office and O'Connell Bridge. He sent orders now that the men at these posts were to erect a barricade across Lower Abbey Street to help protect the GPO headquarters from the direction of the Amiens Street railroad station. If the British were to dispatch reinforcements from the north, they would arrive through Amiens Street. Under the direction of George Plunkett, one of those three brothers of Mrs. Dillon, a squad of men pushed into the street huge rolls of newsprint commandeered, by the authority of the Irish Republic, from an *Irish Times* warehouse. They augmented these rolls with whatever articles of furniture, machinery, merchandise, or trash they could find in the shops along Abbey Street. From the smashed window of Keating's cycle shop they hauled out bicycles and even a motorcycle to add to the pile.

People began to gather and watch in fascination. One of the curious bystanders said to another, "Jaysus, isn't that a lovely bike?"

A second said, "Would you look at the bloody eejits throwing it away."

A young lad darted out of the crowd, grabbed the bicycle under discussion and ran off with it. There was a rush forward as others got the idea. Plunkett and his men tried with their hands to protect their dwindling barricade but it looked as if they would fail until a few shots, just over the heads of the acquisitive citizens, proved at least temporarily efficacious. The sullen crowd retreated, grumbling, as more items were added to the junky bulwark, and the whole mess was bound together with wire, woven in and out between the various items until they held firm. When the barricade was completed, two men were stationed behind it, not so much to await the arrival of the British as to discourage the still sullen spectators from cutting the wires and carting it all away, piece by piece.

The outposts protecting the GPO had been occupied without bloodshed but not without incident. On the corner across the street from the bridge, Seamus Robinson, Seamus Lundy, and Cormac Turner were interrupted by a policeman during their efforts to enter Hopkins and Hopkins jewelry shop. They had just forced an opening through a hall door when the officer, on bridge duty, became curious about the motives of three men breaking into a jewelry shop. As he approached, Cormac Turner stepped forward to meet him and ordered him to halt.

The officer was at first disinclined.

"Halt or I'll run you through," Turner promised, tickling him with a bayonet.

The officer seemed suddenly to understand what was in progress. "Oh, I see," he said. "Well, you boys needn't worry about me. I won't interfere. In my opinion, it's a matter for the military."

The three insurgent soldiers were just entering the building when a party of British Lancers came trotting along the quay, escorting several wagonloads of stores from the harbor, presumably to Phoenix Park. The Lancers looked down disdainfully from their horses at the Volunteers but did not stop.

Meanwhile, four more Volunteers had taken Kelly's gunpowder store on the Bachelor's Walk corner directly across O'Connell Street, so that unknown to the Lancers riding past, rebel guns now commanded not only O'Connell Bridge, the broadest and most strategically important in the city, but also the very pavement on which their horses trod. One or two rounds of fire from Hopkins and Hopkins and from Kelly's "fort," as it was called, could have wiped out that small company of Lancers. The order to fire was withheld, however, due to previous instructions from Connolly. It would be unwise to engage and alert the British needlessly before the Post Office headquarters was fully prepared to resist attack.

In the Post Office, preparation and fortification continued. O'Rahilly, besides discharging his duties as munitions officer, took command of the top floor, perhaps because he was still too angry at the other leaders to wish to be near them. Downstairs, Joseph Plunkett's aide Brennan Whitmore, after making the rounds of the windows, reported to Plunkett and Pearse that few of them were properly loopholed. It seemed to him that despite their months of training, the men were appallingly ignorant of the elementary principles of fortification. They thought it was enough to break the glass in a window, put a book or two up on the sill, sit down behind it, and wait. There were too few officers to tell them otherwise. Pearse, with Connolly's concurrence, ordered Whitmore and Michael Collins to go from window to window, making sure each rifleman protected himself as well as possible. Whitmore, glancing out a window on the south side, saw British officers still watching from the Metropole Hotel across the narrow street. They now looked puzzled and concerned. They were no longer laughing. Whitmore, gathering up piles of books, records, and mailbags, loopholed one of the windows, then stood by while each of the three men stationed in the corner room did another. He found it diffi-

cult to make them see that because they were on the corner they
also had to protect themselves against cross fire. When he was
finally satisfied, he moved on to the next room.

In one room, a man sat at his window, his homemade bombs
lined up in a row before him, lighting his pipe and blithely dropping the used matches as he waited for action. A large stock of
the homemade bombs and grenades had been distributed
throughout the building. Reserve ammunition had been stored in
several rooms O'Rahilly had decided were the least vulnerable to
enemy fire. On a huge table behind a partition in the great
ground-floor room was an array of daggers, bayonets, pikes, and
assorted weapons, some of them so curious as to be beyond all
understanding.

Among the men, there were already rumors of great victories
in other parts of the city, of the archbishop's house in Drum-
condra being attacked by the British, of Cork, Kerry, and
Limerick in revolt, of some of His Majesty's Irish regiments joining the Republican ranks, of strong Volunteer forces from country regions marching on Dublin, of a German submarine sinking a
British transport in the Irish Sea, of Turks and Germans landing
at Waterford. Though the Germans were at the moment quite
busily engaged in the Battle of the Marne, they had been expected, through the good graces of Sir Roger Casement (a dis-
tinguished and famous Irishman once knighted by Queen Victoria but now a devoted Republican), to provide substantial help
to the Irish cause. And in fact, a German ship, the *Aud*, due to
arrive with arms for the Irish, had managed to run the British
blockade successfully, arriving Holy Thursday at Tralee Bay,
loaded with the 20,000 rifles, 10 machine guns, and a million
rounds of ammunition on which the insurgents had been counting.
But thanks to an extraordinary series of mixed signals and messages sent too late, the insurgents were expecting the ship Sunday,
and had no one on hand to unload its cargo. Consequently, the
British got to the *Aud* before the Irish. The ship with its guns now
lay at the bottom of the sea, scuttled by the Germans just outside
the entrance to Queenstown harbor. And as for Roger Casement,
a cryptic story in Easter Monday's edition of a Dublin newspaper,

the *Freeman's Journal*, revealed his fate to the few men in the Post Office (Pearse, Connolly, MacDermott, Clarke, Plunkett, and a handful of others) who were privy to what had gone before. They already knew, through their private sources, that the arms cargo was lost. The story in the *Freeman's Journal*, many copies of which were circulating in the Post Office, confirmed their belief that Casement was also lost. The story was from Tralee, though it was dated "London, Friday," and had been passed by the British censor:

> News reached Tralee this evening, says a Central News message, that a collapsible boat containing a large quantity of arms and ammunitions was seized about four o'clock this morning at Currahane Strand by the Ardfert police. A stranger of unknown nationality was arrested in the vicinity and is detained in custody. Where the boat came from, or for whom the arms were intended is at present unknown.

Insurgent sources in Tralee had informed their Dublin superiors that the stranger of unknown nationality was undoubtedly Casement and that he had come ashore from a submarine that must have accompanied the *Aud* into Tralee Bay. Thus ended the alliance between the Irish insurgents and Germany, an alliance that had been doomed from the start, perhaps, by the vast differences between the Germans and the Irish, both in temperament and in ultimate aims. Casement long before leaving Germany had made clear his disenchantment with the German military establishment. And James Connolly, on a sign he had posted above the door of his Liberty Hall union headquarters, had fairly well expressed the attitude of the insurgent leadership: "WE SERVE NEITHER KING NOR KAISER BUT IRELAND."

In his union publication *The Workers' Republic*, Connolly had written: ". . . the instinct of the slave to take sides with whoever is the enemy of his own particular slave-driver is a heathy instinct and makes for freedom."

Side by side in the Post Office there were men who believed all the rumors and others who believed none of them, men who could not conceive of the rebellion failing and others who could not conceive of it succeeding. A Volunteer like Sean Gallogly, who had come from Glasgow to fight in this war of Irish liberation, had an unfailing faith in final victory. One like John O'Connor, who had come from London to be a part of it, had no such illusions. Though he tried to keep morbid thoughts from his mind, he could not avoid the conviction that the cause was hopeless and that he himself had little chance to come out alive.

An uneasy rapport existed in the Post Office between the labor union members, who belonged to Connolly's Citizen Army, and the men from slightly higher economic or social levels, who belonged to the Volunteers. Though Connolly had said that morning, "There are no longer Volunteers or Citizen Army, there is now only one army, the Irish Republican Army," men on both sides were aware of a class barrier, erected by past generations, which still divided them. When a Citizen Army man, in his working clothes, addressed a Volunteer as "comrade," that uncustomary word, offered no doubt as a token of solidarity, served instead to emphasize differences neither side could forget. A week before, Connolly had also said, in his last lecture on tactics to the Citizen Army, "The odds against us are a thousand to one. But if we should win, hold on to your rifles because the Volunteers may have a different goal. Remember, we're out not only for political liberty, but for economic liberty as well. So hold on to your rifles." To Connolly, Ireland was the people—exploited, underpaid, badly housed, and badly nourished thanks to a greedy, unfeeling establishment, which was not altogether English. To Pearse it often seemed that Ireland was the beautiful myth of Cathleen ni Houlihan and the heroic myth of the Gaelic warrior Cuchulainn. And though Pearse's social and economic views had been deeply influenced by those of Connolly in recent years, Connolly could hardly regard him, or any of his associates, as dedicated socialists. Connolly had once said to Pearse, "The idea of Ireland means nothing unless it helps the people of Ireland." It would be hard to know whether or not Pearse got the message. Pearse felt so deeply the romantic reality of Ireland that he sometimes seemed to consider her people important mostly as instruments of her glorification. There was no doubt that he willingly relegated himself to such a purpose.

An intermittent stream of vans, trucks, automobiles, carrier bicycles, and carts began pouring through the great wooden gate on Prince's Street now as men who had been sent out on commandeering missions returned with what they could procure from the shops in the area. (What the commandeering parties procured first were vehicles on which to carry away whatever else they might procure.) Though they concentrated on foodstuffs, they did not pass up such items as blankets, mattresses, and empty containers in which to store water, against the possibility that the British might cut the supply.

At the Metropole Hotel, just opposite the Prince's Street gate, they found a rich source of food and bedding, which, however, the manager was loathe to surrender. When the Volunteer in charge of the requisitioning party removed his cocked hat and said, "I must ask you to show me the way to your provisions," the manager surveyed him indignantly but did not budge.

The young insurgent repeated his request, somewhat less politely.

The manager said, "Suppose I refuse?"

The insurgent took hold of his arm. The manager, looking outraged, said, "Take your hands off me."

The insurgent, tightening his hold, said, "If you don't cooperate, I'll take everything I find. And I'll take you, too."

The manager was still furious when the requisitioning party left, despite the receipt the young Volunteer had given him promising compensation by the "Irish Republic." Some people who contributed goods at gunpoint to the Republican cause were paid off in cash, but the majority were given receipts because the insurgents had enough cash for only a small part of their needs. Sean T. O'Kelly, who went out on a commandeering tour (after supervising the transfer of more munitions from Liberty Hall to the GPO), found deep resentment among the merchants as he moved from shop to shop, filling carts with bread and milk. When he handed them receipts, to be honored at some future date by some future "Irish Republic," their resentment turned to fury. One of the more speakable things they called him was "thief," a designation with which he felt inclined to agree. The gun in his hand did nothing to help him overcome the guilty conviction that he was simply robbing people of their property.

The crowd had now grown to such alarming proportions in O'Connell Street that a group of priests got together to try to disperse it. They were stepping bravely into a vacuum left by a sudden scarcity of policemen. Their strategy was to link hands, thus creating an unbroken picket stretching from one side of the wide thoroughfare to the other. Then, counting on the Irish reluctance to show disrespect for the cloth, they would walk from one end of the street to the other, forcing the crowd to fall back and dissolve before them. This amusing strategy worked— to a point. As the black, moving fence of priests advanced up O'Connell Street, the mob kept retreating and squeezing into a succession of doorways and side streets. But alas, before the priests had swept their way to the top of the street, the groaning crowds they had compressed into the byways had already spilled back out to refill the space behind them. Undaunted, the priests reversed their picket and came sweeping down the street. The result was the same. They made one more attempt to dissolve the overwhelming mob, then gave up in confusion and despair.

As word began to circulate in Dublin that an uprising was, indeed, under way, some Volunteers (though disappointingly few) who had been led by the countermand order to suppose that nothing was going to happen, hurried to the General Post Office to take part in whatever was happening. Liam McNeive, for example, a Liverpudlian Irishman who was a member of the Irish Republican Brotherhood as well as a Volunteer, had helped bring a company of Volunteers from Liverpool to take part in the uprising, but there was such limited communication even among IRB men that he and his group, having read the countermand order, decided to go to the Fairyhouse races. It was only when they reached O'Connell Street to get transportation to the track that they learned the uprising was in progress and got into it.

Another group from the Dublin suburb of Rathfarnham arrived at the Post Office late, about 1:15 P.M., having gone first to Liberty Hall. As it happened, they chose a dangerous moment to come. Their arrival coincided almost precisely with the approach of the first British troops to the Post Office—a company of Lancers that charged down O'Connell Street on horseback from the north.

The coincidence was as confusing as it was frightening to the Rathfarnham lads. As they approached the building, expecting perhaps to be greeted by cheers from their comrades inside, they were greeted instead by a wild chorus of shouts.

"Lancers! Lancers! The Lancers are coming!"

The ill-uniformed, overloaded Rathfarnham boys knew that they were not Lancers and could never be mistaken for such; they looked up anxiously to find out what provoked the cries and saw the company of proud British hosemen, still two or three blocks away but bearing down toward them. Instead of continuing toward the front door of the Post Office, the Volunteers sensibly ducked into Prince's Street and tried the first door they saw there. It was locked.

Someone inside, behind a fortified window, shouted, "Who are you? Where do you come from?"

When they identified themselves properly, the man inside looked for the key to the door but couldn't find it.

Someone else inside called out, "Watch yourselves! The Lancers!"

A panicky Rathfarnham sub-officer, determined to meet battle properly if he couldn't escape it, shouted to the men, "Line up! Line up!"

A cooler voice from inside said, "Don't line up! Get in here, you bloody fools! Through the windows!"

Though the Rathfarnham men took to this idea eagerly, it was not as simple as it sounded because the windows in that part of the building had not been broken thoroughly. Jagged edges threatened anyone intending to crawl through. A dozen rifle butts attacked the glass as voices inside kept shouting, "Hurry! The Lancers!" Finally the men scrambled over the sills, though many of them were cut and bleeding. And two who failed to make it before the charge of the Lancers had to be carried into the building later, one the victim of a stray bullet, the other shot in the stomach by his own rifle.

The troop of knightly Lancers, their backs erect, approached proudly at a canter from the top of O'Connell Street in columns as straight as their lofty, ceremonial lances. Carbines still holstered, heads fixed high, they declined even to acknowledge the presence of the Dublin rabble and the company of scruffy Rathfarnham Volunteers scurrying out of sight to safety in front of them. They had not been sent to acknowledge. The function of British Lancers was to be acknowledged. The street was their parade ground and anyone within view of them was to recognize that they were the British Empire on parade.

About a hundred yards north of the Post Office, the troop broke columns smartly, fanned out across the street and came to a halt. As the jingle of their trappings ceased, a deep silence fell over the whole street.

Out of a doorway came a Dublin voice shouting, "Look out fer yerselves! The bowsies will mow you down!"

No Lancer even turned his head. One of the horses lifted a front hoof, clopped it on the pavement. Another horse whinnied. The colonel in charge glanced ahead to the right and left at the sandbagged windows in the Post Office and in some of the shops across the street. He raised his eyes toward the rooftops, stared at the two strange flags on the Post Office masts. He saw in the middle of the street ahead a tram the insurgents had overturned for use in the construction of a barricade. The colonel stiffened, reached for his sword, raised it high, and gave a command. The Lancers, still in formation, charged forward.

Inside the Post Office and on the roof, the shouting and confusion had given way to fearful, feverish silence as forty riflemen, their barrels resting on the ledges, began to realize that this revolution to which they had pledged their lives was now approaching the moment when they must fire real bullets into human flesh. They were about to attack a uniform they had known since early childhood as the prime symbol of civil authority. They might have been less nervous had it not been for these minutes they had to wait and think.

On the upper floors, The O'Rahilly spread the word that they should hold their fire until they heard the command. On the ground floor, Connolly spread the same word. The approaching Lancers were now in full view of the men on the roof, whose eagerness to fire was tempered by admiration for the advancing horsemen. They must have known that the insurgents had them in their sights, yet on they came. Though the moment might call for a careful, door-to-door infantry approach, that was not the Lancers' style. Proud cavalrymen should show their strength and courage in the open.

They reached Nelson's Pillar, just opposite the Henry Street corner of the Post Office. The insurgents' plan was to let them come even farther, put them under every gun in the building. But as the squadron passed the pillar, one of the insurgent riflemen lost patience. A shot rang out. Then another. A ragged volley followed as most of the men decided that it was pointless to wait any longer for a command.

Four Lancers toppled from their saddles, three of them dead as they hit the ground, the fourth wounded. A wave of shock passed over the proud troop, as if every man in it had been hit. The ranks broke. What had been a precisely disciplined unit became a milling mass of horses and men, neither charging the unseen enemy nor continuing on out of range, but simply bunching together at the mercy of the insurgents. By some miracle of chance, however, the insurgents' guns became at that moment more merciful, or less accurate, than anyone could have imagined. As the horse of one of the dead Lancers pushed its nose against its master's lifeless body, another ragged volley issued from both sides of the street. The horse fell dead on top of the man's body. Another horse also fell, unseating its rider, but miraculously, no more Lancers were hit. The colonel gave a hasty order to regroup and they retreated at a gallop in the direction from which they had come, the unhorsed Lancer making his way on foot along the sides of the buildings to safety.

An urchin ran into the street and picked up the carbine of one of the fallen men. A shawlie emerged from a doorway and tried to grab it from him, but he was too quick for her. After a raucous exchange of words, she tried again to get the gun away from him. This time the boy swung it at her, clubbing her on the side of the head. As she fell, screaming, he sprinted with the carbine to one of the front windows of the Post Office.

"Here yiz are!" he shouted, flinging it inside.

When the insurgents realized their victory, they cheered as if they had routed the whole British army. One of them, watching the Lancers retreat, shouted, "Look! The Leapordstown races!"

Another said, "If that's the way they attack a fortified building there's some hope for us yet."

The insurgents were not without casualties, however. A rifleman in a building opposite the Post Office was killed in the cross fire, obviously by one of his own men: the Lancers had not fired a shot. And there was the Rathfarnham Volunteer, a sixteen-year-old boy, who was wounded by a stray bullet as he waited his turn to climb into the Post Office. That bullet, too, must have come from a comrade's rifle. There was also the Rathfarnham Volunteer who, in the excitement, accidentally fired his rifle into his own stomach.

The British army came close to losing another man by chance. A bullet from across the street entered the Post Office and just missed the head of the captured lieutenant whom Michael Collins had bound and placed in a phone booth. The lieutenant's bonds were cut now and he was sent, still trembling from his unpleasant experience, upstairs to join the other prisoners.

Although the retreat of the Lancers buoyed the spirits of the men in the Post Office, the three dead bodies and the mortally wounded fourth Lancer victim being carried away by ambulance from the street outside certified in the minds of the insurgents what most of them had already assumed—that the full wrath of England must now descend upon them. Perhaps the Lancers had been sent simply to serve notice on these mischievous subjects that they had better go home and behave before it was too late. After the way the Lancers were received, no one could doubt that it was now too late. They had better be prepared.

Because the Lancer charge had demonstrated the importance of the roof, both as a lookout and as a sniper's perch, several new

men were sent there with rifles, shotguns, and grenades as they
arrived at the Post Office. A few of the roof men were already
finding targets for their bullets, which was ingenious of them
since, as far as anyone else could see, no British soldiers were in
sight. Throughout the building, windows until now unbroken
were smashed and fortified. A makeshift barricade was erected to
protect the Prince's Street gate as a hurried procession of trucks
and carts kept moving through it, loaded with commandeered
supplies. The tempo of activity increased and so did the noise as
officers barked out an unending stream of orders. There were so
few officers that each one, it seemed, had to issue enough orders
for three or four, especially Connolly. He even found time to
order Sean T. O'Kelly out on another errand.

"Take as many copies of the proclamation as you can carry,"
he said, "and post them up around the city."

"Where do we get the paste?" O'Kelly wanted to know.

"Go to hell and make it."

O'Kelly went to the basement of the building, where he found
buckets, brushes, ladders, two hand carts, and a sack of flour with
which to make the paste. Off he went again into the streets of the
area with 200 of the broadsides to post.

Meanwhile, something had to be done about the two Volunteer
gunshot victims. There were no doctors on hand and no infirmary had been set up, so Volunteer Joseph Cripps, who had
been a druggist's assistant, was relieved of his rifle (also a camera
he had brought along when he heard that the uprising had actually begun) and given instead a Red Cross armband. After
helping remove the two wounded men to Jervis Street Hospital,
he returned to help bandage the Rathfarnham men and others
who had been cut by broken window glass.

"Damn those windows," he said, faced with one jagged wound
after another, "they're more dangerous than the British army."

The casualties of the first two hours demonstrated so forcibly
the need for more medical supplies in the Post Office that Cripps
was dispatched on a commandeering mission to the pharmacies in
the area. When he couldn't find everything he needed at the first
shop he favored (Hayes, Conyningham, and Robinson on Henry

Street), he went up the block to another shop and loaded a cart with bandages, slings, disinfectants, and drugs, mostly painkillers. He returned to the Post Office in time to come to the aid of an officer, Lieutenant Liam Clarke (unrelated to Tom Clarke), who had just proven that the homemade grenades, with which every man was oversupplied, actually did explode. Clarke was holding one when it exploded in his face. The result looked at first like tragedy. Patrick Pearse, accompanied by his younger brother Willie, who was often at his heels, rushed to the scene and bent over the wounded man, concerned for his survival. But when the blood was wiped away, Clarke proved to have suffered no more than facial wounds, at which his friends rejoiced, then gradually began to feel uneasy.

"So much for those bloody cannisters," one of them said. "If it didn't blow Liam's head off, the divil little use it is to us."

As Pearse ordered Clarke to the hospital, despite the man's insistence that he stay and fight, some of his comrades took a selection of the "bloody cannisters" out onto the street to test them. When they set them off, against the base of Nelson's Pillar, the foundation did not even tremble, nor was the stone chipped. The only result was a fast-spreading rumor up and down O'Connell Street, and eventually throughout Dublin, that "those eejits are trying now to blow up the pillar."

The whole incident served no other purpose than to call to the attention of a sniper on the Post Office roof a target that would at least pass for an English military man in the absence of any flesh-and-blood English soldiers. The sniper took a pot shot at Lord Nelson, standing firm upon his lofty pedestal, and plucked the nose from his face.

Joseph Plunkett's strength was waning again to such an extent he had to go upstairs and rest, leaving Brennan Whitmore in charge of the table from which Plunkett operated as military planner and communications officer. Before giving way to his exhaustion, however, Plunkett had received from outposts in other parts of the city a series of reports, which he found, on the whole, satisfactory. Every few minutes now, dispatch riders were arriving at the GPO on motorcycles, delivering their messages.

The most exciting report, not yet confirmed, was that several Citizen Army men under Sean Connolly (unrelated to Commandant General James Connolly) had attacked Dublin Castle, the seat of British government in Ireland, had shot a guard, and were apparently in possession of that huge, rambling complex of structures. These men had been assigned to make only a hit-and-run attack on the castle, for it was presumed to be too well guarded to take and too large to defend, then go on to their primary objective, City Hall, which was nearby. It was almost too good to believe they could have taken the castle.

Another Citizen Army detachment under the command of two of James Connolly's close associates, Michael Mallin and Countess Constance Markiewicz (a fanatical Irish patriot despite the un-Irish flavor of her name), had taken St. Stephen's Green and was preparing for attack from any direction.

At the Four Courts on King's Inn Quay, men under Edward Daly (Tom Clarke's brother-in-law), after taking the building, had encountered the company of Lancers escorting supply wagons from the harbor at the North Wall toward Phoenix Park —the same company the Volunteers at O'Connell Bridge had allowed to pass unchallenged. These Lancers had not been so fortunate a second time. Daly's men had opened fire on them, killed two, and driven the others into a building on Charles Street, where they were presently under siege. The wagons they were escorting had apparently been loaded with ammunition.

At Portobello Bridge, a group of Citizen Army men protecting St. Stephen's Green had engaged British troops stationed in Portobello Barracks and were getting support from Thomas Mac-Donagh's unit, which was already in control of the huge Jacob biscuit factory dominating Camden and Aungier Streets.

A party of about twenty men had taken the Mendicity Institution near Usher's Island on the south bank of the Liffey and hoped to hold the difficult position for at least four or five hours, long enough to give the Four Courts garrison time to get established.

Eamonn Ceannt, with only 42 men, had taken over the 52-acre South Dublin Union, a workhouse between the Rialto Bridge and

James's Street, but could hardly be expected to hold it long unless he got reinforcements. And at Boland's mill, Eamon De Valera with 120 men was prepared to cut off the route between Dublin and the harbor at Dun Laoghaire (then Kingstown), where British reinforcements might arrive.

Reports were coming in so rapidly now that it was difficult to distinguish them from the rumors, which were coming in even more rapidly. One minor officer in charge of a position near the Post Office sent in so many messages that Connolly was moved to say, "If that man were standing on his right foot, he would send me a dispatch to inform me he planned shortly to put down his left foot." But both Connolly and Pearse found encouragement in the reports, despite indications that the turnout of men everywhere had been disappointingly low. MacNeill's countermand order had taken an irreparable toll.

As the crowd in O'Connell Street increased so did the problem of managing it. The chief commissioner of the Dublin metropolitan police, having learned that several of his men had been shot, had promptly ordered all the others, the entire force, withdrawn from duty, leaving the streets of the city in the control of either the insurgents or the mob, whichever might prove stronger. Sentries at the front door of the Post Office looked unperturbed as a constant stream of people walked back and forth past them, sometimes brushing against them. Only when the door seemed about to be blocked completely did the sentries push forward, their rifles clutched horizontally in front of them, to gain more room. Occasionally someone would shout, "Here come the soldiers again!" causing short bursts of panic, which would quickly subside when no soldiers were forthcoming.

A man wheeling a bicycle and dressed in working clothes forced his way up to one of the Post Office windows and asked: "What is it you boys're doing in there? Guarding the place against the Sinn Feiners?"

He was not the only person confused by the bizarre proceedings. Clusters of people from O'Connell Bridge to Parnell Monument exchanged rumors, argued their theories, took sides. A University College student named Ernie O'Malley, later to become an Irish revolutionary hero himself but at this time not yet interested in the nationalist movement, arrived in O'Connell Street and asked a man what was causing all the commotion.

"Those boyos, the Volunteers, have seized the Post Office," the man said. "They want nothing less than a Republic." He paused to laugh at the idea. "They've killed some Lancers but they'll soon run away when the soldiers come."

O'Malley watched a detail of men on the Prince's Street side carrying heavy bundles into the building. A man standing beside him said knowingly, "Explosives." Another detail was unloading vegetables. On the roof, sentries patrolled to and fro. As couriers arrived on motor bikes, guards emerged to clear paths for them through the growing crowd.

Up the street, near Nelson's Pillar, lay the Lancers' dead horses, one with its feet in the air. A man standing by said, "Those fellows," pointing toward the Post Office, "are not going to be frightened by a troop of Lancers. They mean business."

A woman sat on the rump of one of the dead horses, her shawl around her head, wisps of hair straggling across her dirty face as she swayed drunkenly and sang:

> Boys in Khaki, Boys in Blue,
> Here's the best of Jolly Good Luck to You.

As people stopped to read the Republican proclamation still held down by stones near the base of the pillar, some looked serious, others laughed or sniggered. O'Malley smiled as he looked at it, then stopped smiling as he read it and began to feel the force of its eloquence.

Patrick Pearse was now standing in front of the Post Office in his green uniform, wearing his green soft hat, his saber dangling from his side as he watched the crowd. Someone shouted his name. He seemed not to hear.

A close friend of The O'Rahilly, Desmond Fitzgerald, arrived on the scene with his wife as Pearse was standing there. Fitzgerald, whose education and accent were English, nevertheless had just served a prison term for Irish revolutionary activity. O'Rahilly had come to pick him up the day he was released from prison, less than a month earlier, and had told him he thought the uprising would take place soon. "Things are moving fast," he had said, though he did not know exactly how fast since he was not privy to the inner councils of the Irish Republican Brotherhood. When it became apparent, late in Easter Week, that the IRB faction planned the uprising for Eastern Sunday, O'Rahilly, like the other more moderate leaders of the Volunteers, was horrified at the scheme—especially at the timing, because in his opinion (and he was the organization's munitions procurement officer) the Volunteers and the Citizen Army, with the resources they had at hand, would make a laughable force to send against the British military, at least until the German aid they expected had definitely arrived. By Easter Saturday, when it became known that the German aid would not arrive, an uprising the next day was unthinkable to him.

Fitzgerald had seen O'Rahilly Easter Sunday evening on the latter's return from his automobile trip to the country spreading the countermand order. O'Rahilly had then expressed his relief that there would be no immediate uprising. He seemed certain of it. Yet on Monday morning, a few hours before the uprising, when Fitzgerald went to his home to tell him it was scheduled to proceed anyway, O'Rahilly had been philosophical.

"If the men are determined to have a rising," he had said, "nothing will stop them."

After Fitzgerald left on bicycle to inform MacNeill of this latest development, O'Rahilly had gone in his car to Liberty Hall. As Fitzgerald and his wife approached the Post Office now, they suspected they would find him there. They saw the Republican flag flying from the roof and Pearse standing on the street outside.

Fitzgerald said to his wife, "This is worth being wiped out for."

Pearse, when he saw them, came forward. He looked, to Fitzgerald, graver than usual. Though there was something of elation in him, there was also a heavy air of responsibility.

Whatever elation Pearse felt may have arisen from the castle report or from seeing this friend of O'Rahilly apparently answering the call to duty. Perhaps it was still not too late to hope the rest of the Volunteers would join the rebellion. He welcomed Fitzgerald warmly.

"O'Rahilly is on the top floor," he said. "I want you to go upstairs with him, as his adjutant." Then, turning to include Mrs. Fitzgerald, he added, "We had some great news a few minutes ago. I understand the Citizen Army has captured the castle. Do you know what you could do? You could take the boys a flag. Imagine an Irish flag flying from the castle."

While his wife hurried off with a brand-new tricolor tucked under her arm, Fitzgerald gaped in wonder and dismay at the great bustle of strange activity inside the Post Office. As he looked around at the apparent chaos, he was greeted by friends and acquaintances who must have been as surprised to see him as they had been to see O'Rahilly. He also encountered, to his amazement, a pair of Swedish sailors who said they had come to join the rebellion because they didn't want to miss a chance to fight the English. They were prepared to fight until Thursday, when their ship was scheduled to leave. They had apparently been taken seriously. They were posted at a window. Other men at other windows were singing the "Soldier's Song." Some were exchanging banter with the girls passing in the street. Guns went off, presumably by accident, but without causing much concern. Fitzgerald made his way as quickly as possible through this incomprehensible ground-floor scene and hurried upstairs to find O'Rahilly.

When he reached the top floor, O'Rahilly saw him and came forward, his smile arising in his eyes and spreading to his entire face.

"They were determined to have a rising," he said, "so here we are."

Fitzgerald asked, "How long do you think we can hold out?"

"By a miracle," O'Rahilly said, "we might last for twenty-four hours, but I don't think we'll go that long."

Fitzgerald considered this estimate extremely optimistic.

After O'Rahilly had shown him through the upper part of the building, including the second-floor commissary, which was now filling up with stacks of commandeered food, they sat down to try to establish some kind of order. They decided that Fitzgerald should handle the provisions and mess; no one else had shown any inclination to do so. O'Rahilly's efforts so far had been toward getting the upper-floor windows manned and fortified, posting snipers and lookouts on the roof, and handling the disposition of weapons and ammunition as they arrived. He had been forced to post guards at the door leading to the roof to prevent the men below from coming up on sightseeing tours. Every few minutes someone on one of the lower floors, or even on the street, would shout, "Here comes the military," and in the scramble to be ready in case it might be true, more guns would go off. It began to look as if one would be safer outside the building than in it.

While O'Rahilly and Fitzgerald talked, Fitzgerald's wife returned from her flag-delivering mission with a harried look on her face and the flag still in her hand. Whoever told Pearse the Citizen Army boys had taken the castle, she said, ought to go have another look. She had arrived there and hurried up to one of the entrances assuming they had possession, but she had soon found herself facing a bayonet in the hands of a khaki-clad British soldier. With the Irish flag under her arm, she had retreated as discreetly as possible. She could assure one and all that the British were as much in control of the castle as they had been for hundreds of years.

O'Rahilly showed no sign of surprise. He appeared not to have believed the report in the first place. He did not pretend to be happy with any part of what was going on around him. The insurgent forces were pitifully small, inadequately armed, and, as it was now obvious to anyone who had been downstairs in the Post Office, dangerously undertrained. The country was not yet in sympathy with their aims and was not likely to support them. It had been a great mistake, in his opinion, to precipitate the uprising at this moment. It was only a matter of hours before they should all be wiped out.

Despite his romantic commitment to Irish independence, O'Rahilly was essentially a life-loving man who favored practical methods and found no satisfaction in courting death simply as a gesture of protest. The head of a County Kerry clan (hence the title "The" O'Rahilly, which he assumed), he had embraced the Gaelic and Republican movements as a young man (he was now forty-one), and it was he who first conceived the idea of founding the Irish Volunteers. Because he had an independent income of £900 per year, he could afford an automobile (which he actually owned jointly with one of his sisters) and was therefore considered wealthy by most of the other Republican leaders. He used to take trips through the countryside, tossing pennies to small children with admonitions in Gaelic to be good, gathering young people around the car in the evening to sing or tell jokes in Gaelic. His own Gaelic was not as good as theirs, and that became one of the jokes. In latter years his Gaelic had improved because he had no timidity in using it and because, through foreign travel, he had developed a facility with languages. He had once designed a modification of the Gaelic alphabet. He had also designed the Dublin house in which he lived with his wife and five children and had made with his own hands some of the furniture in it. During a sojourn in America, he had invented an automatic warning gate for railroad crossings.

After the Volunteers were organized, he had taken charge of the task of arming them, and in doing so, he had sometimes spent more of his own money than he could afford. He had recently said to a friend who was a priest, "I suppose, father, I'll be accounted a fool from the worldly point of view. I am giving this movement all my time, all my thoughts day and night, my money as far as I can. I do not suppose I'll ever have a fortune to leave my children, but one thing I shall try to leave them—the memory of a father of whom they need not feel ashamed."

As a result of his devotion to the movement, he had developed a close friendship with Patrick Pearse. He felt now that despite their differences about when, how, and under what circumstances an uprising should take place, Pearse had betrayed that friendship by going ahead secretly and withholding from him the IRB plans. It seemed clear to him that neither Pearse nor the other leaders thought he would have the courage to appear when the fighting began. They must have considered him simply a rich dilettante playing at revolution. He was also outraged at their apparent kidnapping of his friend Bulmer Hobson. That was a matter he would have to settle soon, but for the moment he didn't want even to speak to any of them. When he and Fitzgerald had worked out what seemed to him satisfactory arrangements for managing the upper floors of the building, he sent Fitzgerald downstairs to get their approval.

Pearse was so receptive to O'Rahilly's arrangements that Fitzgerald could sense in him the deep guilt and embarrassment he must feel about O'Rahilly.

"Isn't O'Rahilly a marvelous man?" Pearse said.

When Fitzgerald, changing the subject, asked him if there were any prospects of victory, Pearse hesitated, then spoke in general terms about the situation without making any cheerful or exaggerated predictions. Though he had accepted the necessity of living a lie by withholding from O'Rahilly and the rest of the moderates the plans for the uprising, he could not bring himself to tell an outright lie even at a time like this, when, as commander in chief, he had almost a duty to stimulate optimism. As their conversation came to a close, he said once more, "Isn't O'Rahilly a marvelous man?"

When Fitzgerald reported to Tom Clarke, he found him clearly elated at the realization that Irishmen, however few in number, had actually risen in arms against England, that this generation was not going to pass meekly without reasserting the Irish right to self-government. He was not, on the surface at least, bitter or vindictive in his attitude toward the English, despite those fifteen years in British prisons, during which he maintained his sanity by copying the entire Old and New Testaments twice in shorthand. He was simply afire with zeal for Irish independence. He was bitter, however, toward his fellow Irishmen and fellow Republicans who had propagated the countermand order. And that bitterness perhaps included O'Rahilly. Yet time and again he assured Fitzgerald that of all men he admired O'Rahilly.

"What do you think of our chances of victory?" Fitzgerald asked him.

"Imagine what a fight we could have put up," Clarke said, "if there had been no countermand order."

He did not say, however, that even under those circumstances they could have hoped for victory. About their outlook as it stood, he made no predictions.

After reporting to Clarke, Fitzgerald located James Connolly, who quickly approved of whatever O'Rahilly thought best for the upper floors of the building. Fitzgerald and Connolly talked for only a short time, because Connolly was busy and Fitzgerald could not speak to him freely, never having met him before. Fitzgerald felt it would take very little under the circumstances to make Connolly angry.

Pearse walked up to Fitzgerald with a sizable sheaf of ten-pound notes, accompanied by the Volunteer who had laid hands on the manager of the Metropole Hotel.

"This young man has been out commandeering food," Pearse said. "Since you'll be in charge of provisions, will you go back with him to the places from which he took things and settle accounts."

When Fitzgerald and the Volunteer entered the Metropole, they found the manager still indignant.

"That young man assaulted me," he said.

The young man said, "I did no such thing."

"You did. You took hold of me."

"I don't call that an assault."

Before Fitzgerald had time to settle the argument, another man took hold of his arm, pulled him aside, indentified himself as a newspaper reporter, and asked for a statement.

The manager grabbed Fitzgerald's other arm and said, "I won't accept this kind of treatment."

Fitzgerald began to explain he had come there to pay for what the requisitioning party had taken.

The newsman again asked him for a statement. The manager became more indignant. The Volunteer smiled sheepishly and shrugged. Fitzgerald, becoming impatient, escorted the reporter out of the hotel, then forced upon the manager the amount of money he had coming and hastened to depart.

The swelling O'Connell Street crowd was beginning to develop an ominous character. As people became gradually aware of the withdrawal of the police, a mood of license, fostered by contempt for the play soldiers who had captured the Post Office, began to permeate the festive atmosphere. Bitterness was added to the contempt when women out of the slums lined up at the side door of the Post Office, where they had always collected their "separation money." They presented a problem for which the insurgents had no happy solution.

"Separation money" was the term used for the stipend the British government offered to those whose sons or husbands were serving in His Majesty's armed forces. Because there were about 150,000 such Irishmen in 1916, most of them from poorer families, the gathering of shawl-enshrouded slum women at the Post Office door was soon sizable and restless. But there was only one thing to tell them.

The sentries at the door kept trying to explain, "You're no longer ruled by the English. You're citizens of the Irish Republic now. There'll be no more separation money."

This patriotic message was not well received. As its full purport sank in, a rich Dublin patois began to fill the air.

"Bastards!"

"Lousers!"

"Shite-hawks!"

"Bowsies!"

"Wait till the military gets here. They'll take care o'yiz."

"Wait till me husband comes back from France. He'll take care o'yiz all by himself."

The sentries tried to be polite. "Please go away," they said. "There's nothing we can do."

The mood of the women was not improved by an unfortunate incident that took place about three o'clock. A young Volunteer was sorting a basketful of supplies at a Henry Street window when one of his homemade grenades (packaged in a Meadowland cigarette tin) fell out of the basket and down behind a pair of hot pipes. It began to sizzle; smoke arose from it. The soldier turned in fright to run, thought suddenly about the danger to the men around him, came back and rooted behind the hot pipes until he got hold of the cigarette tin, then flung it out the window into the street, where the shawlies were gathered, shouting for their separation money. Luckily, it was about as effective as most of the other homemade grenades. When it exploded, it reduced the women to silence for a moment, but it did not injure any of them. And its explosion was a mere rumble compared to the furious uproar that followed, as the women quickly concluded that the bloody Sinn Feiners were now out to kill them all. Their fury seemed to raise them beyond fear. They bombarded the men in the Post Office with a salvo of obscenities and showed no inclination to disperse. A woman at the edge of the crowd, who was apparently not one of them, made the mistake of objecting to their language. She soon found herself in a hair-pulling fight with a shawlie who objected to her objection. The men in the Post Office windows, relieved at this diversion of the crowd's attention, cheered the clumsy battle.

The O'Rahilly climbed up to the roof to inspect the snipers' positions, and moving from man to man, he warned each not to fire without orders. One of the men pointed out to him a British officer in the tower of the Amiens Street station, three blocks away, looking toward them through field glasses.

"You needn't worry about him," O'Rahilly said. He pointed to Nelson's Pillar directly in front of them, with the admiral's statue standing high on its pedestal. "His Lordship here will screen you if they fire this way. So don't fire at them. You'll give away your position."

Then, as he turned to leave he added, perhaps in sober recollection of all the wild shots taken at the Lancers, "Besides which, you'd probably miss him anyway."

That glimpse of one British uniform two blocks away left O'Rahilly with the question that was eating at everyone in the Post Office. Where were the British forces? Why hadn't they attacked? Perhaps they had been twice deceived. When they sent the Lancers prancing down the street, they must have thought they were dealing with only a handful of men. And when they learned how the Lancers had been received, they must have decided, just as wrongly, that they were dealing with an army. It was amusing to contemplate the British general staff planning an attack against a few pathetic men scattered around Dublin, as if they were planning an attack against ten German divisions on the western front. But if the British were deceived about the strength of the insurgents, O'Rahilly was convinced they would not be long deceived. They had only to send one man walking past the Post Office in civilian clothes to find out how ill-prepared the insurgents actually were. By nightfall, the British would have the situation analyzed and the attack would come. O'Rahilly was certain of that.

A restless, impatient mood was beginning to permeate the entire Post Office as everyone wondered at the continued absence of British troops. The insurgents, though almost all innocent of battle, were now reconciled to it and ready for it. Although they might dread it, they were eager to get on with it, to get it done. Waiting for action tightened their nerves, especially since they knew so little about what was happening outside the immediate vicinity of their makeshift fortress.

Connolly, aware that he had to have instant communication with the roof of the building if he was to receive any warning of British troop movements, assigned a Volunteer named Liam Daly to improvise a telephone line. Daly had once told him he was a phone operator, and it was soon apparent he knew what he was doing. Within a short time he had Connolly talking to the men on the roof. It was not from there, however, that the first definite indication came of the British closing in on the Post Office.

At 3:30 Connolly sent a small contingent of men south across O'Connell Bridge to reinforce the pitiful garrison that for a while had been thought to hold the Castle but was now known to be holding the nearby City Hall with some difficulty. The men advanced westward along Fleet Street in the belief that the Dublin telephone exchange there had also been taken earlier by some of their comrades. Unfortunately, the telephone exchange apparently had been inadvertently overlooked. At Temple Bar, a few friendly civilians who were out to watch the fun told the insurgents they were heading for trouble. They could not long

doubt the reliability of this information. As they moved along
Fleet Street, a rude barrage of rifle fire greeted them from the
exchange. They fell back into the nearest doorways to consider
strategy. Another, more convincing, barrage of bullets bit into
the pavement in front of them to help them make up their minds.
Prudently the small squad of insurgents returned to the Post
Office with the sad news that the plan to capture the telephone
exchange had gone awry and that the enemy was firmly lodged
there, just a few short blocks away.

Convinced now that a British attack was imminent, Connolly
sent fifteen commandeered vehicles with written orders to evacuate the indefensible Liberty Hall and transfer to the Post Office
all the supplies and munitions still stored there. The Post Office
was gradually filling up with latecomers, so he was also able to
send small detachments to augment MacDonagh's forces at
Jacob's biscuit factory and the pocket garrison occupying
Gilbey's distillery on Fairview Strand. Scouts reported back to
him that the men on their way to the distillery encountered fire
from British infantry advancing toward Annesley Bridge and that
after a short skirmish the British had retreated. Connolly was
pleased but not deluded by this surprising bit of news.

While the insurgents expected O'Connell Street to become a
battleground at any moment, the crowds that swarmed back and
forth across its broad expanse considered it more of a play-
ground, a fairground, a treasure ground offering infinite tempta-
tion now that the police had retired. Since noon these people had
been pouring forth from one of Europe's most dismal slums to
stare greedily into the shop windows at the expensive dresses and
suits, fur coats, watches, jewels, cameras, liquors, shoes, linens,
and hundreds of other beautiful items they had often dreamed of
owning. What was to prevent them from owning such things
now? Not a policeman in sight. If the dirty Sinn Feiners could
walk into shops and carry things away, why shouldn't the
"dacent" citizens of Dublin do the same? At least that would put
things in the right hands—keep the bloody rebels from grabbing
everything. These notions must already have seeped into hundreds of minds by the time the first shop window, at Noblett's

candy store, directly across O'Connell Street from the Post Office, cracked and shattered under the acquisitive pressure of the mob.

Neither the shards of glass that rained into the windowful of candy nor the jagged edges of glass still jutting from the window frame gave pause to the grasping hands reaching for forbidden sweets. Shawlies with elbows almost as sharp as the glass and urchins nimble enough to scoot around them (using their hats as containers) jostled and grabbed for the spilling piles of candy until dozens of bleeding fingers and wrists had speckled the chocolates, mints, fruit bonbons, and Turkish delight with drops of red. The sight of blood in no way diminished the crowd's appetite for the candy.

A drunken old woman shouted, "They're raiding Noblett's," and the cry spread down the street.

Hundreds who heard it came charging to the scene, increasing the pressure of human bodies in front of the shop to such a point that people on their knees, picking up stray pieces of candy from the sidewalk, were unable to get back to their feet. The stampede to reach this now-dwindling fountain of free sweets became so frantic that lives were endangered. People cried out in panic as they were squeezed helplessly against each other or against the sides of buildings, scarcely able to breathe. A calamity was averted only because someone in the throng had either the good sense or the perversity to shout, "The soldiers are coming!"

Like a sponge compressed to its inner limits then let go, the mass of people suddenly expanded in all directions as everyone scrambled for safety. Into North Earl Street and Henry Street and all the side streets they raced, but the largest segment ran down O'Connell Street toward the bridge. Because the Lancers had arrived from the top of O'Connell Street, there apparently was an assumption that the next visit from the military would come from the same direction.

When the candy-chewing people at the bridge, after an impatient wait, still saw no sign of soldiers and realized the warning cry had been just another false alarm, they returned to Noblett's in earnest and, as if angered at being so shamefully deceived, went through the display window into the shop itself, which they proceeded to strip down to its last bonbon.

It quickly became obvious that Noblett's had too little to satisfy the entire mob. Candy was, after all, a childish objective. Adults wanted more substantial items. Fortunately, there were enough shops to satisfy every taste, and there were no longer any fears or inhibitions about breaking and browsing in them. Dunn's hat shop was the next to go, and Frewen and Ryan hosiery shop, and the Cable boot company, and the Lemon company, another confectionary. Men threw away their ragged caps and strutted out of Dunn's in silk toppers, boaters, or bowlers. An urchin came out wearing a variety of hats (all too large for him), one on top of the other. The first person he approached knocked every one of them off his head. Women standing in the street raised their skirts to daring heights so they could pull, up their unwashed legs, the first silk stockings they had ever worn. After admiring the feel of stockings, they donned their new satin slippers or knee-high Russian boots. Two women emerged from the Cable boot shop fighting each other for possession of a large box, which proved to contain a variety of shoes. The woman who prevailed found to her annoyance that they were all for the left foot. As more hats came forth from Dunn's, the men began playfully knocking them off each other's heads; before there was time to pick them up, in case anyone were so inclined, urchins would scurry in to kick them down the street like footballs. But while some of the looters went playfully and aimlessly on their free shopping rounds, others were more serious and systematic, carrying away wholesale lots of goods on their backs or in carts. If, between them, they didn't clean a shop down to its bare shelves in a half-hour, it could only mean they held that shop's merchandise in low esteem.

From the windows of the Post Office, the insurgent leaders watched first in disbelief, then in horror, as this scene began to develop. Was it possible that so many people—the very people they were offering their lives to emancipate from British rule—could shamelessly show themselves to be such a disgrace to Ireland? The Irish insurgent movement had become, in recent years, almost puritanically scrupulous. The policy of giving cash or receipts for commandeered provisions was an example. In addition, the men were trained to have the highest respect for life, property, and womanhood—including English womanhood. And they were urgently discouraged from drinking. They had been warned that if so much as a bottle of stout were removed from any premises they might occupy during the rising, they would be held severely accountable for it. Too many Irish rebellions in past centuries had been subdued because of drunken leaders or drunken informers.

A frown of pain covered the face of Patrick Pearse as he watched this licentious carnival. He said nothing. When others turned to him, apparently expecting of him some miracle that would erase the scene before them, he looked away as if to hide the anguish on his face. The rapine horrified him not because he lacked sympathy for these ragged, greedy slum dwellers or because he was unaware of the poverty that might be blamed for their exesses but precisely because he knew their condition. In the pages of an IRB publication called *Irish Freedom* he had written a short time before:

> My instinct is with the landless man against the lord of lords, and with the breadless man against the master of millions . . . I calculate that one third of the people of Dublin are underfed, that half the children attending Irish primary schools are ill-nourished. Inspectors of the National Board will tell you that there is no use in visiting primary schools in Ireland after one or two in the afternoon; the children are too weak and drowsy with hunger to be capable of answering intelligently. I suppose there are twenty thousand families in Dublin in whose domestic economy milk and butter are all but unknown; black tea and dry bread are their staple articles of diet. There are many thousand fireless hearthplaces in Dublin on the bitterest days of winter . . . Twenty thousand families live in one-room tenements. It is common to find two or three families occupying the same room; and sometimes one of the families will have a lodger!

He had been convinced these people would see ultimately, in the struggle for independence, an opportunity to enrich their meager lives. The rebellion was an occasion to which he had expected they would arise. Even the most abject poverty could not explain to him their failure to comprehend the transcendent importance and glory of this day in Irish history.

Whereas the outbreak of looting stunned Pearse, it offended Sean MacDermott. Though he was so badly crippled that every step gave him severe pain, he nevertheless came rushing down from the second floor of the Post Office in a rage and, supported by his cane, limped across the street into the thickest crowd of looters, demanding, then reasoning, then pleading with them to stop disgracing the fight for Ireland's freedom. They were too busy even to pause and laugh at him.

O'Rahilly's men on the roof poured buckets of water onto another mob, which was directing its attention to the Henry Street shops. Riflemen on the first floor fired two volleys over the heads of these people, all to no avail.

As James Connolly looked out at them, he had more reason for bitterness and frustration than anyone else in the Post Office; these were his people, the depressed working class to whom he had devoted his life as a labor organizer. When he fought for Ireland, Connolly was fighting for Ireland's poor. In his book *Labour in Irish History*, he had written: "Only the Irish working class remain as the incorruptible inheritors of the fight for freedom in Ireland." It was becoming painfully evident now that some of the people he championed had a more liberal concept of freedom than Connolly himself. He reacted to their behavior with the anger of a father toward errant children. When commands and threats and volleys over their heads proved to no avail, he sent Sean T. O'Kelly out to deal with them at the head of a dozen men armed with rifles and police batons.

O'Kelly launched his hopeful project on the other side of O'Connell Street from the Post Office at Clery's department store, whose gates and doors had already been jimmied open and windows smashed. Clery's was a large establishment offering a wide variety to the collective ambitions of the mob. When O'Kelly and his men entered, they might have thought they were breaking in on a spring clearance sale in which the customers, forced to shift for themselves without benefit of salesgirls, made their selections impulsively, with no more concern for sizes than for prices. People were grabbing up the unprecedented bargains by the batch. When O'Kelly ordered them to stop, they paid no attention. When his men began persuading them, with batons, that they ought to stop, they did so reluctantly, making hurried exits with what they had. Some ran upstairs, the baton-wielding Volunteers following them like avenging floorwalkers. Conversation was hasty but pungent.

"Bloody Sinn Feiners, yer a disgrace to yer own people."

"The soldiers'll bate yer heads in when they get here."

"Don't touch me. I'm an honest citizen, lookin' aroun' fer me wife."

"You bastards can take what yiz like, I see, but a mother with six little ones can't even be left with a few trifles God put in her way."

After a campaign of shoving and skull tapping, accompanied by a chorus of yelps and curses, O'Kelly and his squad finally cleared everyone out of Clery's and moved on to the next shop that needed their attention, but by the time they had cleared three or four more establishments, they looked back to find Clery's again overrun. People were swarming like bees through the street, loaded with treasure. Never had anyone seen them so industrious. In hopeless resignation, O'Kelly and his men finally returned to the Post Office to face Connolly.

"You couldn't manage that job," O'Kelly said to him, "with 200 men."

Connolly asked, "Did you shoot anybody?"

"Only over their heads."

"That'll do no good at all," Connolly said. "Unless a few of them are shot, you'll never stop them. I'll have to send someone else to do the job right."

But having made the remark, he did nothing to effectuate it, turning instead to some other matter, leaving O'Kelly to stand there sheepishly as if he had somehow failed the cause of Ireland by failing to shoot a few looters.

A priest from the Pro-Cathedral, blazing with anger, came into the Post Office to protest the looting, as did Ireland's most prominent pacifist, Francis Sheehy-Skeffington, but neither could offer a practical suggestion for stopping it, and they didn't stay long. Sheehy-Skeffington went into the street and tried for some time to reason with the crowds. It was not an effective method. The looting continued.

Despite the chaos outside, a semblance of order was beginning to emerge inside the Post Office. Latecomers were still arriving, some of them to be reassigned to the various garrisons throughout the city. Commandeered provisions and supplies by the truckload were filling up every available room and unused corner. Desmond Fitzgerald had begun selecting people for mess-hall duty, though he had not yet found anyone who knew how to run so large a commissary. And on the ground floor, a munitions section had been set up to load shotgun cases, pass out ammunition, handle explosives, and inspect rifles. The inspection and adjustment of rifles had become a matter of life and death. Many of the latecomers were quite inexperienced in handling firearms. One whole company, thirty-five to forty men, had arrived with their rifles loaded and the safety catches of some apparently off. People in their vicinity had found life a gamble for a while. Most of the insurgent guns were old, with temperamental triggers, and demanded gentle care even in experienced hands. With alarming frequency, bullets were still flying around the building at random. An eighteen-year-old Volunteer named Ernest Nunan, whose father (an Irish Republican Brotherhood member in England) had sent him and his brother Sean to Dublin for the uprising, was stationed at a ground-floor window when he felt moisture on his body. He looked down to find it was his own blood. He couldn't understand how it had happened, for he had felt no impact or pain. Apparently one of the flying bullets had grazed him. He had the wound dressed and returned to duty.

The O'Rahilly's sister Anna came into the Post Office, asked for her brother, and was directed to the top floor. They talked awhile. She did not favor his participation in the uprising, especially under the conditions that prevailed. O'Rahilly, however, had no intention of deserting the fight. He wrote a hasty note to his family and gave it to her to deliver. On her way out of the Post Office, she encountered Patrick Pearse.

She took hold of his arm and said, "This is all your fault, you know." Then she turned and left. Pearse gazed after her, silently absorbing the blow she had dealt him.

About five o'clock, the first members of the Irish Volunteers' women's auxiliary, Cumann na mBan, began arriving in their smart green uniforms with white and orange sashes, properly militarized by the addition of Sam Browne belts plus knives and revolvers. They had reported to the Citizen Army unit in St. Stephen's Green, but there were already several girls in service there, so they were sent on to the Post Office. Pearse assigned some of them to the hospital section and sent the others upstairs to the commissary, where Desmond Fitzgerald was looking for all the help he could get.

Among Fitzgerald's lesser problems were the prisoners taken so far—the British lieutenant who had been tied up in the phone booth, where he had missed by an inch stopping a stray bullet, and the enlisted men who had been forcibly relieved of their task of "guarding" the Post Office with empty rifles. Though the insurgents now designated these men prisoners of war, they allowed them, with characteristic Irish generosity, the freedom of the second floor. Three of the prisoners had shown their appreciation by offering to help in the commissary, but the lieutenant and one of the men were less cooperative, thanks to their thirst. The lieutenant had gotten hold of what must have been a sizable supply of brandy. By this time he could scarcely stand on his feet, yet he kept demanding more. Fitzgerald refused. The lieutenant insisted. Fitzgerald began to lose his patience. Finally, with tears in his eyes, the lieutenant pleaded for more. Fitzgerald began to see that terror made the man drink. Pitying him and embarrassed for him, Fitzgerald turned away.

While the officer continued to shout for brandy, the only truculent enlisted man shouted for stout.

"I'm one of Jim Larkin's men," he insisted. "Is there no stout for one of Jim Larkin's men?"

Since Jim Larkin was James Connolly's predecessor as head of the Transport and General Workers' Union, his "men" were more likely to be in the Irish Citizen Army than in the British army. Fitzgerald kept saying there was no more stout, but the man had already taken too much of it to be convinced.

Meanwhile, the Scottish sergeant of the Post Office guard, who had been grazed by a bullet when the insurgents invaded the second floor, had returned from the hospital where his wound was dressed. Though he need not have come back to the Post Office, he insisted on doing so because that was where he had been assigned. He seemed puzzled and offended to find himself a prisoner now, when he was only doing his duty. Peering out one of the windows, he saw a priest in the street trying to exert some influence over the mob.

"I'm no religion no more!" The sergeant exclaimed. "Look at the people of Dublin coming to rescue us, and the priest pushing them back."

Louise Gavan Duffy, a friend of Pearse's who had worked for him as a teacher at St. Ita's, his school for girls, and who had been one of the founders of Cumann na mBan, arrived at the Post Office, not because she had received a call to duty but because she had heard the fight was on and the place was in rebel hands. She looked for Pearse, knowing none of the other leaders, and quickly found him on the ground floor.

"I don't agree with what you're doing," she said. "The way things stand, you haven't a chance of success."

He listened courteously, looking deeply into her face as she spoke. When she was finished he said, "Are you here to stay and help us?"

"Yes, of course. If there's to be a fight, I want to be in it."

"They need you upstairs in the commissary," he said.

Joseph Plunkett, back on duty now, refreshed after his rest but still pale and weak, called for Fergus O'Kelly, who had received rudimentary instruction in the use of a wireless at the Plunkett family estate in the Dublin suburb of Kimmage, where many of the Volunteers from England had been trained. As communications officer, Plunkett was distressed at the insurgents' uncertainty of contact with each other and with the world at large.

The motorcycle couriers who were now carrying messages back and forth between the various garrisons would no longer be able to move so freely when the British forces began occupying and barricading the streets. Meanwhile, it was important to tell the world that the capital of Ireland was, for the first time in 750 years, in the hands of Irishmen. That message had to be gotten through, especially to the United States, from which much of the Irish Republican Brotherhood's financial support and direction came. Plunkett ordered O'Kelly to take a squad of men, occupy the school of telegraphy on the other side of O'Connell Street, and get its equipment into working condition. The assignment was not expected to be easy, for British authorities had closed the school at the beginning of the European war to prevent the possibility of its being used clandestinely for German purposes. Key parts of the institution's wireless apparatus had been dismantled and removed; the doors had been sealed.

Plunkett needn't have bothered with the crippled equipment in the wireless school had it not been for a disastrous incident the previous week, Good Friday night, which was reported in Monday's edition of the *Freeman's Journal*, on the same page as the cryptic story about the capture of the "stranger of unknown nationality," who was actually Sir Roger Casement. To all but the leaders of the insurrection, the second story was as puzzling as the Casement story. It was dated "Tralee, Saturday Evening" and headed:

KERRY TRAGEDY
THREE MEN DROWNED
TWO BODIES RECOVERED

A tragic accident is reported from Killorglin. Three men, whose names are unknown, motoring from Limerick, were drowned in Ballykissane Quay, near Killorglin last night, the motor having jumped over the bridge into the river.

Tralee, Sunday

The bodies of two unknown men were recovered from the River Laune near Killorglin last evening. They are described as of the labouring class. Each had a revolver and some rounds of ammunition and the Sinn Fein badge. The body of the third victim has not been recovered yet.

The story of the three men drowned at Ballykissane was the story of another missed opportunity in the preparation for the rebellion. By Monday the insurgent leaders had heard from their contacts in County Kerry all the frustrating details of the tragedy. Good Friday morning, Joseph Plunkett and Sean Mac-Dermott had sent five men on a mission to Cahirciveen, Waterville, where there was a government wireless station. They were to take the station, dismantle the equipment, then set up the transmitter in Tralee, in the hope of contacting the *Aud*, the German munitions ship expected Saturday or Sunday. The fact that the *Aud* had arrived Thursday and on Friday morning was already settling into the depths outside Queenstown harbor doomed this primary aspect of the mission to failure from the start, but it need not have foreclosed a secondary benefit, the possession of all the radio equipment Plunkett so badly needed now in Dublin to set up a dependable communications system.

The five men Plunkett and MacDermott had sent on the mission separated into two cars when they reached Killarney. In one car was a local driver who did not know the route to Cahirciveen, plus three of the five men, only one of whom claimed to know the route. As they passed through Killorglin Friday night, they took a wrong turn and headed unknowingly toward Ballykissane, where the road ended, abruptly, at the end of a pier on the River Laune. Apparently without ever suspecting they were on the wrong road, they drove off the end of the pier into deep water. Only the driver survived. When he emerged from the water, he fell into the right hands, fortunately for the insurgents, and had so far managed to escape questioning by the police. But the opportunity to capture the government wireless equipment at Cahirciveen had gone down with the three men who drowned. Therefore it was with only a forlorn hope that Plunkett sent Fergus O'Kelly across O'Connell Street to work on the crippled equipment at the wireless school.

O'Kelly took with him six men, including John O'Connor, who was a qualified electrician, and Arthur Shields, a prominent Abbey Theatre actor who later became internationally famous, as did his brother Barry Fitzgerald, both on the stage and screen. Breaking into the building, O'Kelly and his men found that the school's apparatus, a 1½ kilowatt ship's transmitter and receiver, had been disconnected but apparently not altogether dismantled. The antenna on the roof had been pulled down and all parts removed except the poles and the clamps to support them. But when O'Connor began, with commandeered equipment, to rebuild and restore the antennas, he soon found out where the British were. Snipers' bullets from south of the Liffey, at or near Trinity College, began skipping and whistling past him on the roof. The restoration of the antenna had to be postponed until the dead of night.

Meanwhile, O'Kelly, noticing that the building housing the wireless school was dominated by the pagoda dome of the Dublin Bread Company building two doors away, sent a message to Connolly suggesting that the DBC building also be occupied to protect the wireless. Connolly went even further. He sent men to occupy the entire block of buildings directly across O'Connell Street from the GPO.

Late in the afternoon, one of the snipers on the Post Office roof got hold of a copy of the just-released proclamation issued by Lord Wimborne, the viceroy, which was now circulating through the building. The sniper began declaiming it, in the stentorian tones he thought appropriate for a viceroy, to a pair of fellow snipers on the roof of the Tower bar across the street.

Whereas an attempt, instigated and designed by the foreign enemies of our king and country to incite rebellion in Ireland, and thus endanger the safety of the United Kingdom, has been made by a reckless, though small body of men, who have been guilty of insurrectionary acts in the city of Dublin:

Now we, Ivor Churchill, Baron Wimborne, Lord-Lieutenant-General and Governor-General of Ireland, do hereby warn all His Majesty's subjects that the sternest measures are being, and will be taken for the prompt suppression of the existing disturbances and the restoration of order:

And we do hereby enjoin all loyal and law-abiding citizens to abstain from any acts or conduct which might interfere with the action of the Executive Government, and, in particular, we

warn all citizens of the danger of unnecessarily frequenting the
streets or public places or of assembling in crowds.

Given under our seal, on the 24th day of April, 1916.

Wimborne

"Ah, he's an ould cod," one of the listeners shouted. "Send us
more grenades."

Early in the evening, most of the leaders, O'Rahilly not included, had tea together in the GPO commissary. Clarke and
MacDermott questioned men who had been out during the afternoon about reactions to the uprising in other parts of the city. At
the mention of looting, the leaders did not conceal their anger,
frustration, and even personal sorrow. But they laughed as Sean
T. O'Kelly told them stories of his adventures commandeering
supplies. Pearse did not participate in the laughter. He would stay
awhile, then leave, then return. Sometimes he had short,
whispered talks with MacDermott, Clarke, or Plunkett. With
him at almost all times now was his younger brother Willie.
After everyone had eaten, the doctor who had performed throat
surgery on Plunkett two weeks earlier arrived to examine his
patient. The others, sensitive to the serious, even terminal, nature
of Plunkett's tubercular affliction, politely left the room. The
doctor stayed on alone with Plunkett for almost an hour, talking
in a surprisingly casual way about the uprising.

Pearse, in the meantime, was increasingly worried about any
men in the Post Office who might not be ready spiritually for the
very strong possibility of their deaths. They had no chaplain: the
Republican movement at the time was no more popular with the
clergy than it was with the majority of Irishmen. Most members
of the Volunteers had been instructed by their immediate commanders in the days before the uprising to get to confession and
communion before Easter. Indeed, British intelligence agents, had
they been sufficiently alert, could have predicted a military show-
down of some sort simply by counting male heads in Dublin
chapels Easter Saturday evening. The confessionals had been full
of men and boys that night, all anxious to get themselves into a
state of grace by morning, because they had heard convincing
rumors about the "maneuver" scheduled for the next day but had

not yet heard about MacNeill's order countermanding it. Pearse could feel satisfied, therefore, that the majority of the men who came out for the uprising, despite the countermand, had received the sacraments within the previous two or three days and were therefore ready to meet their maker if that eventuality should arise. Yet there were some who had missed their opportunities, and this was a matter of extreme concern to Pearse, who had himself gone to Dominick Street church Easter Saturday morning, at one of his few free moments during that hectic weekend, and talked a priest there into giving him holy communion even on the one morning of the year when Catholics do not ordinarily receive it. When he learned there were men in the Post Office who had not even gone to confession recently, he sent a messenger to the Pro-Cathedral, just two blocks away, to ask for a priest. Father John Flanagan, a curate attached to the archdiocese, answered the call at nine o'clock and was given a room at the ground-floor rear of the Post Office, where he was kept busy hearing confessions until 11:30.

In the streets, the looting continued through the evening hours, for there were many shops still unplundered. Even those establishments near the Post Office that had been fairly well emptied kept drawing gleaners and children who made the rounds in search of worthwhile items that might have been overlooked. Some of the children had found a batch of fireworks in one of the shops and were setting off as dangerous a display as they could contrive near the Cable boot shop, next door to the Imperial Hotel and across the street from the Post Office. At 9:30, the shop was in flames and a crowd had gathered to watch it burn. The fire was gaining momentum on the lower floors when one man in the crowd, William Redmond-Howard (who happened to be a nephew of John Redmond, leader of the Irish party in the British Parliament), noticed a light behind a curtained window on the top floor. It occurred to him, as it had apparently not occurred to anyone else, that people might be living up there unaware of the disaster developing beneath them. He ran to the stairway door of the building, found it locked, and, when he got no response by pounding on it, called for help from the crowd.

The shoulders of three men against the door brought no immediate result. However, their noise did. An angry man put his head out of a top-floor window.

"What the hell's going on down there?" he demanded.

"The place is on fire!" Redmond-Howard shouted, quite unnecessarily now.

"My God!" The man cried. "There are women and children here!"

Finally the stairway door opened and Redmond-Howard led the charge to the top floor, through the smoke and perilously close to the flames. Within a short time, all the able-bodied people were out of the building. Then, however, the rescuers found themselves confronted by a more difficult case—a woman in labor who was so distraught she refused to leave her bed. They made the almost fatal mistake of arguing with her. They were still arguing with her, and losing, when the fire brigade arrived. The captain wasted no time in discussion. He simply told his men to remove her. Though part of the staircase had caught fire by now and the screaming woman fought them all the way, the firemen managed to carry her downstairs to safety.

This dramatic scene concluded, the crowd settled down to watch the firemen fight the flames, which they did to such advantage that some of the onlookers must have decided they had better take measures lest they run out of entertainment. By the time the brigade had the Cable boot shop fire under control, a few of the boyos on the sidelines had managed to start a second one, in another shoe store nearby.

In the Post Office, the concern about communications continued to nag Plunkett and Pearse. The wireless Fergus O'Kelly and his men were trying to repair in the school across the street would not be ready until morning at best. Meanwhile, there were only the most wishful of rumors about reactions to the uprising in country districts. Did anyone outside Dublin even know it had actually begun? Had any of the Volunteers outside Dublin risen in support? It might make a difference. About this time, a group of older Volunteers who had awaited the call at a meeting place in Parnell Street and a company of thirty Hibernian Rifles (an independent nationalist group affiliated with the Ancient Order of Hibernians) who had waited in a house on Frederick Street arrived at the Post Office eager to serve the cause. Among the Hibernian Rifles was a man named J. J. Walsh who knew Morse code. He sat down at the telegraph desk on the second floor and, posing as a government superintendent, began sending out queries about the uprising in the hope of receiving some news in return. But the few bits of information he was able to pass on to Pearse and Plunkett were so sketchy that they both realized the only hope of continued contact with the outside world was through that wireless across the street.

Pearse also talked to Connolly about the imminent danger of attack from the Amiens Street railway station, three blocks east of the Post Office. Troop trains were rumored to be arriving at Amiens Street now in a steady stream from British garrisons all over Ireland. Connolly expected the attack to come via North Earl Street, which led directly from Nelson's Pillar toward the station, especially since a barricade had already been erected across Abbey Street, the one other likely route along which British troops might advance toward the Post Office. Connolly said Earl Street had to be blocked immediately. Pearse, accepting his judgment, sent him Brennan Whitmore to direct the job. When Whitmore reported to Connolly, ten men assigned to work under his command had already been drawn up in a single rank opposite the front door of the Post Office. In addition to their arms, they carried crowbars, hatchets, saws, hammers, and whatever other tools they had been able to find. Connolly's orders to Whitmore were brief: "Take these men over to Tyler's boot shop and prepare to defend the place. But first, I want you to build a strong barricade across Earl Street." Connolly paused to look hard at Whitmore and the men behind him. "You will defend the position," he said, "to the last."

Whitmore studied his little decade of men, all complete strangers to him. He would know them well enough soon. Meanwhile, he feared that they might lack confidence in him, for he was also a stranger to them. Nine of them were members of the Citizen Army; the tenth, a singer, Gerald Crofts. As Whitmore and his ten headed out from the Post Office across O'Connell Street, the looting seemed to have subsided while the crowd was busy watching the second fire. Though the street lights were on and people were strolling back and forth, the scene looked unreal. No tram cars. A throng of silent spectators huddled in front of a burning building. Two dead horses lying on the pavement just above Nelson's Pillar. The street littered with items of merchandise that hadn't come up to the standards of the looters.

Whitmore's group had no trouble entering Tyler's; the looters had been there before them to open the premises. When they went into Earl Street to build the barricade, they soon drew a crowd like the one that had complicated the barricading of Abbey Street in the afternoon. Though the items used in the barricade had been lying around since the looting began for anyone to carry away, they apparently developed no value in the eyes of the crowd until they became part of the insurgents' fortification, whereupon there was such a rush to grab them that the barricade kept disappearing almost as fast as it was built. Finally, Whitmore decided to stand over it with his automatic drawn. Yet this was a friendly crowd, even when deprived of booty. Some people went so far as to volunteer their help in the beaverlike construction. Whitmore began to wonder, though, whether their help was worth the trouble of answering their incessant questions. What surprised him most was the eagerness of so many of the men to join the insurgents. The new flag of Ireland flying from the Post Office seemed to have touched them. Some pleaded with tears in their eyes to be allowed to enlist. Whitmore could have increased his garrison to 200 men had he known them to be sufficiently trained and trustworthy, but the rule was strict—only members of the Volunteers or Citizen Army were eligible for acceptance. So Whitmore's little squad continued the big job into the night with occasional assistance but no recruits.

About ten o'clock, The O'Rahilly came down from the top floor of the Post Office to the commissary on the second floor—but not to eat. He wanted to talk to Sean MacDermott and Tom Clarke, who were still there chatting with several other men, all of whom retired to another part of the room when they saw the serious, almost glowering intent on O'Rahilly's ordinarily cheerful face. Now that O'Rahilly had done everything within his province in organizing the defense of the building, the time had come for him to settle a matter that had been biting into his soul since the previous Friday. He was determined to find out what had happened to his friend Bulmer Hobson: if he had actually been kidnapped, and if so, by whom, and where he was being held. If anyone had kidnapped him, it would most likely have been under orders from MacDermott, a man whose methods were sometimes Machiavellian. MacDermott was remarkably skillful at manipulating people, at using them for his own purposes. Within the revolutionary movement few seemed to resent his methods, because his purposes were irreproachable. Everyone was convinced he was using himself just as ruthlessly for the same purposes. No one ever doubted MacDermott's willingness to die for Ireland. And in any case, most of the people with whom he dealt were either won by his persuasiveness, charmed by his disarming smile, or virtually hypnotized by the penetration of his wide, deep-set eyes. A superstitious man might call his eyes evil. A woman would be more likely to call them soulful. When, in spite of all his winning attributes, MacDermott was unable to manage a man (as must inevitably be the case with a man like Hobson, whose independence matched his perception), he was capable of almost any other methods that might, from his viewpoint, be necessary. O'Rahilly had confronted Pearse about Hobson's disappearance, but it was not Pearse's kind of action. It was MacDermott's. Under the circumstances MacDermott might have felt quite justified, from his viewpoint, in removing Hobson from circulation. As the clandestine plan for the uprising developed during Easter Week, Hobson had posed a greater threat to it, and to the secret IRB faction behind it, than any other man within the Volunteer organization, including O'Rahilly or even MacNeill. Hobson understood the IRB faction because he had once been part of it; having then become, in effect, the leader of the moderate faction, he wielded an influence that had to be neutralized.

Hobson was a thoughtful and highly educated Quaker from Belfast who had been a member of the Irish Republican Brotherhood's Supreme Council, the editor of its publication *Irish Freedom*, and the elected representative of its Leinster chapter, which included the entire Dublin area. Once Tom Clarke's closest protégé, he had gradually moved out from under Clarke's influence as MacDermott had moved in. He now agreed with MacNeill and O'Rahilly that the best way to use the Volunteers was as an instrument of threat and of passive resistance that would eventually, by continued pressure, force the British to relinquish their hold on Ireland. Hobson was the first to sense that the IRB faction within the Volunteers planned to convert the all-Ireland Easter maneuver into an uprising. On Palm Sunday, speaking at a Cumann na mBan meeting in Parnell Square, he cautioned the Volunteers to maintain and strengthen their organization in the hope of influencing the peace conference that must follow the European war. Then he hinted that certain people might be planning something foolish. It was not enough, he warned, to make a futile military gesture and leave behind one more failure to add to the Irish tradition.

"No man," he said, "has the right to sacrifice others merely that he might make for himself a bloody niche in history."

When he spoke Palm Sunday, Hobson was acting merely on suspicion. As yet he had no definite information that the maneuver scheduled for the following Sunday was to become an insurrection. But four days later, the evening of Holy Thursday, he learned that Patrick Pearse had issued orders to some men in the Dublin suburb of Bray, concerning the destruction of a railway bridge there. Hobson, feeling that his suspicions had been confirmed, took a taxi to MacNeill's house, got him out of bed, and accompanied him to confront Pearse with the evidence of his duplicity. It was on this occasion that Pearse had said to MacNeill, "Yes, you are right. A rising is intended." The very next night, Good Friday, Hobson had disappeared.

If MacDermott was keeping Hobson under arrest someplace, O'Rahilly did not intend to let him get away with it any longer. Though a good-natured man, O'Rahilly was capable of terrifying wrath when aroused. MacDermott, aware of this, nevertheless listened with outward calm as O'Rahilly demanded to know if he knew where Hobson had been taken.

MacDermott said yes, he knew.

O'Rahilly, his anger rising, made it clear that for MacDermott's sake Hobson had better be alive and well.

MacDermott assured him that Hobson was quite comfortable. No harm had come to him.

O'Rahilly, under tight control, conveyed the suggestion that he would not be able to say as much for MacDermott unless Hobson were released immediately.

The conversation between the two men became animated though not loud. Tom Clarke listened but seldom spoke. The men on the other side of the room, including Sean T. O'Kelly, could make out very little of what was said. When O'Rahilly had sufficiently impressed his message on MacDermott, he turned to leave. His face was set with severity and determination as he walked away from MacDermott and Clarke, but he broke into his usual smile as he stopped to joke with the other men, near the door.

When O'Rahilly left, MacDermott and Clarke talked privately at length. Finally, MacDermott called O'Kelly over to them.

"Sean, I want you to go up to Martin Conlon's house in Cabra Park," he said, "and release Hobson."

After getting the address of the house, in North Dublin, O'Kelly said, "Don't you think it would be wise to give me a written order?"

MacDermott took a page from a small diary in his pocket and wrote on it: "Sean T. O'Kelly to release Bulmer Hobson." As casual as if it were merely a grocery list, but with MacDermott's initials under it, O'Kelly knew it would be enough. Off he went on his latest errand. As he left the Post Office, the second blaze, across the street, was now under control and the mob had returned, after a restful interlude of fire watching, to the more exciting business of looting. They had finally visited a jewelry shop that for some time had been too forbidding and were now bartering with each other gold watches for diamond rings, cameo necklaces for pearl brooches. O'Kelly turned away from the scene and hurried on his mission. Heading north toward Cabra Park, he heard shots piercing the misty night air throughout the city, from every direction.

Brennan Whitmore and his men on Earl Street had found a large coil of flexible wire, which they used to bind their strange collection of junk together into a barricade and also to keep the mob from stealing it, item by item. The barricade completed, they secured the doors and windows of the Earl Street buildings nearest Amiens Street. Then they began the tedious and seemingly endless job of knocking holes in the walls between buildings from the Pillar Café to the Imperial Hotel. While they were at it, an old man who owned a pub in one of the buildings came to Whitmore and said they were doing needless work. The roofs, he said, offered more mobility and better vantage points for riflemen. He took Whitmore to the roof of the building that housed his pub, explained to him a very detailed plan for defending the entire block, then gave him the keys to the pub and told him to take what he pleased from it.

"God keep you and guard you," he said.

"But, where," Whitmore wanted to know, "did you ever develop so many theories about defending rooftops?"

The pubkeeper's wrinkled face broke into a wistful smile. "We thought out all these roofs and their uses," he said, "in the old Fenian days."

Whitmore thanked him and shook his hand. The old man's rooftop plan was practical enough for the Fenian days, forty or fifty years before, but would it work against the twentieth-century machine guns and artillery the British would soon bring into play?

James Connolly, on the ground floor of the Post Office, was in an expansive mood, and perhaps with sufficient reason. As the first day of the rebellion drew to a close, he could look with some satisfaction upon its accomplishments. The Republic had been declared. Insurgents occupied key positions in so many parts of Dublin that it might almost be said they controlled the city. They had used the day well, entrenching themselves in these positions. And in their few encounters with British troops, they had come off victorious. A Citizen Army man came to Connolly with a report that made him smile.

"Listen to this," he shouted. "The Citizen Army has captured King George and Lord Kitchener"—he paused—"in the Henry Street waxworks."

When the laughter died, an unsmiling Volunteer standing near Connolly said, "But, sir, what are our chances of winning?"

Connolly replied quickly, before his true feelings had time to show. "Oh, they're beaten!" he said. "I tell you, we've beaten them!"

A thin drizzle was falling as Bulmer Hobson, released from house arrest, walked slowly down O'Connell Street on his way to his flat in the southern part of the city. He felt let down, empty, saddened, and also somewhat amazed at what was happening, even though he had been the first to detect the signs that it was imminent. As he approached the GPO, there was the barricade of junk on Earl Street and the abandoned tram car, and the dead horses near the Pillar, and the discarded merchandise everywhere littering the street—a fur stole, a toy gun, empty bottles, shoes, hats, a violin—and groups of looters still moving drunkenly in and out of shops, looking for more. A young shawlie, pretty even through the dirt on her face, with a baby's head sticking out of her black wraparound. Another girl, not so pretty, prancing in front of three men in a plumed hat and a satin dress too small for her. A pack of children playing tag at midnight.

At the GPO, rifle barrels protruded aimlessly from the glassless window casements. Shadowy figures moved about in the dim candlelight inside. Hobson had many friends in that ghostly building—and some former friends, bringing to a catastrophic end his dream of an Ireland that would win independence by winning respect. Hopelessly resigned, he stood for a while across the street from the Post Office, absorbing the entire sadness of the day and the days and weeks and years leading to it.

He thought of the gun-carrying guards who had held him prisoner since Friday in that house back there—men he had known and liked for years—and the way he had laughed and said,

"You're a lot of fools," when they had first told him he would not be allowed to leave.

He thought of Sean T. O'Kelly, who had come to free him with a note from MacDermott, and what a cute little fellow Sean was (though such a dull speaker he would clear the hall if you gave him the rostrum), and the classical nerve of the man to suggest, having freed him, that he should join the fight.

He thought most sadly of his dear friend The O'Rahilly, who had (he gathered from O'Kelly) demanded his release, and he was as troubled as he was perplexed to learn that O'Rahilly was in that building with the others when he could have so little enthusiasm for what was happening there.

He thought of honest, simple but perfervid Tom Clarke, whose zeal for Ireland had ignited himself and all the others, and of his own years as Clarke's closest friend before the rise of Mac-Dermott.

He thought of MacDermott, hopelessly crippled but devilishly clever, whom he had introduced to the movement in Belfast many years before, whom he had carried to the hospital when polio struck, but who now saw him as such a dangerous enemy.

He thought of Connolly, who had said to him a few months previously, "The Irish working class is a powder magazine. If you drop a match it will go up," and to whom he had said in return, "Since you must deal in metaphors, Connolly, I'll tell you what the working class is—it's a wet bog. You drop a match and it will land in a puddle." Here was Connolly's working class on O'Connell Street tonight, raping the shops, reeling about in an alcoholic orgy.

And he thought of Patrick Pearse, alone even in a crowd. He was reminded of how often he had heard Pearse say, "Bloodshed is a sanctifying thing, and the nation which regards it as the final horror has lost its manhood." He was reminded also of Pearse's play *The Singer*, in which he said, "One man can free a people as one Man redeemed the world. I will take no pike. I will go into the battle with bare hands. I will stand up before the Gall as Christ hung naked before men on the tree." No one would ever again doubt that Pearse meant what he said. But was he right?

Could he and this pitiful band, by facing the British army alone with their bare hands, by shedding their blood for Ireland, actually make it a free nation? Bulmer Hobson did not believe so. Yet he found himself hoping so. He could not sustain any rancor against these old companions who had mistreated him. He simply thought they were mad.

11. *Tuesday, April 25*

THE short, restless sleep of The O'Rahilly was broken by a volley of machine-gun fire from someplace in the southern part of the city. British, of course. The insurgents had no machine guns. O'Rahilly, as munitions officer, was painfully aware of that. But they would be well acquainted with machine guns before long. The British would soon be putting them through an intensive familiarization drill.

O'Rahilly opened an eye to the dull gray light that timidly announced day at the glass-free, top-floor windows of the Post Office. He put his hand to his face, thoughtlessly smoothed back each side of his wide mustache, then turned over on the hard mattress and sat up. How long had he slept? Not long enough. He must write another note to the family. Yesterday's note was perhaps not the last he would ever write after all. He stood up, stretched, and went into a nearby room where he looked into the wide-open eyes of his friend, Desmond Fitzgerald.

"What happened to your schedule?" Fitzgerald asked him. "I thought we were to be wiped out yesterday."

O'Rahilly laughed. "So we should have been," he said. "It's

against all the best military rules that we're still alive." The laughing smile faded from his face. "But don't worry. It won't be put off for long."

He walked over to a window, exercising reasonable care to avoid exposing himself to fire, and looked down on O'Connell Street, free of looters now but littered with thousands of pounds worth of soiled and broken merchandise they had stolen only to discard. They would come back after it, no doubt, as soon as their drunkenness wore off and they ran out of fresh shops to loot.

He moved from window to window, inspecting the men installed behind stacks of books and mailbags and office supplies. Some of the men were wrapped in blankets, and a few shivered though the temperature was warm for Dublin. It hadn't gone below 50 degrees all night. Nerves might account for some of those shivers. It was difficult to sit and wait for a fight. Would the blasted British never attack? Each man had a bowl of ammunition and a pile of homemade grenades ready for them when they did.

Downstairs, Pearse and Connolly, who had taken turns trying to rest on mattresses during the night, were now up and at work —Pearse polishing the prose of his first communiqué, Connolly inspecting the men at their posts, encouraging them, giving them instructions, assuring them that all signs pointed to victory. He had been up since four, when he sent a man off to Wexford, on the southeasternmost tip of Ireland, to make sure the Volunteers in that area were aware of the uprising in Dublin. Despite the cheerful optimism he maintained in front of his men, he was desperately aware of the need for all Ireland to rise. Only if the British were forced to spread themselves thin throughout the country did the rebellion have any chance at all.

While he brooded about ways to increase public support for the cause, Connolly was approached by a group of his own Citizen Army men who didn't seem to be quite with it. They asked his permission to leave the building.

"Why?" he asked. "Where do you want to go?"

"Now that the holidays are over," said their spokesman, ingenuously, "we have to go back to our jobs."

At seven, a contingent of men from Maynooth, who had attempted to sleep through the night in Glasnevin Cemetery, arrived at the Post Office tired, bedraggled, and hungry. As they entered the building at the rear, the first sight to meet their eyes was a man who had been wounded the day before. He was now in great pain, twisting, writhing, pleading for comfort. After this introduction to the nature of warfare, the new recruits staggered upstairs to the commissary, where tea and buns were offered to those who still had stomach for breakfast. Thereafter, they were led back downstairs to the armorer's department, presided over by a Citizen Army man named Jim O'Neill, who issued them bombs—the usual tin cans full of explosives, with sulfur-covered fuses.

"All you do is strike a match," he said, "touch the fuse, count to three, and throw it."

Some of the boys looked doubtful. Connolly appeared and they came to ragged attention as he issued instructions to them. A few minutes later they were on their way, as a unit, to help the besieged garrison at City Hall. And less than a half-hour after that, they were back in the Post Office, having encountered invincible British firepower as they reached the Exchange Hotel on Parliament Street. Connolly, listening to their report, could almost feel the ring of British troops closing in on the Post Office. He could not yet figure out, though, why they were so slow to attack. Had they overestimated by that much the strength of the insurgents?

Another, more immediate problem nagged Connolly. That grasping, chattering malodorous mob that had sunk back into the slums shortly after midnight would be pouring forth again any minute now to take advantage of whatever loot and entertainment the day might offer. There had to be a way to cope with those people. Suddenly inspired, he sent a detail of men out in front of the Post Office with a roll of barbed wire, which they were to stretch across O'Connell Street at each end of the building. It would, he hoped, clear at least the area directly in front of the building and prevent the constant parade of curious people past it. Unfortunately, there happened to be just enough barbed wire to stretch once across, chest high, at the Prince's Street end of the building. Looking around for wire with which to fence off the other end, the men spotted the tram cables overhead, suspended from iron standards. With grenade explosions they undertook to bring down the standards. They succeeded in attracting a small crowd of people; by some miracle, they even succeeded in shaking down a length of cable. But the standards withstood the homemade grenades as easily as Nelson's Pillar had done the day before. It was becoming apparent that fire crackers in the hands of urchins could do more damage than these tin-can bombs. Hadn't a crowd of kids burned down a shop with fire crackers the night before?

The tram cable was soon extended, and when the work was done, two peculiar-looking wires, one thick and heavy, the other barbed, neither very taut, stretched hopefully across O'Connell Street from the corners of the Post Office. They looked as if they would be about as effective as the priests who had formed a picket in an effort to roll back the crowd the day before.

Among the morning's first visitors to the Post Office was a postman, who came, as he had been doing every morning for years, to pick up the mail for his route. When he presented himself at the employees' entrance, the puzzled sentry barred him with a bayonet and said, "Go home. There's no mail today."

"No mail? Sure, why not?" the man wanted to know. "It's a Tuesday."

"There's a revolution on. That's why not."

"Since when is there no mail of a Tuesday?"

"Since yesterday."

"But yesterday was Monday."

The sentry, unable to confute the man's logic and running short of patience, advanced on him with bayonet. "You heard me say there was no mail. Now, will you feck off? Go home!"

Prodded from behind, the postman slowly retreated, mumbling about what the people on his route would say when they got no mail.

Among the men in the Post Office a new set of rumors arose to greet the new day. There was talk of a general uprising in Galway and in Limerick, and there was talk about all the talk being nothing but a lot of talk. Rumors were so thick and contradictory at breakfast that the only thing on which everyone could agree was the low quality of the food. Desmond Fitzgerald, laughing at the complaints even though he knew them to be justified (he hadn't yet organized the kitchen to his satisfaction), said to one of the grousing Volunteers, "Do you think I'm obliged to serve four-course dinners to you, when some of you never had a decent bite in your lives before? Even if you are here to die for Ireland, eat that crust of bread." Although he did not believe they could hold out for long, Fitzgerald was already well aware that in case they did last awhile, his responsibility was to make sure the food did likewise.

Sean MacDermott was ready to back him up if he had any problems with the men. Though MacDermott had no rank, either military or civil, within the new government, he was heard when he spoke and he was obeyed when he gave an order. He had the knack of bending people to his will with just a few quick, firm words. He also knew more of the men personally than any other insurgent leader because he had been for several years the full-time, chief organizer throughout Ireland of both the Volunteers and the Irish Republican Brotherhood. He was so persuasive he could almost make the men believe they liked the food. But he couldn't make himself believe it. His taste was a little more sophisticated than that of most Irishmen in his day and from his social background. Just before the uprising, he and a group of his closest friends, knowing what was to come, had pooled all their money one evening for what they assumed would be their last excellent meal. They went to Jammet's, a French restaurant, the finest in Dublin, and ordered the works. MacDermott could at least look back fondly on that exquisite dinner as he ate the tasteless, overcooked food in the Post Office. It could not have been very easy for him, however, to tell the men around him how fortunate they were to be eating so well.

MacDermott was also helpful in dispelling rumors among the men, but the rumors were flying so fast that it would have taken a thousand MacDermotts to keep ahead of them—especially the wishful rumors of uprisings around the country. The men in the

Post Office so fervently desired all Ireland to rise with them that they felt a compulsion to convince themselves it was actually happening. The falsified "official" telegraph queries brought replies from Cork, Limerick, and Thurles, but they still were not reassuring. No uprisings or even disturbances were reported in any of those places. When these messages were relayed to Connolly and Pearse, they passed them off, perhaps because they were longing even more fervently than the men for a general uprising. In Connolly and Pearse, contradictory hopes and expectations were at work. They fully expected defeat and death. They almost counted on defeat to bring them ultimate justification and triumph. Yet they could still dream of victory. They fought to win and they desperately wanted the entire country to support them.

Connolly had written, just a month earlier, in *The Workers' Republic*: ". . . generations, like individuals, will find their ultimate justification or condemnation not in what they accomplished but rather in what they aspired and dared to attempt to accomplish . . . By aspiring to reach a height, the generation or individual places its soul unassailably upon that height, even should its body be trampled in the mud."

Pearse, at an IRB meeting, had once said, "If one man must die for the freedom of Ireland, that man shall be me." To which Tom Clarke and Tom MacDonagh said, "And me," and Sean MacDermott said, "And all of us."

They even courted defeat, in a sense (as their plan of action indicates), because in their sober moments they were quite certain that their best chance to prevail ultimately would be through their own annihilation. Yet the dream of military victory was too tempting to relinquish entirely, so they played out their drama as if it had more than one possible ending.

Pearse could easily believe the entire island would rise momentarily to his cause because it was inconceivable to him that his fellow Irishmen were devoid of the zeal for nationhood that consumed him. His nationalism grew out of what he called a "mystical birthright," which made him speak to the souls of men as well as to their minds. Even when he got no answer from their minds, he continued to believe he had reached their souls and at the proper time they would respond. But unfortunately for him, in the Ireland of 1916, the appeal of nationalism moved only a minority of men. The little island had settled comfortably into what Pearse might call an "insidious web" of British wartime prosperity. Most Irishmen were better off now than they had ever been. Business profits were the highest in history. Farm produce was in great demand. Thousands of people who had never before been able to find jobs were working, and those who still had no jobs were welcome in the British armed forces. Even the slum families were benefiting financially from the war by sending sons and husbands into the forces, thus becoming eligible for the weekly "separation money." A substantial majority of Irishmen absolutely opposed rebellion. Their elected representatives in the British Parliament, led by John Redmond, had pledged Ireland's support to England in the war against Germany and were actively encouraging Irishmen to join up and fight for His Majesty in France. To reach the souls of all these people one had first to get past their pocketbooks. That was a hard fact for anyone as zealous as Pearse to accept. He continued to anticipate good news from the country as he concluded his first communiqué and sent it to the print shop in Liberty Hall.

After he finished writing, Pearse went outside and across O'Connell Street to inspect the Earl Street garrison. Brennan Whitmore and his men, having worked all night on their barricade and on the fortification of the buildings facing toward the Amiens Street station, were preparing the buildings on the Post Office side of the block. Whitmore had also stationed two riflemen on the roofs as snipers. An occasional shot would ring out, then there was silence except for the distant spitfire of rifles south of the Liffey, around City Hall. There were people on Earl Street and O'Connell Street now, gawking curiously or gossiping in clusters, but yesterday's riotous mob had not yet re-formed. Pearse chatted for ten minutes with Whitmore and congratulated him on the work that had been done. He seemed gratified by the situation in the rest of the city. A report had just come in about heavy fighting at City Hall and the *Daily Mail* office, which the

City Hall garrison had occupied, and the report was no doubt true, for he could hear heavy gunfire from that direction, but he had reason to be confident the boys there could take care of themselves. Whitmore said nothing. After an empty pause, Pearse, as if he had decided he ought to leave this little group with one more morale booster, suddenly said, "And Wexford is up."

Whitmore did not ask him where he had gotten that information. Pearse returned to the Post Office, and Whitmore's ten-man garrison returned to work.

Connolly had sent people out to bring in more guns and ammunition, stored in secret dumps throughout the city. Two men, Pat McCrea and M. W. O'Reilly, had taken a car to the largest of these storage depots, in Parnell Square, and returned with such a heavy load that the car's engine seemed about to expire as they rolled it slowly up to the Prince's Street gate. Even the Cumann na mBan girls, of whom there was an increasing number as the morning went on, were put to work bringing in guns from various hiding places. Within the folds of their long dresses it was possible, though not easy, to conceal weapons. When they were not delivering guns, the girls also delivered messages to the outposts. Movement within Dublin was still amazingly easy if one avoided main streets and obvious trouble spots. One courier, Ignatius Callender, made ten trips between the GPO and the Four Courts garrison.

Because Connolly was not yet satisfied with the siege preparations in the Post Office, huge rolls of newsprint were pushed and guided across O'Connell Street from the *Irish Times* warehouse in Lower Abbey Street. It took three or four men to stand up each of the rolls at vulnerable places near the Post Office doors and corner windows. Connolly also instructed his junior officers, of whom there was still a woeful shortage, to make sure the riflemen at all windows were alert. The sound of gunfire from the City Hall area was so insistent now that one could not imagine that the British would wait much longer before attacking the Post Office.

A woman approached the Henry Street side of the building and opened her black shawl to reveal beneath it a sack containing perhaps as many as a dozen bottles of stout, which she had liberated from a public house across the street. It was obvious, as she staggered toward the Post Office windows, that the stout in the sack was not the only stout she was carrying. With a bleary smile on her face, she pulled out a bottle and offered it to one of the riflemen inside. He looked tempted but declined.

"What kinda men are yiz, anyway?" she cried. "Will ye not even take a drink with a lady?"

She offered the stout to a second, a third, and a fourth man as she wobbled and weaved from window to window. All declined. Finally she came to a man with more thirst than caution. Without so much as a backward glance, he reached out for the bottle she offered and uncorked it. He was putting it to his lips when it was knocked from his hand by an officer making his rounds.

"You know the regulations," the officer shouted to him and to all within earshot. "The next man who takes a drink without permission will be shot without warning."

The trickle of recruits arriving Tuesday morning included one who was desperately needed—Jim Ryan, a medical student within two months of his final medical examination. Captain Sean Doyle, a nonmedical officer who had been doing his best to take care of the sick and wounded in the absence of a doctor, put Ryan to work, but not immediately in the Post Office. He asked him to look after some civilians in nearby Moore Street who were ill but couldn't get to a hospital. Joseph Cripps, who had spent the previous day commandeering medical supplies, accompanied Ryan on the mission.

"What kind of war is this?" Cripps remarked. "We need a military hospital, so we're running a clinic for civilians. And without a doctor."

Fortunately, Ryan was close enough to being a doctor to know what to do for the ailing civilians. But could he do it? He called out prescriptions and Cripps ran off to the nearest pharmacy to fill them. What Cripps brought back was not exactly what Ryan had ordered, but it was close enough. Among those he treated there was no serious illness. They all needed soothing and reassurance about the excitement around them as much as they needed medicine, so he gave them calm words as well as pills, and they blessed him before he left them. As a fledgling doctor, he had found out something important about himself. He had a good bedside manner—something he would need in the days ahead.

The O'Rahilly, looking tired, rumpled, and soiled, came down to the second floor of the Post Office, found Desmond Fitzgerald, and, with a sigh, settled into a chair near him.

"If only they had held this thing off until we were ready," he said.

Fitzgerald nodded. Both men were so aware of the mistakes already made in judgment, in tactics, in execution that it was pointless to discuss them at length. The question of timing was paramount, of course. Had the rising been held off long enough for proper planning, O'Rahilly would have joined it with his entire heart. But who had decided Easter was the only time? It sounded like one of Pearse's messianic notions. The resurrection of Ireland. Or was it the result of Connolly's endless pressure? He simply couldn't wait. He had wanted to rise in January. The fact of the uprising seemed more important to him than its success. What had happened at that three-day January session between Connolly and the IRB boys? They had apparently talked him out of rising immediately, but at what cost? He had apparently forced a promise from them to rise by Easter. What made them suppose, though, that they could get away with committing all 9,000 members of the Volunteers without even informing the president of the organization about their plans? If they thought they would be able to handle MacNeill, they had slightly misjudged him. They should have kidnapped him, too, when they kidnapped Hobson. And how could they have failed to make connections with the German munitions ship? If it arrived in Tralee Thursday night, why was there no one on hand to unload it? Apparently they hadn't expected it until Saturday. Could there have been that much of a misunderstanding? Not until Friday had they even sent men down to set up radio communication with it. And then to have those men drive off the Ballykissane pier, after the Germans had already scuttled their ship to keep the guns out of British hands—it was too much to contemplate. All those precious guns, the only hope the uprising ever had, sitting on the bottom of the Atlantic, simply because there had been no men on hand to unload them at Tralee Thursday night.

O'Rahilly was convinced that, under the circumstances, he had been right to talk MacNeill into issuing the countermand order Saturday. Without the German guns and ammunition, it was suicide to face the power of the British military. Why couldn't Pearse and Connolly and Plunkett see that? The strategy Plunkett had worked out in his military plan for the uprising did not seem destined to revolutionize warfare. Why had they decided to make the Post Office their central stronghold? Merely because it was on the city's principal street? Sandwiched in between all the downtown buildings, it would not be easy to defend, nor did it command any strategic area around it. Why hadn't they taken Trinity College and the Bank of Ireland? They might then, at least, have created a bottleneck. Who was it that forgot to destroy the telephone exchange? In an hour, they could have cut the government's communications all over Ireland. And what about the Castle? There were rumors in the Post Office that the Castle could have been taken Monday, that it was virtually undefended when Sean Connolly and his men made their hit-and-run attack on it. But it was somewhat late now to agonize about all that. They had cemented themselves into a purely defensive position; nothing was left to do but wait for the slaughter and meet it bravely. If only one could find some justification for leading all these good young men and women to the slaughter. O'Rahilly was unable to conceal his depression, but Fitzgerald marveled at him for not speaking of the one thing that must have disturbed him most—the fact that he had left a devoted wife and family to give his life in an action that not only lacked the assent of his own judgment but had been provoked by men who had shown him no respect.

"Have you heard anything from the family?" Fitzgerald asked.

"I got a note out to them yesterday," O'Rahilly said. "I'm sending another today." After a moment he turned away from

Fitzgerald, stood up, and, without looking back, headed for the stairway to the top floor.

James Connolly had reason to feel troubled. Those reports from the country, however unreliable they might be, were not reassuring. There were other reports even less so. British troops were said to be arriving at Amiens Street, Kingsbridge, and Westland Row by the trainload from all over Ireland. Would they dare strip the country garrisons if there were signs of trouble outside Dublin? And the pitiful insurgent forces at City Hall and the *Daily Mail* building across the street from it were now completely isolated, with British units pounding them from all sides. He disliked even to listen to the reports his couriers brought him. Concerned about the vulnerability of the Post Office from the direction of Amiens Street, he went out to inspect the Earl Street barricade and was shocked at the flimsy appearance of it. In a loud, questioning voice he called for Brennan Whitmore, who was emerging from a nearby building, having been told of Connolly's approach.

"Whitmore, what's the good of this thing?" Connolly demanded. "It'll never withstand a charge. Schoolgirls could knock it over."

Whitmore smiled. "If you think so, sir, try it."

Connolly gave it a kick, then grabbed hold of a chair leg protruding from it and yanked with all his strength. The barricade didn't budge.

"It's interlaced with wires," Whitmore pointed out.

Connolly examined the work closely, allowed a momentary smile to cross his face, then, sobering, pointed to a shoe shop on the opposite corner. "Have you occupied that building?"

"I don't have enough men."

Connolly thought about this a moment. He might easily have replied that he had the same problem himself, but he said, simply, "Good luck."

He shook hands with Whitmore, then turned and strode back briskly toward the Post Office. Whitmore, gazing after him, reflected sadly on the magnitude of the task ahead of him and ahead of all of them. Whitmore had no illusions. The chances of military success seemed to him outside the bounds of reasonable calculation. Yet when he looked at men like Connolly, he could still dream of miracles.

Back in the Post Office, Connolly stopped to dictate some orders and to talk to his secretary, Winifred Carney, a woman with a sharp eye and a sharp tongue, who was not altogether pleased with what she saw around her. Totally devoted to Connolly, she tended to compare the other leaders to him unfavorably—especially Joseph Plunkett, whose style was too dramatic and mannerisms too effete for her. The bangle on his wrists and the large antique rings on his fingers did not fit her picture of military masculinity, nor did the bandage on his throat and his hopelessly low state of health make her feel he was able to handle his responsibilities. She said as much to Connolly, as she had perhaps said before. He became impatient in a husbandly way (though their relationship was quite proper; the years had given it a certain married quality), and with a smile on his face to soften the insistence in his voice, he said to her, as if once and for all, "Joseph Plunkett can do and wear what he pleases. And as for military science, he could teach us all a thing or two. He's a clear-minded man, and he's a man of his word."

It was characteristic of this Irish rebellion that a man like Plunkett, a poet, should be its chief military strategist. (Three of the signatories to the Republican proclamation, Pearse and Thomas MacDonagh as well as Plunkett, were poets.) Plunkett was not a professional poet any more than he was a professional military strategist, but his verse had merit and he had the flamboyance often associated with poets. The fancy bangle on his wrist was one of his most loved possessions, for it had been given him by his fiancée, Grace Gifford, whom he had already married in his heart though not in church and whom he had made the chief beneficiary in his will. The huge antique ring on his finger was intended as a gift for her if he saw her again. Winifred Carney may have been overly concerned about his personal flair and the jewelry he wore.

A matter of much greater concern about Joseph Plunkett was the question of his general qualifications for the role he had

chosen. Despite Connolly's confidence in him, his lack of experience as a military tactician made him a questionable choice
for the job. About planning a campaign, he knew only what he
had read in books and what he had been able to evolve from an
active imagination. Yet he had remarkable confidence in his military ideas. During a 1915 trip to Germany in behalf of the Irish
Republican cause, he was said to have caused a member of the
German general staff to exclaim: "That blowhard Plunkett!
Imagine! He was trying to tell us how to conduct the war!" In
the Plunkett family it was said that the general plan of the uprising was one Joe worked out as a boy while mapping imaginary
battles with playmates. Whether or not this was true, he had
reason to wish, by Tuesday morning, that he had worked out
some alternative plans.

The most promising aspect of the original plan—his intention
that they wage guerrilla warfare against the British—had been
abandoned because the bulk of the Volunteers hadn't yet joined
the uprising. Now, with no sign of disturbances in the country to
hold British garrisons there, the insurgents' positions in Dublin
were in danger of being quickly engulfed by a flood of British
troops from all over Ireland. And without a radio, Plunkett had
no hope of driving those British troops back to their posts by
fomenting local actions. Nor could he send out calls for German
or American help.

The radio at the Marconi wireless school across the street from
the Post Office was not yet in working condition despite a whole
night's labor, which was interrupted only by occasional sniping.
Though the antenna and transmitter were ready to be tested, it
seemed pointless to begin broadcasting before sunset, for the
wireless transmitters of 1916 had, for some unknown reason, very
limited daytime ranges. Even if the transmitter were working,
however, it would be of little use inasmuch as the receiver at the
school was completely dead, its batteries apparently having de
teriorated. Plunkett, in his capacity as communications office₁,
spent much of the morning and much of his waning strength
trying to solve this problem. Finally, in frustration and exhaus-

tion, looking as if he were at the point of death, he went upstairs to the commissary and sat down with Desmond Fitzgerald.

"I must have a rest," he said, but instead of resting, he began a long account of his 1915 trip to Germany for the IRB, and his negotiations with the German government and general staff. It was all news to Fitzgerald, who was not an IRB member and therefore not privy to its secrets. He found the story so fascinating he considered taking notes on it, then abandoned the idea since he didn't expect to live long enough to pass on the information.

The O'Connell Street scene began to pick up as the morning progressed. Sightseeing crowds of proper Dubliners had come downtown to find out what all the turmoil was about, inspect the barricades, descry both the lack of police and the absence of the military. The town was filling up with troops. Why didn't they come here where they were needed and put this nonsense down? Well-dressed people glanced disapprovingly at the Post Office with all those rifle barrels protruding from its windows and silhouetted figures behind the rifles. Pretty girls listened intently as their escorts explained the intricacies of the situation. Discussions began and knots of people gathered around to argue about what should be done. Everyone deplored the looting that had been so rampant the previous day except the looters themselves, who were beginning now to reappear, many of them already drunk, in their newly acquired and ill-fitting outfits. Though it was not yet noon, they were already floating on the leftovers of the liquor they had snatched the night before. One "ould one" who had abandoned her shawl in favor of a new flowered hat let fly such a stream of profanity in the direction of the Post Office windows (she hadn't forgotten how those bowsies had robbed her of her "separation money" the day before) that gentlemen with ladies on their arms quickly moved away. And there were few smiles on the faces of the men in the windows who heard her. The atmosphere throughout the Post Office was becoming more serious as the men continued to wonder, with increasing tension, when the British attack would begin.

The only established Dublin newspaper published Tuesday was

the *Irish Times*. When copies began circulating in the Post Office, the men read it eagerly, but if they were expecting a voluminous story about themselves, they were disappointed. In its six pages, the *Times* included, first of all, one of the most essential ingredients of any Irish newspaper: a long horse-race story, in this case the account of the Fairyhouse races the day before. It included also a piece on the D'Oyly Carte company (which had opened at the Gaiety Monday night), a detailed description of a meeting of the Irish Traders' Assistants' Association, and a short editorial in praise of the Spring Show. On the editorial page were two brief recognitions of the rebellion. One was a reprinting of Lord Wimborne's proclamation announcing that "the sternest measures" were being taken. The other was a one-paragraph report under the headline:

SINN FEIN RISING IN DUBLIN

Yesterday morning an insurrectionary rising took place in the city of Dublin. The authorities have taken active and energetic measures to cope with the situation. These measures are proceeding favourably. In accordance with this official statement, early and prompt action is anticipated.

If the insurgents wanted a more comforting report about themselves, they could get it from a brand-new newspaper that appeared at noon—*Irish War News*, the official journal of the "Republic." A four-page sheet printed at Liberty Hall, it was dated "Dublin, Tuesday, April 25, 1916," and offered at a price of "One Penny." Its front page featured an article entitled "If the Germans Conquered England," which had also been the title of an earlier article in the London *News Statesman*. *Irish War News* suggested that the *New Statesman* article must have been "a very clever piece of satire written by an Irishman," because it drew a picture of England under German rule "almost every detail of which exactly fits the case of Ireland at the present day."

On the back page was a story of more immediate interest under the headline "STOP PRESS! THE IRISH REPUBLIC." What followed was Patrick Pearse's first communiqué. It began: "[Irish] 'War News' is published today because a momentous thing has happened. The Irish Republic has been declared in Dublin . . ." After briefly describing the events of the previous day, the communiqué went on to a somewhat imaginatively optimistic description of the prevailing situation:

> At the moment of writing this report, (9:30 A.M., Tuesday) the Republican forces hold all their positions and the British forces have nowhere broken through. There has been heavy and continuous fighting for nearly 24 hours, the casualties of the enemy being much more numerous than those on the Republican side. The Republican forces everywhere are fighting with splendid gallantry. The populace of Dublin are plainly with the Republic, and the officers and men are everywhere cheered as they march through the streets. The whole centre of the city is in the hands of the Republic, whose flag flies from the G.P.O. . . . Communication with the country is largely cut, but reports to hand show that the country is rising, and bodies of men from Kildare and Fingall have already reported in Dublin.

Perhaps buoyed up by his own words, Pearse went to the commissary and asked Desmond Fitzgerald how long the food supply would last.

"For how many men?" Fitzgerald asked.

"A little over 200."

Fitzgerald, who was completely comfortable in discussions of English literature or Catholic theology, found himself quite bewildered by the whole subject of restaurant management. But fortunately for him, a Liverpool Irish girl named Peggy Downey, who was vacationing in Dublin when the rebellion began, had come to the Post Office and offered her services. Because Peggy was an experienced caterer, she was not only accepted but immediately appointed chief cook. When Fitzgerald went to her and relayed Pearse's question, she took a quick inventory.

"With rigid economy," she said, "we have enough for three weeks."

Returning to his commander in chief, Fitzgerald said, "With rigid economy, we have enough for three weeks."

"Then exercise rigid economy," Pearse said. "We may be here that long."

Though startled by Pearse's apparent optimism, Fitzgerald obediently took steps to tighten the belts of everyone in the Post Office. He now had five Cumann na mBan girls working in the kitchen, plus two British prisoners who had volunteered their services. The work was fairly well organized. All he had to do was figure out what to tell his hungry diners when they complained that they weren't getting enough food.

By noon, the respectable element in the O'Connell Street crowd was beginning to give way to the hordes pouring out of the slums in the hope that today would be another yesterday. Though these people didn't like the revolutionaries, they loved the revolution. If this was what Irish freedom meant, they wanted their fill of it. Even the fact that they had been deprived of their separation money annoyed them only slightly now that everything they had ever wanted was so readily at hand. Food was not as plentiful as it should be, but that was unimportant as long as liquor remained in such good supply. Men and women stood in the street, their heads tipped back, bottles to their mouths; every few minutes another empty smashed against the pavement or the side of a building. Often the shattering bottles were not empty. It didn't matter. There were several pubs in the area that had not yet been looted. From time to time, the crash of a large pane of glass would indicate that another establishment was falling, and a sizable section of the crowd would run in the direction of the noise. But the coldly rapacious mood of the day before was largely absent. This was a day to celebrate the gains of yesterday. Liquor seemed to diminish the acquisitive drive and, at least temporarily, to soften the bitterness of the mob toward the rebels. Even when someone shouted, "Dirty bowsies!" or "The Tommies'll bate yer bloody heads off!" to a passing squad of insurgents, it was without much rancor. Laughter and gaiety took hold of people, and occasionally someone would break into a dance.

The most amazing incident took place in the center of O'Connell Street. A girl with an armful of lingerie (and perhaps also a skinful of liquor) began stripping off her clothes, item by item, until she was totally naked. A hush came over the crowd as people shook their heads and blinked their eyes to make sure their senses were not deceiving them. Here was a sight much rarer in Ireland than a rebellion. A woman naked in the street! Hesitantly they gathered around her, almost afraid to watch her as she tried on the various items of newly acquired finery, one after another, tossing away those she didn't fancy. For a while, no one spoke.

Finally, a man coming up to see what was happening cried out, "Mother of God, she's naked!"

Another said "Would you look at the bloody whoor? Has she got no morality at all?"

A middle-aged woman wearing new shoes, a new dress, and a new hat said to the woman next to her, "It's a mortal sin, that's what it is. Th'Almighty God'll sthrike her dead!"

A man with a pleasantly drunken smile sighed, "If only me own wife had a figure like that!"

Two women near him turned away in shocked silence. A voice toward the rear shouted, "Will no one stop her? Police! Police! Is there not a policeman in the entire city of Dublin?"

All policemen had been withdrawn from duty the previous day, as everyone knew. Though the cries of outrage continued, no one interfered with the girl, and few people left the scene (despite the fact that a gentle rain had begun to fall) until she had finished her indecent fashion show.

At about one o'clock, the well-known Francis Sheehy-Skeffington emerged from the Post Office with a bundle of broadsides under his arm, a paste pot and brush, and as many walking sticks as he had been able to find. He had gone to the Post Office to inform Pearse and Connolly of a plan he hoped would reduce looting and restore some degree of order to the civilian population.

Though Sheehy-Skeffington was an ardent nationalist, he could not participate in the uprising because he was also a pacifist. There was no cowardice in his unwillingness to take up arms. The previous day he had walked into a cross fire of bullets in the hope of helping a British officer who, he had been told, was bleeding to death on the pavement near the castle. He said afterward he could not let anyone bleed to death while he was in a position to help. He was regarded in Dublin as a gentle, harmless man with peculiar ideas who loved debate and espoused causes. As a student at University College, he defeated classmate James Joyce, already a literary aspirant, in an election for the auditorship of the "Literary and Historical" debating society. When Francis Skeffington married Hannah Sheehy, they took each other's names as a token of belief in equal status for women.

Though pacifism was one of the causes Sheehy-Skeffington espoused most passionately, he had been outraged almost to the point of violence by the looting and carousing Monday in the center of Dublin. He had remonstrated and reasoned with the looters to no avail. Already today they had broken into several shops, including Frewen and Ryan's emporium. He was determined to take positive action to stop them.

After leaving the Post Office, he looked around for likely places to put up notices, then walked over to the William Smith–O'Brien monument in O'Connell Street and set to work with his paste pot. An open-mouthed crowd gathered around to read his message:

> When there are no regular police on the streets, it becomes the duty of citizens to police the streets themselves and to prevent such spasmodic looting as has taken place in a few streets. Civilians (men and women) who are willing to co-operate to this end are asked to attend at Westmoreland Chambers (over Eden Bros.) at five o'clock this (Tues.) afternoon.

Though howls of ridicule and laughter greeted his idea, Sheehy-Skeffington was unperturbed. As a habitual dissenter, he was accustomed to ridicule. He had even carried his dissent so far as to leave the Catholic Church seven years earlier. If he could endure the reactions that produced in Dublin, how could he be touched by the raucous remarks of these unfortunate gurriers from the slums? He moved on in search of respectable people and encountered a friend, the writer St. John Ervine, who patiently listened to his plan for a civilian constabulary that would put crime to flight with walking sticks. Ervine smiled at the thought of his pacifist friend taking up arms of any kind and at the image of him flailing at the devil with a cane. "Good luck," he said, but at the offer of a walking stick for himself, he declined. Undaunted, Sheehy-Skeffington went on pasting up his notices and offering walking sticks to friends, priests, reliable-looking strangers. The crowd went on drinking and looting.

Sean MacDermott, as concerned about the insurgents' lack of a doctor as he was about the lack of a chaplain, heard with delight of the arrival of Jim Ryan at the Post Office. MacDermott had been, as it happened, a dear friend of Ryan's two sisters, Mary and Phyllis, the latter of whom was one day to become the wife of little Sean T. O'Kelly and, upon his elevation to the presidency, the First Lady of Ireland. Having become acquainted with young Jim in the Ryan household, MacDermott thought highly enough of him to put him in charge of the hospital, thus relieving for more active duty Captain Sean Doyle, who had been dispensing medical care to the best of a nonmedical man's ability.

Ryan hesitated to accept the post because he was not yet a doctor, but then he went to work quickly, organizing his untrained staff and meager facilities into something approximating an infirmary. The only qualified assistant he had was a fellow medical student named Dan McLaughlin, who was not even close to earning his degree. The rest of the staff consisted of three or four medical corpsmen, which is to say ex-riflemen on whom Red Cross armbands had been thrust, and a dozen members of Cumann na mBan, who, being women, were therefore expected automatically to be nurses. The space they had available to them amounted to a pair of rooms on the ground floor at the rear of the Post Office. One room was of moderate size with a glass roof. Ryan converted it into a first-aid center. The other, which had apparently been a mail-sorting room, was large enough to accommodate a number of beds, though probably not as many as would be needed. Ryan wasted no time getting these beds made and ready. Like everyone else in the building, he anticipated a brisk demand for them before this day came to an end.

Reports had reached the Post Office of intensified fighting around City Hall, where the British were concentrating in force, and in St. Stephen's Green, where machine guns firing from the upper floors of the Shelbourne Hotel had driven the insurgents out of the park. They had been fortunate to get out. For several hours, they hadn't even dared raise their heads from their trenches. It looked as if the occupation of the green had been another tactical mistake: the whole park was vulnerable from the upper floors of the buildings around it. The men (and women) who had escaped were now occupying the Royal College of Surgeons building on the west side of the green, but whether or not they could operate effectively from this position was questionable. Another report indicated that the British had taken over Trinity College in force. If so, they had virtually cut off the Post Office from the garrisons in St. Stephen's Green, the South Dublin Union, and Jacob's biscuit factory. Although communications remained open to the garrisons in Boland's mill, the Four Courts, and the northern suburbs, the British were applying heavy pressure to all of them, especially the northeastern areas around Fairview and Annesley Bridge. Their strategy was apparent now. They were preparing for a massive, unharried, and uninterrupted attack on the rebel headquarters at the Post Office by first eliminating the outposts.

Tom Clarke and Patrick Pearse were both acutely conscious of this impending assault. It seemed to intensify Clarke's impatience for action. It seemed to deepen Pearse's brooding melancholy. He paced endlessly from station to station in the Post Office until Clarke, finally becoming irked at him, said, "For God's sake, won't someone find that man an office and get him out of the way?"

MacDermott laughed. He and Connolly and Plunkett appeared so calm and optimistic they were able to make at least some of their men feel they were engaged in a promising as well as a glorious enterprise. Sean Gallogly, a guard at the side gate, was filled with the kind of confidence that prevented him even from noticing the signs of growing tension around him. The thought of victory was too sweet for him to relinquish, especially after an incident about midafternoon. He and a companion, seeing a man who looked like a British officer in the O'Connell Street crowd, rushed up to him and took him prisoner. They were right. He turned out to be a British captain who had been propelled to the Post Office either by arrogance, alcohol, or stupidity, or, possibly, by his headquarters, in quest of information about the rebel headquarters. If the British were so careless as to send their officers right into the enemy camp, why shouldn't Gallogly be confident?

There were other men in the Post Office equally sanguine. In the commissary, Desmond Fitzgerald heard a group talking so unrealistically about victory and about the wonderful future that lay beyond it that he became depressed listening to them.

Most of the men did not consider the outlook so bright. John "Blimey" O'Connor, who was going back and forth between the Post Office and the wireless school across the street, trying to find batteries and bits of equipment with which to make the receiver operate, never supposed for a moment that either the radio or the revolution would work. Ernest Nunan, who had been wounded superficially the day before and was now preparing to go out with a group of snipers to the harbor area known as the North Wall, felt that the uprising would have had a chance of success if it had begun Sunday but that as matters now stood they would be lucky to hold out a few days. To Liam McNeive, stationed at a ground-floor corner window looking out toward Prince's Street and O'Connell Bridge, the experience was becoming a matter of frustration. They were fighting an enemy who refused to show his face, yet they seemed to have no plan to seek him out and attack him, to take advantage of his reluctance. They should not be spending their time waiting to be attacked, constantly on the alert. They couldn't get proper rest. Each time they tried to relax for a few minutes, a gun would burst somewhere and they would be on their feet again, expecting Armageddon. McNeive could see the strain beginning to tell on the men around him.

Seamus Brennan, a rifleman from Tullamore who was posted as a sniper on the roof of the Tower bar directly across Henry Street from the Post Office, had misgivings about The O'Rahilly's participation in the uprising. Brennan, like many others, knew of O'Rahilly's role in propagating the countermand order and had not yet been able to put down his resentment against him for it. O'Rahilly had done everything he could to prevent the rebellion from becoming countrywide, and he had thereby condemned it to failure. After he had done that much damage to the cause, why was he even allowed in the Post Office, and whose idea was it to put him in a position of command? From a rifleman's viewpoint there were some things about this army difficult to explain. But a rifleman wasn't there to explain. He was there to fight. Brennan wished the fight would hurry up and begin.

For Seamus Robinson, Seamus Lundy, and Cormac Turner, holding the Hopkins and Hopkins jewelry store building at the O'Connell Bridge corner, the fight had already begun. British snipers from the Trinity College buildings across the Liffey two blocks away kept their post under such constant pressure that Turner made his way to the Post Office to ask for a high-caliber rifle with which to fight back.

Connolly, looking calm and cool, said in his deliberate, slightly Scotch-Irish accent, "I'll do better than that, man. I'll send you a crack shot." He sent a Citizen Army man named Andy Conroy, whose accuracy from the roof of Hopkins and Hopkins soon slowed, though did not stop, the fire from Trinity.

At three o'clock, Connolly heard a boom that could not fail to shake him, at least momentarily, as it shook everyone in the Post Office. It was the distant boom of an artillery cannon in the northern suburbs. The sound seemed to come from the Phibsborough–North Circular Road area. Connolly could scarcely believe what he heard. Artillery was the one weapon he had been certain the British would not use. He had told his fellow conspirators many times, "No capitalist government will use artillery and destroy the property of its own capitalist class." He was so much a Marxist he had no doubt about it. Yet the rumbling boom, repeated now, had the sound of an eighteen-pounder. No one could deny that. Where were they using it, though? Not in the center of the city, where they would destroy the highly valuable commercial property of the wealthy capitalists. Not in the southern section of the city, where they might damage the homes of those wealthy capitalists. But in the modest Phibsborough section, where they could only destroy lower middle-class houses. They would never shell O'Connell Street. Connolly remained certain of that.

Wild stories were rampant throughout the Post Office now and especially in the commissary. Many of the men, having no special duties except to wait for the British attack, came upstairs to while away their time, drink a cup of tea, talk to the girls in the kitchen. These men brought with them all the rumors a building-ful of troops could invent or collect in a day. The Germans had landed a force somewhere. No one could name the exact location because a dozen places had been mentioned. German submarines, a whole fleet of them no doubt, were in Dublin Bay. Everyone but the British seemed to know that. Jim Larkin (the labor leader whom Connolly succeeded and who had gone to America) was on his way home at the head of an army of 50,000 Irish Americans. People who heard these stories believed them so eagerly that Desmond Fitzgerald became distressed. He looked for Patrick Pearse and found him in the street outside the Post Office, gazing sadly at the spectacle of his fellow Irishmen, drunk on stolen liquor, brazenly showing off their stolen finery. Up and down the street people were still surging in and out of ransacked shops, indifferent to the snipers' bullets that occasionally zinged past them. The barbed wire and the strand of cable extending across O'Connell Street sagged so loosely that people stepped over them, scarcely inconvenienced. Despite the rain, which was falling more heavily now, girls strolled past showing off their smart new tweed outfits and their expensive fur coats as if the Easter Parade of two days earlier had not yet ended. Silk vests and knickers stuck out of the pockets of some of the coats. Quite a few people had put on their new clothes over their old so that soiled, black underwear showed beneath white lace and filthy shirts beneath bright, clean jackets.

Fitzgerald stood watching Pearse, saying nothing, identifying with the pain that showed in his face. The more he saw of Pearse, the less resentment he felt against him for the way O'Rahilly had been treated. The very presence of Pearse, his quiet, brooding suffering dignity, his fearless, irrevocable, absolute commitment to his cause, wiped out all lesser considerations about him. In his face was etched the heavy, Christ-like responsibility he had taken upon himself for the men around him and for all Ireland. Despite his political inexperience, his military innocence, and his evident impracticality, he was the mystical heart that pumped blood into this rebellion, and he knew it. The fate of every human being around him bore down on him; he was relieved only by the knowledge that Ireland had actually risen once again in arms, had again punctuated her claim to freedom. The uprising would no doubt result in his death, but it would also vindicate his generation of Irishmen, and it would spark the coming generation to finish what was beginning here.

Fitzgerald stepped up closer to him, got his attention, and said, "There is an assortment of outrageous rumors among the men."

Pearse nodded. He was well aware of the rumors.

"They come into the commissary with endless stories, filling my people with such impossible hopes it makes me want to cry."

Pearse said nothing for a moment. As Fitzgerald was finding out, he was a man to whom few hopes seemed impossible. Then he said, "I quite agree with you. There are many false rumors."

Fitzgerald said, "I would like to tell my people the most hopeful thing that is known for certain at this moment. Is there anything to suggest we may get outside help?"

Pearse hesitated, then said, "Smoke has been seen in the bay. We honestly believe there are submarines."

Fitzgerald waited. "Is that all?"

Pearse said, "That's all."

It was little enough, but it was more than Fitzgerald had expected. They lapsed into silence, watching the greedy mob at work up the street. The looters were traveling in packs now. A gang of them would swarm into a shop, then come trailing out, one after another, with arms full.

Fitzgerald said, "Is there no way we can stop all this thievery?"

"We can shoot them," Pearse said, but Fitzgerald felt no conviction in his voice.

A short time later, Brennan Whitmore, standing at the Earl Street corner, saw James Connolly pacing back and forth in front of the Post Office. Concerned about the looters, he sent a messenger across the street to ask Connolly for permission to deal drastically with them. Though Connolly, like Pearse, had talked about shooting a few of them, he now said, by return messenger, "Leave them alone unless they attack you."

Whitmore had become exasperated with them because they had started a fire in a boot shop in the center of the block of buildings he and his men occupied. Had it not been for the speed with which the Dublin fire brigade arrived to put it out, the fire might have eliminated their entire position, undoing all their fortification efforts. Constrained by Connolly's order, Whitmore shrugged and watched the passing scene.

A girl came weaving toward him and began to climb over the barricade he and his men had built. He rushed up to stop her but she would not be stopped.

"Are ye tellin' me I can't go home be way of Earl Street?" she said. "All me life I've gone home be way of Earl Street."

She resumed her perilous climb over the chairs, barrels, mattresses, and junk that formed the barricade. An old man who had donned a silk hat and wrapped a fur boa around his neck shouted an obscenity at her. She paused long enough to shout a few at him in return, then resumed her climb, made her way down the other side, and continued on in the direction of Amiens Street.

A boy who looked about twelve years old came along wearing a new golf outfit, somewhat too big for him, but complete—plus fours, a cap, brogue shoes, even a bag with a set of clubs. He teed up a ball on a mound of dirt, selected a club, took a few practice swings, then stepped in and drove the ball half a block down the street. As it sailed into a crowd of people he turned to a bystander and said, in the appropriate accent, "Bunkered, by Jove."

Connolly could find little comfort in reports from his outposts. Hearing nothing for some time from the Citizen Army men at City Hall and the *Daily Mail* building, he sent Sean T. O'Kelly to find out who was in control there. O'Kelly returned, by a circuitous route, with a short answer: "The British." The battle was over. The British had paid a high price, more than twenty dead, but they now controlled the whole section around Dublin Castle and were cleaning out the entire area south of the river around Dame Street and Trinity College. At four o'clock, the pressure became too heavy for a detachment of men Connolly had stationed in Westmoreland Street, just south of O'Connell Bridge. They withdrew to the Post Office as British soldiers made their way up to the bridge, staying, however, out of sight of the Post Office riflemen. A strong British detachment had also moved out from the Amiens Street station to repair the rebel-damaged Great Northern Railroad tracks, and fierce fighting was in progress around Annesley Bridge. The sound of gunfire there could be heard at the Post Office, but the outcome of that battle was still in doubt.

Joseph Plunkett had, by this time, abandoned all hope that the wireless in the Marconi school across the street would be useful for tactical communications. The receiver battery was dead beyond recharging and no replacement for it could be found. The transmitter, however, was operative, and it would be useful to tell the outside world about the rebellion. At 5:30 P.M., therefore, the Irish insurgents became probably the first people in history to broadcast news by radio. James Connolly composed the dispatch and sent it across the street. Fergus O'Kelly, in command at the wireless school, retained for himself the privilege of transmitting the news that an Irish Republic had been declared, with a provisional government in Dublin, and that the army of the Republic had taken possession of the city.

A portion of that army was at the time in the process of retreat toward the Post Office from the Fairview–Annesley Bridge area in the northeastern section of the city. The first of these retreating troops brought with them a batch of five prisoners, including a British army doctor, Lieutenant George Mahoney, who was a Cork Irishman home on leave from duty with the Indian army medical service. He had been stopped in an automobile at an insurgent roadblock. His uniform gave him away though he had tried to hide it under a civilian overcoat. His capture was a potential stroke of good fortune for the insurgents. At last they had a doctor. Now they had only to persuade him, despite his prisoner status, to go to work in their "hospital."

The possession of prisoners had been both an advantage and a danger to this first group coming in from Fairview. As they left the Annesley Bridge area, the British khaki uniforms in their midst saved them from enemy fire, but as they neared the Post Office, those same uniforms began to draw the fire of insurgent snipers. Connolly, who had been expecting the contingent, called a halt to the firing, though not before a few men had suffered minor wounds.

The insurgent forces in the Phibsborough area to the northwest of the Post Office were also retreating now as shrapnel destroyed their barricades at the North Circular Road and Cabra Road railway bridge, but few of them were able to make it to the Post Office. They reported that many had been taken prisoner, and most of those who escaped were withdrawing in the only direction left open to them, northward toward Glasnevin Cemetery.

Lawrence's, a large photographic and toy emporium in upper O'Connell Street that had miraculously escaped looting the day before, came now to the attention of the crowd. But the cameras were not the principal attraction. Lawrence's offered something even more exciting: fireworks. The fun began when a few of the boyos brought out armloads of pryotechnics and created a huge pyramid in the middle of the street. They covered the pile with wood shavings, then set fire to the shavings (not an easy task at the moment, for the rain was increasing) and stood back to watch the display. It was more spectacular than all the combined gunfire in the rebellion up to the moment. Sky rockets, Roman candles, star showers, firecrackers went off in an enormous, bursting bouquet of flame. When the blaze of color fizzled out, it was difficult to imagine a fitting encore, but the crowd managed. People began exploding more fireworks inside the store, with the inevitable result that the building was soon on fire; the spectacle of sky rockets and Roman candles shooting forth from the windows added not only bursts of color but elements of danger to the flames consuming the premises. When the firemen arrived, they had to keep ducking the fireworks to get at the fire. A party of Volunteers came from the Post Office to help them fight the blaze, but to little avail. As the crowd cheered, the building continued to burn.

Sniping against insurgent positions in O'Connell Street was increasing, though not enough to inconvenience the crowd. From the Amiens Street station tower, from the roofs of Trinity College, and from a shop on the south quays came intermittent rifle fire, especially against the three-man garrison at Hopkins and Hopkins jewelry store. A bullet intended for one of these men hit a woman who was walking past the building. By the time anyone could get to her she was dead.

A group of insurgent soldiers in the street became so exasperated at the looters they arrested one of them as an example to the others; took him to Desmond Fitzgerald, who was more or less in charge of prisoners; and accused him of theft. Fitzgerald, not knowing what to do with the man, went to Pearse for instructions. When Pearse heard the story, he seemed to have forgotten his earlier talk about shooting the looters.

"Ah, the poor man," he said, "just keep him with the others."

As Fitzgerald passed through the main hall downstairs, he noticed Joe Plunkett at his map table and went over to talk to him. Plunkett looked appallingly ill but seemed cheerful, even happy, as he studied his maps. While they talked, Pearse, looking exhausted, joined them. Though the three men chatted for a few minutes about subjects like books, food, and the rain outside, it was soon evident they could not abstract their minds from the circumstances around them. Fitzgerald, convinced it was only a matter of hours before they would all be dead, wanted to ask Pearse how long he thought they would be able to hold out, but although it was a question one could ask O'Rahilly, it was not an easy question to ask Pearse, who spoke about the rebellion as a glorious thing in itself, regardless of its outcome or achievements.

Plunkett said, "There is no limit to what we might have achieved if all our original plans had gone forward unchecked."

Pearse agreed with him, yet neither man suggested that, even in that event, they might have expected military victory. To Fitzgerald, the very fact that the conversation returned so often to what might have been was an admission by both men that they knew what was going to be.

Fitzgerald wanted to ask why they had persisted in the date of the rebellion even after they learned that no outside help would materialize aside from the shipload of arms, which also did not materialize. He was unable to phrase the question even when the subject of the arms ship did arise.

Pearse said, "Those guns were not a gift, you know. They were bought and paid for." He spoke as if he wanted to make it clear in everyone's mind that the rebellion was the work of Irishmen alone and that no outsiders had inspired it or even taken a significant part in it.

"If we accomplish nothing else," he said, "we shall at least breathe new life into the cause of Irish nationalism." For Pearse, that would be enough.

For most of the men in the Post Office the pressure continued to mount. After a day of waiting, constantly on the alert, they hadn't even seen the enemy. It was worse than fighting. They hadn't slept the previous night and needn't count on sleeping this night, because as soon as they dozed, the attack was certain to begin. The British had no doubt been waiting for darkness to set in. Then why didn't they come? It was dark now. But it was lashing rain. They wouldn't attack in the rain, would they? Sure, and why not? It's the officers who order an attack and they needn't get wet. This would be a perfect time to attack, in the midst of a blinding rainstorm, when no one would expect it. So everyone had better expect it.

The hours passed, however, and so did the heavy rain, without an attack from the British. Pearse spent the evening seated on a high stool at the counter just inside the main GPO entrance. He was writing, polishing, and repolishing a manifesto to the people of Dublin. By the time he finished, the rain had abated and the mobs, which had run for cover, were again swarming up and down O'Connell Street. Though the firemen were still fighting the blaze at Lawrence's, the battle there had already been lost. The building was doomed. Pearse emerged from the Post Office with an escort, glanced up and down the wide thoroughfare, then marched out to Nelson's Pillar. The previous day, when he read the proclamation of the Republic, he had been heard by a sparse gathering of listeners who didn't recognize him and hadn't even heard of him. Twenty-four hours of notoriety had made a difference. People knew him now. When he appeared, a large audience pressed in around the pillar. He began reading in his slow, intense cadence:

> The Provisional Government to the Citizens of Dublin. The Provisional Government of the Irish Republic salutes the Citizens of Dublin on the momentous occasion of the proclamation of a SOVEREIGN INDEPENDENT IRISH STATE now in the course of being established by Irishmen in arms.
>
> The Republican forces hold the lines taken up at Twelve noon on Easter Monday, and nowhere, despite fierce and almost continuous attacks of the British troops have the lines been broken through. The country is rising in answer to Dublin's call, and the final achievement of Ireland's freedom is now, with God's help, only a matter of days. The valour, self-sacrifice, and discipline of Irish men and women are about to win for our country a glorious place among the nations.
>
> Ireland's honour has already been redeemed; it remains to vindicate her wisdom and her self-control.
>
> All citizens of Dublin who believe in the right of their country to be free will give their allegiance and their loyal help to the Irish Republic. There is work for everyone; for the men in the fighting line, and for the women in the provision of food and first aid. Every Irishman and Irishwoman worthy of the name will come forward to help their common country in this her supreme hour.
>
> Able-bodied citizens can help by building barricades in the streets to oppose the advance of the British troops. The British troops have been firing on our women and on our Red Cross. On the other hand, Irish regiments in the British Army have refused to act against their fellow countrymen.
>
> The Provisional Government hopes that its supporters—which means the vast bulk of the people of Dublin—will preserve order and self-restraint. Such looting as has already occurred has been done by hangers-on of the British army. Ireland must keep her new honor unsmirched.
>
> We have lived to see an Irish Republic proclaimed. May we live to establish it firmly, and may our children and our chil-

dren's children enjoy the happiness and prosperity which freedom will bring.

Signed on behalf of the
Provisional Government

P. H. Pearse
Commanding in Chief the Forces of the Irish
Republic, and President of the Provisional
Government.

A fanciful document but an understandable one, coming from
a commander in such circumstances. To acknowledge the situation as it actually existed would be to admit there was no hope
and no point in continuing. For the sake of his troops as well as
the populace, he had to let his imagination overrule the facts; nor
was it difficult for a man like Pearse to do so. Completely gov-
erned, as he was, by his dream, he could easily believe every
word he had written.

As for those sections of the manifesto suggesting order and self-
restraint to the populace, he may as well have saved his words.
That part of the populace to whom he was addressing himself
became bored even before he finished reading and began drifting
off up the street in search of new shops to loot.

Pearse himself returned to the Post Office, where, shortly after
midnight, he was confronted by depressing evidence of the wish-
fulness of his words. Sixty-six men, routed by the British from
the suburb of Fairview, arrived at headquarters for rest and reassignment. They got very little rest. First, Pearse addressed them
in the public office just inside the main entrance.

"Dublin, by rising in arms, has redeemed its honour," he said.
"It has redeemed an honour forfeited in 1803 when it failed to
support the rebellion of Robert Emmet."

After listening to Pearse, the men were marched upstairs to the
commissary, where they were served huge slabs of cake. Then
they were divided into three parties, the first of which was dispatched to the Imperial Hotel on the other side of O'Connell
Street and the second to the Metropole Hotel just across Prince's
Street, while the third was kept in the Post Office. Connolly, who

had taken charge of the reassignment, designated a lieutenant named Oscar Traynor as commander of the Metropole detachment.

Traynor was reluctant. "I'm not qualified for the job," he said.

Connolly stood directly in front of him and stared at him fixedly. "Is it enough," he said, "that I tell you you're qualified?"

Traynor saluted, called the men to attention, and marched them away.

It appeared now that the men in the Post Office and in the various strongpoints around it could settle down and get some sleep. But it was not to be so.

First, a warning arrived from Mrs. Tom Clarke, who had heard from an informant that the British planned a night airplane attack on the Post Office. Unlikely as the possibility seemed, Connolly and Clarke decided to put more riflemen on the roof.

Then, about half past midnight, a party of excited civilians came bursting into the Post Office to inform Connolly that hundreds of British soldiers, from Phoenix Park, were nearing Parnell Square at the top of O'Connell Street, just two blocks above the Post Office. If so, the encirclement of the insurgent headquarters was complete, and undoubtedly the long-awaited attack was now imminent. The British must have decided to make their assault at night because the cost of a frontal attack on the Post Office in full daylight would be prohibitive. They perhaps thought that at night they would have the element of surprise as well as the cover of darkness in their favor. They would soon discover how wrong they were.

After dispatching several scouts, including the ever-ready Sean T. O'Kelly, to find out if the British were, indeed, advancing in force, Connolly called the Post Office and its outposts to full alert. Men to whom sheer exhaustion had finally brought sleep were shaken awake and sent to their stations. Muscles tightened, mouths went dry, and, as Connolly ordered all light extinguished, all noise eliminated, voices could be heard in the darkness mumbling, "Jesus, Mary, and Joseph," and, "Hail Mary, full of grace . . ." No one doubted that the fight to the finish was finally about to begin. The British would come on, wave after wave, as they had at Balaklava, caring nothing for their losses, which would be enormous. They might eventually prevail, thanks to their overwhelming numbers, but before they did, they would know the full fury of Irish bravery. At every window two or three riflemen crouched, and behind the riflemen, more men, sometimes women, with grenades in hand. Old Tom Clarke grabbed a gun and chose a window. At last he was going to get some of his own back for those fifteen painful, almost maddening years of hunger and silence and solitary confinement in British prisons. Through the raindrops, softly falling now, 200 pairs of eyes peered out, scanning the dimly lit streets, expecting at any moment to see a wave of onrushing khaki. Rifle barrels turned toward each sound in the night. And when at last footsteps were heard on the pavement, the tension became almost explosive. Then suddenly a man, alone, came around the corner and walked toward the Post Office across Henry Street. For a moment his life wasn't worth a farthing as dozens of guns zeroed in on him. But just in time, someone shouted, "Hold your fire, boys—it's Sean O'Kelly," and his friends laughed as little Sean came running into the building. He had been to Parnell Square and found no British there.

The letdown spread through the Post Office as this word circulated. Just another false alarm. Impatient mutterings arose. Men put down their guns, stood up, and stretched, cursed the British. They began moving away from the windows, calling for light as they stumbled over each other in the dark. How many more false alarms could there be? How many more times would they be routed out of sleep and sent to the windows to wait . . . for nothing? The grumbling did not last long. The men were too tired. They stretched out and tried again to sleep. But only a few had managed it before they were rushing once more to the windows. The other scouts had begun returning, all with the same information. The British were, indeed, coming. They were approaching Parnell Square in force, though they had not yet arrived there. And they were undoubtedly ready to attack.

Again, Connolly called an alert. Again the tension mounted. But again the British took their time. They arrived at Parnell

Square, just out of sight of the Post Office. They stopped to study the situation. They deployed their forces. To Connolly's scouts, they showed every sign they were preparing an advance. Yet the minutes passed into hours without their moving forward. And as dawn approached, 200 exasperated, sleepless, red-eyed insurgents were still staring out from the windows of the GPO, watching for khaki.

III. *Wednesday, April 26*

At eight o'clock Wednesday morning, the ominous boom of an artillery shell opened the eyes of those who, despite the recurring alerts, had managed to doze off at their stations in the General Post Office and in the nearby insurgent strongholds. The sound, from the east, somewhere along the river, puzzled the insurgents as much as it disturbed them because they occupied no positions in the area from which it seemed to come. It was not a loud boom. It was far enough away so that some of the men were not even frightened by it or by the second explosion, which followed quickly. But these rolling, rumbling blasts were close enough to dry the throats of those who recognized them and close enough to stimulate a new batch of rumors. Some of the men believed they were hearing German submarine guns attacking British ships in the harbor. Most of them, however, were not so optimistic. The first credible rumor to arise was that the British were shelling Liberty Hall, the headquarters of James Connolly's Irish Citizen Army and of his Transport and General Workers' Union, to which most of the Citizen Army men belonged.

This rumor proved to be true. Insurgents stationed in the Hopkins and Hopkins jewelry store and in the Kelly gun store, both at O'Connell Bridge, soon got word to the Post Office that a British gunboat had come up the Liffey as far as Butt Bridge and was lobbing shells into the square, stone structure that had become such a symbol of resistance to British rule. It was above the front door of Liberty Hall that Connolly had emblazoned the words "WE SERVE NEITHER KING NOR KAISER BUT IRELAND!" It was in Liberty Hall that the Citizen Army held its meetings. It was from there that the "Army of the Republic" had marched, Monday noon, to the Post Office. The target was too obvious a one for the British to ignore. Ironically, however, they were destroying a building for which the insurgents no longer had any use. The only man Connolly had left there was the caretaker, whom spectators could see fleeing to safety soon after the first shell burst. And the only answer the insurgents could make to the eighteen-pound-shell fire was the trivial shotgun fire of the three-man garrison in Hopkins and Hopkins. Had the gunboat been able to come upriver as far as O'Connell Bridge, these men might have wished they had held their fire, but fortunately for them, Butt Bridge blocked the way and they weren't even close enough to attract the attention of the big guns.

The men in the Post Office were stunned, not by the fate of Liberty Hall but by the dawning awareness that their stronghold must now expect the same fate.

A young Citizen Army man turned to an older Volunteer beside him and said, "General Connolly told us the British would never use artillery against us."

To this the Volunteer replied, "He did, did he? Wouldn't it be great, now, if General Connolly was making the decisions for the British?"

The sound of artillery against Liberty Hall might have been a shock to a less dedicated and self-confident man than James Connolly. He had indeed been free with his Marxist assurances that the capitalistic British government would never destroy the property of its capitalist subjects. When big guns boomed in Phibsborough the day before, he could point out that they were destroying not the property of capitalists but the homes of working people. And even now, with the big guns thundering in downtown Dublin, he could point out that they had chosen as a target not a commercial building but the headquarters of Irish trade unionism. When he heard the guns and realized that Liberty Hall was the target, Connolly went to the Post Office roof to see what he could see. Because Liberty Hall was out of view, even from the roof, the most important thing he saw was the alarm on the faces of his riflemen as they listened to the explosions.

"Don't be frightened," he told them. "When the British government starts using artillery in the city of Dublin, it shows they must be in a hurry to finish the job."

If he intended this to convey a notion of British desperation in the face of insurgent strength, he could quickly see that the men were not convinced. As an extra boost to their morale he added, "There are probably some forces coming up to help us."

They were as eager to believe this as he was, and the rumor of German support quickly began another journey from mouth to mouth through the Post Office. Connolly himself wanted so desperately to believe it that he began to think even the British believed it. On his return downstairs, he explained the British use of big guns to Willie Pearse as an indication that they expected German intervention and wanted to quell the rebellion before the Germans arrived.

As for the destruction of Liberty Hall, Connolly could deplore it and nostalgically regret it, but he had no need to mourn it since he had been in danger of eviction from the premises anyway. Though his Citizen Army had been recruited from the Transport and General Workers' Union, of which he was acting general secretary, his policies were not universally applauded by the union rank and file. Dramatist Sean O'Casey, at that time a disgruntled member of the union and only recently resigned as secretary of the Citizen Army, represented a typical attitude toward Connolly among his fellow Marxists. O'Casey felt that Connolly had stepped from what he called "the narrow by-ways of Irish socialism" to "the crowded highway of Irish nationalism." In O'Casey's opinion, "the high creed of Irish nationalism" had become Connolly's "daily rosary," while the "higher creed of international humanity" had lost him. A less impassioned critic might have said Connolly adopted the second creed without discarding the first. Though it was true he now had a much larger vision than Liberty Hall, his primary allegiance was still to the working class. "Our task will only commence," he had told members of the Citizen Army, "when the rifle has done its work." He had indeed embraced Irish nationalism, and he cherished it enough to offer his life for it, but he also saw it as a vehicle for social revolution. Deep in his heart was the firm belief that this hopeless-looking rebellion he had helped provoke would actually spark working-class revolutions all over the world. He could judge the success of a revolution only in proportion to the improvement it brought to the lives of the people. "Someone must look after the interests of the workers," he had said. "The others can look after themselves."

The bombardment of Liberty Hall, as if it had aroused both sides to the need of getting on with things, signaled a sharp increase in hostilities around the Post Office. The sporadic sniper fire that had punctuated the night now grew into angry volleys, first from one side, then the other. Rifle and machine-gun bullets spattered O'Connell Street from both ends as the British began tightening their ring around the rebel headquarters. They moved up slowly and carefully from Great Brunswick Street, south of the river, through D'Olier Street, toward the quays. Unfortunately for them, an insurgent sniper in Kelly's gun store commanded a clear view of D'Olier Street. With one bullet, he flattened the scout of the advancing party. The men behind him ran for shelter in the doorways, and the advance was halted, at least temporarily.

In the Post Office, where no British soldiers had been seen since the outlandish Lancer charge Monday afternoon, unshaven men, and quite a few not yet old enough to shave, peered out the windows along their gun barrels, trying to see where the shots were coming from, where the action was. The streets were deep in broken glass, soiled merchandise, cardboard boxes, bits of window frames, bashed hats, crumpled newspapers. A bullet hit a bowler hat in the gutter, bounced it into the air, and sent it rolling eccentrically along the pavement. Though it was no time for people to show themselves, there were, surprisingly, a few in sight. One person after another would dart across the street, or start across, think better of it, and retreat.

On the top floor of the Post Office, Desmond Fitzgerald encountered The O'Rahilly for the first time since the night before and said, "Still here, are we? I thought we were to be wiped out yesterday for sure."

O'Rahilly laughed and shook his head in wonder at the fact that they were still there. He hadn't much time to talk. If the British were preparing at last to make their charge, he had to be sure the men at the windows and on the roof were ready, despite their desperate need of sleep.

The word was circulating that martial law had been declared in Dublin the night before. Most of the men greeted this news with indifference. Some seemed uncertain as to what martial law meant. One man, apparently still indignant at the looting, exclaimed, "Wouldn't you say it's about time? We've had no law at all around here for the last two days."

There was less confusion than usual in the Post Office this morning, partly because the men were so tired they didn't feel like moving around, but partly also because, after two days, organization had begun to be asserted. The Army of the Republic had even begun to develop a few security measures. People could no longer walk in and out of the Post Office like curious tourists. On Monday and Tuesday, the sentries had passed anyone who looked as if he might be friendly. Today it took a good story to get past the guards. One man whose story wasn't good enough, because he had blended it with too much alcohol, was turned away from the side gate by Sean Gallogly and went reeling toward O'Connell Bridge. He was killed at the corner of Abbey Street by a stray bullet. Gallogly, horrified at the sight of the man's body on the pavement, turned to Patrick Pearse, who was standing nearby, and asked if he should have let the man into the building.

Pearse said simply, "You did the right thing."

Four men who took it upon themselves to leave the building in quest of a secret ammunitions cache were at first barred from reentry when they returned. It was only because they actually had the ammunition to offer that the guard admitted them. They took their haul to Sean MacDermott, who was beginning to look haggard but remained jocular. When he heard about their difficulties reentering the building, he remarked that this was the kind of war a man had to fight his way into. He told them they shouldn't be going out without passes—then he sent one of them out again because the four had not quite been able to carry all the ammunition they had found.

"And if you run into His Lordship the Viceroy, give him me regards."

MacDermott, who was famous for the stories he told, often lapsed into dialect. When he was in Mountjoy Prison in 1915, for making a purposely seditious speech, he helped celebrate the impending release of a fellow prisoner by giving "one of his inimitable dialogues entitled, 'Meself and the Guv'nor!' "

In the Metropole Hotel, just across Prince's Street from the Post Office, Lieutenant Oscar Traynor and his men, battle-hardened by their engagement with the British in Fairview the day before, were now enjoying the luxury of first-class accommodations, though without room service. Aside from the snipers posted at the Abbey Street corner of the Metropole block of buildings, most of the men had comparatively little to do. They watched the bullets bounce off O'Connell Street. They exchanged pleasantries with the men in the windows of the Post Office, and they applauded the bullet-dodging runs between the various outposts on the other side of O'Connell Street. A few of them even ventured out themselves in the hope of furthering the revolution. One eager young Volunteer, for instance, brought in a proper, dignified man in mufti and marched him, at gunpoint, to Lieutenant Traynor.

"I've caught a spy," the Volunteer announced proudly.

The prisoner sputtered in fury.

Traynor said, "What makes you think he's a spy?"

The Volunteer said, "He's a British officer."

"How do you know?"

"Because when I said 'Quick march,' he started off on the left foot."

Gradually the man's indignation subsided enough to let him identify himself. He was in the habit of starting off on his left foot because he was a master at a Dublin military academy.

In Hopkins and Hopkins, at the northeast corner of O'Connell Bridge, Volunteer Cormac Turner finally got around to eating his breakfast after the gunboat stopped shelling Liberty Hall. It was not a conventional breakfast. It was the first meal Turner had ever eaten lying flat on the floor. He and his companions, Seamus Robinson and Seamus Lundy, were somewhat inconvenienced by a British machine gun in the tower of the Tara Street fire station across the Liffey and by a sniper's rifle at McBirney's furniture store, also across the river. Though they were unable to deal effectively with the machine gun, they did manage, after breakfast, to impress the sniper. Through a pair of good binoculars borrowed from the stock of Hopkins and Hopkins, they located him definitely at a central top window. They signaled this information across O'Connell Street to Kelly's gun store, where the Citizen Army's crack rifleman, Andy Conroy, was now stationed with the only rifle in either of the outposts. Though the rest of the men had nothing but shotguns, everyone took aim at the offensive McBirney window except the binocular man in Hopkins and Hopkins. When he saw the sniper's outline appear in the window, he shouted, "Fire!" All the guns erupted at once, and for some time thereafter, nothing was heard from the McBirney sniper.

Having accomplished this much, the three-man Hopkins and Hopkins garrison returned to the job that had occupied them, off and on, for two days—tunneling through the walls of building after building up O'Connell Street toward Abbey Street. They soon reached the Dublin Bread Company building, where they found a party of their comrades using the high, domed tower as a sniping post.

In the Post Office, breakfast was more comfortable, if not sumptuous. As the two girls in charge of the kitchen, Louise

Gavan Duffy and Peggy Downey, got their system developed, the service and even the food began to improve. It was now good enough to become a slight matter of concern to Desmond Fitzgerald, the commissar of the commissary, whose job it was to make the rations stretch. At first, the food had been such that the men didn't want any more of it than they had to have. Now they were beginning to eat for pleasure. Each time he limited their intake, his already waning popularity received another blow.

Fitzgerald was also beviled by one of his prisoners. The British lieutenant who was drunk Monday had managed, by some miracle of supply, to remain drunk Wednesday, in addition to which he was now becoming nervous.

"You shouldn't keep us up here," he complained. "Look at the windows. If we're shelled from this side, we'll have no chance."

Fitzgerald walked away. A few minutes later, another prisoner, an enlisted man, called to him. "I want to be put in another room," he said.

"Why? What's your problem?"

The man glanced at the sodden lieutenant. "When I look at him I do be ashamed to be a man at all."

The O'Rahilly came down to the prisoners' room from the top floor and the lieutenant offered him a variety of complaints—none of which moved him. He was there to question the third officer-prisoner the insurgents had taken, Lieutenant George Mahoney, the British army doctor home on convalescent leave from duty in India. Mahoney, a fair-skinned man, slight of build, was entirely Irish, having been raised in Cork and educated in Dublin. It was useless to interrogate him, because he was not attached to any military garrison in Ireland and could not have divulged any information about British strength or strategy even if he had been willing to do so. It was, however, a friendly interrogation except at the beginning when Mahoney asked: "What do you plan to do with us? Shoot us?"

O'Rahilly, whose conduct was so proper that on Monday he had assigned a prisoner to watch the Post Office safe and bear witness to the fact that it was untouched, flared up now in anger at the suggestion that the insurgents might commit an atrocity.

"Good God!" he said, "don't you know you're all prisoners of war?"

Then, perhaps deciding that Mahoney had not been serious, he regained his sense of humor and they began talking about books. When Mahoney asked if there was anything in the building to read, he said, "I noticed a copy of *The Hunchback of Notre Dame* upstairs. I'll send it down to you."

After O'Rahilly left, Mahoney played cards for a while with the drinking lieutenant and the third officer-prisoner, the man who had been captured when he ventured too close to the Post Office the day before. The card game did not last long because the drinking lieutenant couldn't keep his mind on it. He expected to be bombed, shelled, burned, or shot at any moment, and he wanted to be sure his protests were heard before the event. Once again he shouted for Desmond Fitzgerald. He wanted liquor. When that was refused him, he demanded to be put in a safer place. It was inhuman to make him sit there, helpless, while his own comrades, God bless them, lobbed shells at him. And the fact they hadn't yet done so didn't mean they wouldn't. When the full force of His Majesty's army descended, these bloody potato eaters would all wish they had never heard the word "revolution."

Lieutenant Mahoney, listening to him, winked at Fitzgerald and smiled, but Fitzgerald was becoming too annoyed to laugh.

"All right, I'll take you to the cellar," he said to the lieutenant. "See how you like it."

Surprisingly, the lieutenant said, "Better than here, I'm sure."

Fitzgerald turned to Mahoney and shrugged. "If that's what he wants . . . How about you?"

Mahoney said, "What kind of an army are you running here? If the prisoners get to choose their own accommodations, take me to the Shelbourne."

"I wish I could, but since I can't, come along and see what you think of the cellar." Having learned the night before that Mahoney was a doctor, Fitzgerald had been looking for a casual opportunity to talk to him alone. He wanted to show him their meager, doctorless infirmary and try to enlist his medical aid. He was Irish, after all, even if he did belong to the British army. What a revolution this would be if all the 200,000 Irishmen in the British forces were on the Republican side. As the three men descended into the dark, cold, damp, and musty cellar, Fitzgerald said nothing, waiting for the lieutenant to realize how loathesome it would be to have to stay there.

The lieutenant, however, said, "I'd rather be here than up there under the guns."

Mahoney said, "It's not fit down here for human habitation."

The lieutenant said, "I'll stay." They left him, and on their way back to the second floor, Fitzgerald made sure they passed the infirmary, so Mahoney would see the wounded. Already there were two severe cases. One man had been brought from the roof, shot through the eye, bleeding from a superficial throat wound, and looking as if he were about to die. Another man had been wounded in the abdomen by a bullet from the rear.

When Mahoney saw them, he said, "These men should not be kept here. They should be removed to hospital."

Fitzgerald said, "Removed to hospital? What's the good of talking like that? You know we can't get them to a hospital."

"It's impossible to keep wounds like this from becoming infected if you leave them here."

Fitzgerald shook his head. "We can only do our best for them." He tried to conceal his smile of satisfaction as the doctor in Mahoney overcame the prisoner and he bent closer to the man whose eye socket was now a jagged hole. "And the best we can do," Fitzgerald continued, "is to get you to look after them."

Mahoney did not hear him. He was already too busy with the patient, tracing the course of the bullet, which had taken a freakish route through the eye, down the cheek, along the chest, and finally into the man's leg.

On the Post Office roof, a barrage of rifle fire began about ten o'clock when someone spotted troop movements near the Amiens Street station. The concentrated blasts soon drove the British soldiers to cover, and the volleys in that direction dwindled to an occasional shot whenever a blur of moving khaki came into view. Meanwhile, British snipers, difficult to locate precisely, kept pressing in ever closer to the Post Office and paying special attention to the roof, forcing the men there to move more discreetly and keep themselves out of sight. Just about the time the British targets around Amiens Street disappeared, the men on the Henry Street corner of the roof began to notice more khaki around Parnell Street at the top of O'Connell Street, but as soon as they fired in that direction, the khaki there also disappeared. It was as if the British were teasing them, playing hide-and-seek with them.

The British fire was heavier now than at any time since about 7 A.M., when James Connolly had ordered the raising of the Citizen Army flag, the Plough and the Stars, over the Imperial Hotel. That touch of defiance had attracted an angry outburst of British rifles and machine guns from all directions. Now the fire against the Post Office roof was so steady that the befuddled pigeons didn't know where to land as the bullets whizzed among them. The greatest concentration came from the direction of Trinity College, south of the Liffey, but neither the men on the Post Office roof nor those in the Dublin Bread Company tower across the street could locate the snipers there. So many bullets were flying that even the looters were impressed. They retired to the side streets, which proved profitable enough, for there were still quite a few shops in out-of-the-way places that hadn't yet received their attentions.

Onto the roof at this time, somehow getting past the guards O'Rahilly had posted, came a boy about twelve years old, unwashed, uncombed, and in new but ill-fitting clothes. Before anyone could suggest he had no business there, he endeared himself to the entire company by calling the British every name he could think of, and he could think of quite a few.

"Up the Volunteers!" he shouted. "Come on, me boyos, give it to the bloody shite-heads!"

When several riflemen on the south side unleashed a volley toward Trinity College, he gave a cheer almost loud enough to drown out the gunfire. "D'ye hear that?" he screamed. "They'll all be wiped out before youse are done with 'em. Janey, what I don't wish them limey bastards!"

One of the men turned to him and said, "Hey, what're you doing up here? Scoot, kid, before you get killed."

Just then a bullet hit the roof near the boy's foot. He simply looked down at the spot and with supreme contempt said, "Feck off."

Everyone laughed and there were no further attempts to evict him, although several men tried to talk him into keeping his head down. Fortunately he wasn't big enough to draw any special attention from the Trinity snipers.

Shortly after the boy's arrival, a white-haired old priest made his way to the roof and looked around, incredulous, at the men sprawled out on the tar with rifles pressed to their shoulders. He had walked in from the street, past the guards at the door. No guard in this army would think of stopping a man in a Roman collar. One might almost get the impression that a few hundred British soldiers, dressed as priests, could have walked into the Post Office unhampered and put a sudden end to the entire rebellion. Before the kindly looking old priest had a chance to speak to the men, he spotted the boy.

"Who let you up here?" he said. "This is no place for a lad your age. Go home to your mother and leave the fighting to the men."

To the amazement of the men, the boy showed no respect whatsoever for the authority of the priest. "Walk away from a war like this?" he said. "Bejasus, ye must be daft."

Before anyone could remonstrate with him for such language in front of The Cloth, another rain of British bullets peppered the roof and the boy shouted to the nearest rifleman, "Would ye gimme that gun, I'll plug a few of them feckin' limey bastards! I'll see 'em all in hell, I will!"

Even the priest had to smile. Unable to make an impression on the child, he addressed the men. "I suppose you all know the British army will be at your throats any minute now. Sure look at the bullets already beating down on you like hailstones. God help you, it's a fine fix you've got yourself in, but I want to be sure you're in a state of grace, at least. I'll give you all conditional absolution. Do you hear me? I want each man to tell me, are you sorry for your sins?"

A chorus of "Yes, father" went up from all sides of the roof.

The priest, crouching down, raised his right hand and, making the sign of the cross, began, *"Ego te absolve . . ."* as the bullets whizzed past, punctuating his prayer.

After the priest left, Patrick Pearse and his brother Willie, having braved the cross fire to visit several O'Connell Street positions, arrived on the roof of the Post Office to speak to the men and assess the situation there. They appeared just after the lieutenant in charge, Michael Boland, had issued the latest of many insistent orders to his men that they were to keep their heads down behind their sandbags. The Pearses, apparently indifferent to danger, did not present a good example. They walked from man to man, issuing encouragement, peering out over the balustrades toward the Imperial Hotel across the street, then at the Trinity College buildings south of the river, from which a steady stream of bullets came. Finally, Lieutenant Boland could endure watching them no longer.

He addressed Patrick Pearse. "Will you, for God's sake, sir, get your head down before they blow it off?"

Pearse smiled and thanked the lieutenant for his concern though he didn't actually share it. While he worried about the safety of his men he also accepted and almost welcomed the inevitability that blood would be shed. He harbored such a serenely mystical belief in blood sacrifice as a requirement for nationhood that he had written, in December 1915, about the European war: "The last sixteen months have been the most glorious in the history of Europe. Heroism has come back to the earth . . . The old heart of the earth needed to be warmed with the red wine of the battlefields. Such august homage was never before offered to God as this, the homage of millions of lives given gladly for love of country." He took evident satisfaction in the possibility that his own life might be added to the millions. He had long since decided he would be happy to die in battle if, by his death, he could emancipate Ireland. And he was now convinced that his death, plus the possible deaths of some of his fellow leaders, would, in fact, bring about the emancipation of Ireland by arousing the Irish people. Instead of seeking cover, he stood erect in his green uniform and addressed the men.

"I want you all to know," he said, "how well aware we are that you have been on duty here without sleep since Monday. As soon as possible, we shall get some men up here to replace you. But for now you must carry on. And remember, Ireland can be proud of every one of you."

Willie Pearse, standing by, made one of his rare utterances, to the men near him. "A curious business," he said, in a slow, lisping voice. "I wonder how it will end? I know a lot of good work has been done, but there is a great deal more to do." The men shrugged, not quite certain what had produced the remark. Some of them had never before heard Willie Pearse say anything. He seemed to have spoken simply because he felt a sudden obligation to say something. His brother Patrick, having finished his inspection, turned to leave the roof. Willie followed him.

After the Pearse brothers had left, Lieutenant Boland, who had been a British soldier in the Boer War, shook his head in bewilderment. "It's a mad business," he said to one of the officers under him. "Here we are, shut up in this building, all of our leaders with us, gathered in one place so none of them can hope to escape, and those flags flying over our heads to tell the enemy exactly where to find us when they want us. We should have taken to the hills, like the Boers." He shrugged in resignation. "But we're here now, and we'll just have to stick it."

Across O'Connell Street, on the roof of the Imperial Hotel, the Citizen Army flag raised at 7 A.M. had drawn so much machine-gun fire it was now a tattered rag. At the Dublin Bread Company building, bullets were flying one after another into the cupola of the tower, from which two or three insurgent snipers occasionally replied.

From the corner building at Earl and O'Connell Streets Brennan Whitmore and his men stared out, sometimes toward the Post Office, which was drawing more fire than any other place, and sometimes toward Amiens Street, from which they still expected a frontal attack. Some of the men, overworked and irregularly fed, sprawled out on the floor behind their second-story-window stations and tried to nap despite the increasing noise of gunfire.

A young woman in nurse's uniform appeared from the direction of Amiens Street and came running to their barricade. She scanned the building that housed the men until she saw them peering down at her from the upper windows.

"I've come to help," she called. "How do I get in there?"

Whitmore said, "You don't get in. Go away."

She shouted, "Can you hear me? I want to come in."

"Go away!" he repeated.

"I won't go away! I want to help!"

One of the men said to Whitmore, "Don't let her in. She may be a spy." She had come from the direction of Amiens Street, where British troops were concentrated. And spy rumors were rampant among the insurgents. Whitmore decided to ignore her in the hope she would soon go away, but she remained. Eventually she began calling to him again.

He shouted to her, "You can't come in here and you can't stand down there. You'll be shot."

"I'll stand here," she insisted, "until I'm shot."

She folded her arms and planted herself as if she meant it. He liked her spirit. Some of the men were smiling at her now. He wondered if she was actually a nurse. If so, they would be needing her before long. But if she turned out to be a British agent, then what? Would it make any difference? Once she entered the building, any information she might gather would do her no good because she wouldn't be able to get out. She stood at the barricade, looking up at the building while all these considerations raced through Whitmore's mind. Finally he gave the order and two of the men dropped a ladder to her. Despite the snipers' bullets she attracted, she came scrambling up the ladder; they dragged her through the window and put her on her feet. She dusted herself off, then looked around at the men and broke into a happy smile.

Rolling up her sleeves, she said, "Well now, I'm delighted to be here. What can I do to help?"

In the Post Office, Joseph Plunkett lay on a cot behind the central counter, too ill today to be on his feet, but not too ill to work. His maps were brought to him and he studied them as if he actually thought they offered some way out of the insurgents' dilemma. He thought no such thing, of course. He knew what the military outcome of this rebellion must inevitably be and he accepted it. In one of his poems he had included a couplet that acknowledged and even welcomed the fate he anticipated:

> *Praise God if this my blood fulfills the doom*
> *When you, dark rose, shall redden into bloom.*

Plunkett's health was such that death must soon overtake him in any case. The rebellion offered him, at least, an opportunity to make it meaningful and useful. Like the other leaders, he presumed he would die, either in battle or at the hands of the British army after the battle, and that his death would help arouse the Irish people to carry on the fight for freedom. Yet on days like this he was not sure his frail body would hold out long enough for either the battle or the British to immortalize him. He lay down his maps and envisioned Grace Gifford, whom he loved as if she were Cathleen ni Houlihan herself, the manifestation of the Irish ideal in womanhood and in nationhood—beautiful, sanctified, romantic, and not quite attainable. Why had he set their marriage date so late—the very day he expected to go out and do battle? A strange way to consummate an ordinary marriage, but perhaps a fitting way to consummate a marriage to Cathleen ni Houlihan. And why hadn't he found the time to have the ceremony performed Sunday? It had been a hectic day, due to the countermand order, but had it been that hectic? If there were only some way, he would marry her yet before he died.

Tom Clarke and Sean MacDermott took turns trying for at least a few minutes' sleep. While MacDermott dozed, Clarke moved about the building, commenting impetuously on anything that met with his disapproval, stopping impulsively to talk with the men about the glory of what they were doing. He would die, no doubt, and the other leaders would die, but some of these youths would live on to continue the struggle for independence.

He wished there were a way for him to convey to this fresh, eager generation the total meaning of the life he had spent as a revolutionary. He walked into the infirmary and spoke to Jim Ryan, who was not busy at the moment. Here was a bright young man, soon to be a doctor if he survived—and because he was a noncombattant, he was more likely to survive than some of the others. Clarke sat down and looked into Ryan's expectant eyes.

Thus began a monologue that was to last two hours. "Do you know how many years I've waited for these glorious days?" Clarke said. "When I was sixteen, another lad and myself formed a little group, and it wasn't long after that I joined the Irish Republican Brotherhood. Sixteen years old. 1873. That was forty-three years ago." He talked about those Fenian years of frustration and recited the whole history of the IRB. He told of his first trip to America, then his assignment, by the Brotherhood, to go to England to take part in a dynamiting campaign. He spoke of his betrayal and capture before ever a stick of dynamite exploded, of his life sentence, and of the fifteen years he had spent in British prisons, often in solitary confinement, before he was finally released:

> We lived under a scientific system of perpetual harassment. The officers in charge had a free hand with Irish prisoners. At night if you went to sleep you were awakened by officers banging trap doors at hourly intervals. This went on for years. We weren't allowed to speak. We were put on bread and water as punishment. One by one I saw my friends break down, some slowly, others without warning. We had one fellow named Whitehead. I can't forget the night he realized he was going mad. For an hour, between inspections, I heard him curse England and beseech God to strike him dead rather than let him lose his reason. One day in the iron foundry where we both worked I saw him try to eat ground glass. "Don't you know that'll kill you?" I said. "A pound of it would do you no harm," he said. When they finally released him, they sent him to a lunatic asylum. The same with another fellow who was reported insane after five years and had to spend eight more years in prison before they let him go. But they were treated no worse than the rest of us. We did everything we could to hold on to our sanity. We wrote notes to each other at night. For two or three years they gave me the cold treatment. They took

most of my clothes and put me in an arctic cell. I once had forty days of starvation in that cell. I chewed rags to fight the hunger. After forty days I was so weak I couldn't stand upright. And there were other things I won't even mention. Do you know what I did finally? From the prison library I got a book called *Cassell's Popular Educator*. From that book I taught myself shorthand. Then I spent hour after hour shorthanding the entire Bible, Old and New Testaments. And when I was finished, I started over. You had to do something all the time to keep from going mad.

He told of his eventual release from prison, his second journey to America, his return to Dublin in 1907, the reorganization of the IRB, the recruiting of new, young men, and all the events leading to the uprising. He described the heartbreaking contentions within the Volunteer organization the previous week and enumerated the arguments in favor of rising despite the countermand order. If they had waited any longer, they might all have been arrested and another generation would have passed without a blow being struck. At the same time, with remarkable detachment, he did justice to the most telling points advanced by moderates like MacNeill, Hobson, and The O'Rahilly, who had opposed the uprising.

When he was finished, Clarke looked directly at Jim Ryan and said, "I suppose you know why I'm telling you all this. It's because you're wearing that Red Cross armband. In the final bayonet charge, they may spare you. If they do, if you survive, I hope you'll try to make people understand the seven of us who signed the Republican Proclamation."

James Connolly, who had been out of the Post Office several times during the morning, braving the gunfire to inspect insurgent positions and to seek firsthand information about enemy movements, happened to be in the building when Volunteer Joseph Cripps returned after several trips outside. It was Cripps' responsibility to procure medical supplies, and he was in and out so often Connolly had noticed his comings and goings.

"It seems to me you spend more time outside than in," he said. "Are all those excursions necessary?"

"Yes, sir."

"Well, I don't want you taking chances. They're shooting at us from all directions now. If you must go out, be careful. If you don't have to go out, stay here where you're safe."

Cripps looked at Connolly, whom he had seen outside on several occasions, and said, "What about yourself, sir?"

Connolly scowled, then broke into a smile. "Never mind me. I'll take care of myself."

Connolly was getting only sketchy information from outside now. He knew, of course, that all positions in northern and northeastern Dublin were lost, that Edward Daly's men at the Four Courts were pinned down, that the men at the Mendicity Institution farther west were surrounded, and that those at the South Dublin Union were so outnumbered and under such heavy pressure they could hardly be expected to hold out much longer. The garrison around the castle and City Hall had been eliminated. The St. Stephen's Green contingent had been driven into the Royal College of Surgeons, where they were virtually neutralized. About Thomas MacDonagh's garrison at Jacob's biscuit factory and Eamon De Valera's garrison at Boland's mill he knew very little except that they were still holding their positions. He was anxious to get in touch with the De Valera forces because he had heard, from someone who had slipped through the British lines, that shiploads of troops were arriving at Kingstown (Dun Laoghaire) harbor and were marching on the city along a route that would bring them face to face with De Valera's Mount Street and Northumberland Road outposts. Though De Valera and his men should be warned, it was not likely that any of the men in the Post Office could get through the lines to warn them. Connolly called on two Cumann na mBan girls in civilian clothes, Bridget Grace and Mary Cullen. Bridget, it happened, had a brother stationed in a house on Northumberland Road, which the British would probably pass on their way to the center of the city. She and Mary accepted Connolly's dispatch and instructions, swallowed hard, and saluted. Slipping out a side door, they disappeared into an alley and hurried away on their mission. Connolly, watching them go, might wonder what good his warning would do the handful of men on Northumberland Road. At a time when they needed reinforcements more than messages, a message was all he had to offer. Ah well, it would show them at least that headquarters had not forsaken them.

Connolly was worried also about the men in another insurgent position much closer to him: the Dublin Bread Company tower on the other side of O'Connell Street. No longer able to delude himself about the British intention to use artillery, he had to face the likelihood that the domed tower, with its snipers, would be too conspicuous a target to resist and the men in it would be blown to bits. He sent a messenger across the street with an order that the tower be evacuated immediately.

A short time later, the messenger, having traversed O'Connell Street at his peril, arrived at the Dublin Bread Company building in a state of high excitement. When he regained his breath he said to Fergus O'Kelly, the officer in charge, "General Connolly orders you to evacuate."

O'Kelly was puzzled. "Evacuate what?"

"Evacuate your men."

O'Kelly decided he had heard the man incorrectly. "Would you mind repeating that?" he said.

"General Connolly told me to tell you to evacuate your men."

"You mean all the men?"

"I guess so."

O'Kelly exploded. "For God's sake, you must be daft. Why ever would General Connolly want us to evacuate? We're giving 'em hell from here. Are you sure that's what he said?"

"I just got through talking to him," the man said. "He sent me here."

As they talked, the guns in the tower above them barked continuously. There were now so many British snipers south of the Liffey that the men in the tower seemed unlikely ever to run out of targets. The guns in Hopkins and Hopkins at the corner and those in the buildings between were also keeping up a steady pace. This block of buildings was one of the cornerstones of the Post Office defense. It seemed criminal to evacuate, but an order was not to be ignored. Fergus O'Kelly passed the word along to the men in the several buildings between Abbey Street and Eden Quay. Then he went to the steps of the tower above him in the DBC building.

"Come down out of there, boys. We're evacuating the premises."

As the guns fell silent, he could hear the men ask each other, "What did he say?"

"I said come down. We're evacuating the whole block."

After an uproar of disbelief, followed by refusals, all but one of the men, a Volunteer named Tom Ennis, eventually descended from the tower. Ennis, instead of obeying the order, resumed firing.

O'Kelly said, "Did you hear me, Tom? Come down. That's an order."

Ennis stopped firing long enough to say, "You know what you can do with your bloody order," then his gun resumed its insistent message to the British across the river. But finally, after O'Kelly had shouted three direct commands, he gave in to authority. As he descended from the tower, the heat of his language equaled the heat of his rifle.

As soon as O'Kelly gathered together the fifteen or twenty men from Hopkins and Hopkins, the Marconi wireless school, and the DBC, they began a dangerous and roundabout retreat toward their headquarters. They ran east on Lower Abbey Street, then up Marlborough Street, trying to find an approach to O'Connell Street from which they could dash in relative safety across to the Post Office.

Meanwhile, a Volunteer from the north named Sean MacEntee, who had been sent by Pearse and Connolly Monday to arouse his unit in Ardee, arrived back in Dublin and tried to find an open route to the Post Office. MacEntee, who was destined one day to become Ireland's deputy prime minister, had managed to locate his unit, had undergone a series of misadventures with it, and had then lost contact with it. Finding himself alone, he had made his way back to Dublin to take part in whatever might be happening there. It was immediately evident to him that he would encounter difficulties trying to get through the British lines around the Post Office. Being an Ulster man, he didn't know Dublin's back streets. In Mountjoy Square he encountered a talkative little man who told him, with relish, how the military was giving it to the rebels. Encouraged, perhaps, by MacEntee's northern accent, he also confided what rascals and scoundrels the rebels were, every one of them. MacEntee showed no sign of disagreement. He listened to the man, then said, "Is there any way I could see a bit of the fighting? Something to tell my friends about when I get back home."

"Well now," said the little Dubliner, sizing up the innocent-looking country boy, "it might be arranged."

He led the way down Gardiner Street and along Parnell Street until they came to the Rotunda Hospital at the top of O'Connell Street, where MacEntee got his first glimpse of the battle scene. The guns barking, the bullets bouncing back and forth, and the gray stone bulk of the Post Office topped by two Irish flags defying those bullets filled him with a fervor that culminated all his devotion to the cause of Irish independence. He had to find a way through those bullets and into the Post Office, where he belonged. He noticed that at his feet the pavement was wet with the blood of someone who must have been carried away just a few minutes before. The spit of a bullet chipping a wall above his head enforced the message of the blood. MacEntee, with his new "friend" leading the way, retreated back up Parnell Street. But it was not in that direction he wanted to go. They were getting farther from the Post Office.

MacEntee took hold of the little Dubliner's sleeve. "Is there no way we could get a closer view of the GPO?" he said.

It was a suggestion that might have seemed insane to some men, but not to this one. Excitement didn't come that often. When it did, a person had to take a bit of nourishment from it. Much as he despised the villainous rebels, he couldn't deny they had stirred up a grand Donnybrook. If you could only move in close enough, you might even see a few of the dirty bowsies shot. It was exactly what they had coming, every last one of them. Was it not?

MacEntee gave no indication that he disagreed. Down Marlborough Street they walked to the corner of North Earl Street, which put them, though they were unaware of it, in the no man's land between Brennan Whitmore's insurgent garrison and the British forces at the Amiens Street station. In the intersection lay the body of a woman. Her corpse was sufficient evidence of danger to turn MacEntee's guide around. They retreated back into Cathedral Street, which ran parallel to North Earl Street and also led to O'Connell Street. The gutted remains of Lawrence's toy emporium at the corner of Cathedral and O'Connell Streets was still smoldering from the fire that had destroyed it the previous night, and a crowd of looters scurried in and out the Cathedral Street side, keeping themselves just clear of the O'Connell Street bullet traffic as they salvaged whatever items the fire had missed. One youngster who emerged with a mouth organ was spotted by another who had a stack of celluloid collars.

"Hey, Tommy," he cried, "I'll swop ye ten collars for that French fiddle."

"No ye won't. I don't want yer oul' collars."

"I'll give ye twelve then."

The other boy shook his head.

"Fifteen?"

"I tell ye, I don't want 'em at all."

"Give ye ten then, an' this tie pin, and this injey-ball."

"Let's see the ball. Not much use. It hardly bounces."

"How about this gun?" He produced a toy pistol from his pocket. "And the ball," he added.

The boy with the mouth organ was interested at last. "Have ye any caps for it?" he asked.

The other boy shook his head sadly, perhaps afraid there was no hope of a deal, but the gun had made more of a hit than he realized.

"Gimme the gun, and the ball, and a couple of them oul' collars," said the boy with the mouth organ, "and ye can have this French fiddle."

While he was watching all this, MacEntee heard a commotion and turned to see a group of Volunteers and Citizen Army men (the retreating contingent from the Dublin Bread Company block led by Fergus O'Kelly) running up Cathedral Street in his direction. As soon as they came abreast of him, he realized they were seeking a way across the street to the Post Office. His little Dublin friend looked with evident disgust upon this unshaven, bedraggled collection of men.

He turned to MacEntee. "A dirty-looking crowd."

MacEntee said, "Indeed they are"—and, removing his overcoat, which he gave to a nearby urchin, he said, "Good day," to the little man and joined them.

Though there were some enemy guns raking O'Connell Street from the south, the fire did not seem as heavy as it had been. Fergus O'Kelly decided to chance it. Darting out from the Cathedral Street corner, he zigzagged his way across O'Connell Street. From the Post Office windows a cheer arose as he reached the other side safely. Another man followed O'Kelly, and another, but as each man made the dash, the enemy fire increased until a storm of bullets filled the street. The deadly traffic was soon so heavy it would have been certain suicide to step out into it. Some of the men, including "Blimey" O'Connor, Seamus Robinson, and Tom Ennis, made their way up to the Parnell Monument, where they crossed so quickly they caught the British at the top of O'Connell Street by surprise. The rest of the men, including MacEntee and Cormac Turner, waited in vain for the gunfire to abate. Instead, it was augmented from a new direction, behind them, in Marlborough Street. It was beginning to look as if they might be pinned down indefinitely when a door opened on the south side of Cathedral Street and a woman called out, "Come this way!"

They raced toward her and she led them back through a public house and a billiards room into a tobacco shop that opened onto North Earl Street.

"There's some of your men in the corner building across the street," she said, pointing to the second-story windows from which Brennan Whitmore's riflemen controlled North Earl Street. One of them, Paudeen O'Keefe, recognized Turner among the newcomers who suddenly appeared in the doorway of the tobacco shop. Once again, Whitmore's men lowered their ladder, as they had done earlier for the insistent nurse, and their fugitive comrades in arms darted across the street to climb to safety despite an unflagging shower of bullets from Amiens Street. After Brennan Whitmore satisfied himself that the new arrivals were indeed Volunteers, he made sure they were fed (a meal of cold meat), then assigned them to various duties. Thus, the North Earl Street garrison almost doubled its strength. But unfortunately, the Hopkins and Hopkins—Dublin Bread Company garrison, which had protected the North Earl Street men from the south, was now out of existence, thanks to a misinterpreted order.

Meanwhile, when James Connolly learned that the entire block of buildings from Eden Quay to Lower Abbey Street had been abandoned, he erupted in fury. Fortunately it was not he but Joseph Plunkett whom Fergus O'Kelly encountered when he entered the Post Office after his dash across O'Connell Street.

O'Kelly said, "I received an order to return to the . . ."

Before he had time to ask for an explanation of the order, Plunkett, lying on his cot behind the counter of the main room, looked up and interrupted him. "I know," he said. "Collect your men and go back."

It was like telling him to collect a handful of sand he had just thrown away, but O'Kelly asked no more questions. He gathered together those of his men who had reached the Post Office, and they began the perilous journey back to the stations they had abandoned.

While gunfire continued to increase on O'Connell Street, the looters continued to go about their business in the side streets around the Post Office. The loss of O'Connell Street did not seem to distress them because they had done thorough jobs on most of its shops before the bullets began to interfere with their work.

One old shawlie, pushing a cartful of pilfered merchandise, came to a shop she hadn't noticed before and, seeing a crowd of people inside, decided it wouldn't be right to pass the place without giving it a look. When she entered, she was so pleased with what she saw that she came out with an armload. But alas, as she emerged she found that her cart was gone.

"Could you believe it?" she cried. "The bloody place is full of thieves!"

A wide, muscular man staggered along the street with a pair of bright yellow boots in one hand and, in the other, a large jar that hung by its handle from his index finger. As he walked, the jar bounced lightly against his right thigh. A gun fired and a bullet whistled. The jar split asunder; the liquor in it splashed out, wetting both the man and the pavement. He looked with surprise, then indignation at the jagged neck of the bottle still dangling from his finger. Then he turned toward a man watching in a doorway.

"Jasus!" he said, "not a drop of it left. The wasteful bastards!"

A blind man who tottered out onto Eden Quay was not so fortunate as to lose only a jug of liquor. Emerging from a door near Hopkins and Hopkins, he began feeling his way toward O'Connell Street with his walking stick. From McBirney's furniture shop a shot rang out. The blind man fell, writhing, to the pavement.

A few moments later, an ambulance man emerged from cover and ran into the street to administer first aid. He knelt, opened the injured man's clothing, and put a bandage over the wound. Then he helped the man to his feet and led him out onto O'Connell Bridge in the direction of safety. Gunfire from both sides had stopped now as if everyone were fascinated by the rescue attempt. It appeared that the blind man was destined to be saved. As he and his escort reached the middle of the bridge, however, two more shots rang out from McBirney's. Both men fell to the pavement.

Silence settled over the river for several minutes. Finally, an ambulance drove onto the bridge, picked up the bodies, and sped away. The gunfire resumed.

At two o'clock, the British began occupying the buildings on Aston's Quay almost directly across O'Connell Bridge from the insurgents in Kelly's gun store. The British were also moving up in force to occupy Great Brunswick Street and College Street near Trinity College, just a block south of the river. The men at Kelly's could get occasional glimpses of khaki now, but when they did, they had to shoot so quickly their accuracy suffered. One of them, however, managed to hit a British soldier on D'Olier Street, and a short time later, at 2:30, he had reason to wish he had missed. As if in answer for the man who had been hit, the British rolled a nine-pound gun out into the juncture of D'Olier and College Streets and began lobbing artillery shells up D'Olier Street, across O'Connell Bridge, into the upper portion of Kelly's shop.

The first explosion was so fierce it shook even the Post Office, two short blocks away, convincing some of the men there that a bomb had gone off in the bowels of the building. The second and third explosions made them realize they were again hearing artillery, and this time from a gun much closer than the ones that had blasted Liberty Hall in the morning. On every floor of the Post Office the men looked uneasily at each other. The detonations were so tremendous they sounded as if they were coming from Abbey Street, just a block away. Pearse and Connolly looked out the nearest windows, but the Metropole Hotel blocked their view so they could not see the shells tearing holes in the Kelly building. The men on the Post Office roof had a better view. They saw the blasts and the clouds of dust that rose; they could even see in the distance the mouth of the big gun spitting fire. It was within their range, so they trained their rifles on it and sent volley after volley of bullets toward it, but the men operating the gun were too well covered behind it. The shells continued to riddle the Kelly building, accompanied now by rifle and machine-gun fire from the tower of the fire station south of the river, from the roof of the Custom House, and from windows all along the southern quays.

Inside Kelly's, the men hurried downstairs after the initial shock and huddled in the corners as one explosion after another, sometimes less than a minute apart, tore holes in the building. The thought of answering this kind of bombardment with rifle and shotgun fire was too ludicrous to consider even if they had dared approach the windows. They could only ride out the storm in the hope that enough of their fort would survive to enable them to maintain their position there. But after an hour of shell-fire, with beams, floors, and plaster falling down around them, with more dust than air to breathe, with their ears so battered they could scarcely hear even the continuing explosions, they began to realize that their situation was untenable. By that time, so did James Connolly, who kept getting reports on the shelling from the Metropole Hotel garrison. At 3:30 the men at Kelly's were ordered to retreat to the Metropole. The rain of shells continued, however, for another hour, until the building was nothing but four shattered walls.

After the bombardment subsided, an old woman emerged from a house on Bachelor's Walk, just a few doors west of the de-molished building, and, as if shell-shocked, wandered over to it. Standing on the edge of a pile of rubble, she gazed in at the ruins and shook her head, as if in sorrow. The shouts of people on both sides of the river shook her, finally, from her lethargy. Looking around aimlessly, she raised a feeble hand, then turned and wan-dered off, at a shiftless pace, across O'Connell Street. Until she passed, both sides held their fire.

The machine guns south of the Liffey now began to concen-trate on the Dublin Bread Company building, not yet reoccupied by the insurgents, on the Imperial Hotel, and on the Post Office itself. The rat-a-tat of bullets entering the top-floor windows sounded like bursts of hail hitting the walls. On the Post Office roof, the insurgent snipers spotted the machine-gun positions one after another and concentrated their fire on them. Gradually, the stream of bullets subsided, but whether it was because the machine-gunners had been put out of action or because they were simply resting, the insurgents didn't know.

During the lull, the insurgents heard what sounded like a heavy truck approaching from the top of O'Connell Street. When they turned in that direction, they thought for a moment they were about to be attacked by a contraption from some other planet. Slowly bearing down on them was a huge vehicle with an armor-protected engine and, behind the hood, a rectangular, armored body with tiny slits and circular holes, from which gun barrels protruded. In these days before the introduction of tanks on the western front, nothing like it had ever been seen. Relentlessly it kept coming as the men in the Post Office, shaking off their initial alarm, tried to figure out how to combat it. Having nothing better to do, some of them raised their rifles and fired at it. The bullets made an almost musical sound as they bounced off. Soon, almost everyone in the Post Office with a rifle was firing at it, but to no avail. The armored monster drew closer by the moment.

One man who had not yet fired at it was a Volunteer named Joseph Sweeney. He studied it as it drew closer, noticing the holes and slits in its armor, and in particular the widest slit, a one-foot by one-inch opening in the front of the body. It seemed reasonable to Sweeney that the driver would be just behind that slit. Raising his rifle, he trained his eye upon the narrow gap. One, two, three times he fired. Each time, his bullet struck armor and the vehicle continued to roll forward. A fourth time he fired. There was no sound of impact against metal. The bullet went neatly through the slit. The vehicle rolled a few feet closer, then, as its engine coughed, came to a chugging stop. After several more shots at it, the riflemen in the Post Office held their fire, watching, wondering breathlessly whether its engine would start again. The minutes passed. The big vehicle stood dead in the street. The men in the Post Office looked at each other and began to smile.

Ignatius Callender, who since Monday had been the communications link between the Post Office and Edward Daly's garrison at the Four Courts, surprised James Connolly by managing, late Wednesday afternoon, to make one more successful trip to the Post Office. Other messengers who had gone out on missions Wednesday (including Sean T. O'Kelly) had not been able to get back through the British cordons. Callender (whose mother, as he went off to fight, had pinned a badge of the Little Flower of Jesus on his chest with the remark "You're all right now—the Little Flower will protect you") had made his way from the Four Courts along a series of back streets and alleys, eventually crawling through a hole in the wall of Randall's boot shop on Henry Street, then through a series of holes in several buildings that brought him finally to the Post Office. Before allowing him to give his report, Connolly called together Pearse, MacDermott, and The O'Rahilly to hear him. There was some surprise when O'Rahilly appeared. Until now, he had rarely come down from his post on the upper floors of the building. After hearing what Callender had to say, he could wish he had stayed upstairs.

Having been on the streets quite frequently, Callender knew where the British troops were located. Connolly, eager for the latest information, called for a map on which he could point out the British deployments, but as Callender went over the map, telling how many infantrymen he had seen here, how many he had seen there, it became evident that no map was needed. The British were everywhere.

Callender's report of the Four Courts garrison was only slightly more encouraging. Troops at the Broadstone station were threatening Daly's men from the north. A British sniper in the Bermingham Tower south of the Liffey had accounted for more than twenty casualties already, and no one seemed able to pick him off. A machine gun on the roof of a building was spraying the entire area. Yet morale was high and there was no thought of surrender. When he finished his report and answered their questions, Callender received warm thanks from Pearse and Connolly, after which Pearse and then Sean MacDermott shook his hand, thereby providing the young man with one of the great thrills of his lifetime. Like so many Volunteers, he had long since come under the spell of MacDermott, who knew him by name, could lift his spirits with a smile, and had a way of making him feel important. To Callender, MacDermott, despite his twisted, polio-stricken body, was a special hero among all these heroes. He was brave, commanding, and strong beyond physical strength; yet he was also lovable. And looking now into his eyes, Callender noticed something else about him that was amazing. Despite the chaos and danger around him, he seemed sublimely happy.

The most significant aspect of this gathering of the leaders was the presence of O'Rahilly, for it indicated a softening of his resentment against the others. O'Rahilly was not the kind of man who could long bear a grudge. The approach of almost certain death made it pointless to cherish grievances. If there was still a noticeable uneasiness when he took his place beside Pearse and MacDermott, it arose now not from bitterness but from embarrassment on his side and from an element of chagrin on theirs. His exclusion from their confidence during the planning of the rebellion seemed increasingly shoddy in light of his brave acceptance of responsibility. And his confrontation with Mac-Dermott over the kidnapping of Bulmer Hobson was too recent to be forgotten. Pearse, a less pragmatic man than MacDermott, was especially sensitive in O'Rahilly's presence because he had always tried to be as devoted to his scruples as to his cause. He had praised O'Rahilly lavishly to one person after another since Monday and was pleased to see him arrive for their meeting. It was not easy, though, for a person of Pearse's somber and constricted nature to convey such pleasure.

The North Earl Street garrison, augmented by the men from the Dublin Bread Company garrison, had now taken the Imperial Hotel, directly across from the Post Office, to protect the southeastern flank, which had been left exposed when the DBC men mistakenly evacuated their position. But while this put the North Earl Street men closer to the Post Office, it did not solve the problem of communication with headquarters, for dispatches could no longer be carried across the bullet-swept street. The commander of the garrison, Brennan Whitmore, thought of a solution. While one man held the end of a ball of twine, another man threw the ball across O'Connell Street to the Post Office, where it was run around a post and thrown back. A can was fastened to the twine as a message carrier, and Whitmore had a two-way "telegraph" for communication with his superiors. The invention had only one flaw. The can, moving slowly across the street, was an attractive target for British marksmen. On the can's third trip, it was shattered.

Whitmore was becoming depressed now, though he carefully concealed it from his men. The early excitement of action having passed, he became, hour by hour, more acutely aware that they were all trapped, that they could offer nothing but token resistance as the British moved in to destroy them, that there was no escape, no alternative to annihilation. Why had the rising been planned so badly? Why were they here in Dublin, surrounded, squeezed, and bombarded, when they could be in open country, hitting, running, hitting again, driving the British to desperation? These were such pointless questions now he wished he could blot them from his mind. He saw one of his men fastening a new can to the twine "telegraph," thus creating another easy target for some British rifleman. He went up to the man and took the can away from him.

"For God's sake," he said, "just tie the message to the twine. They'll never see a bit of paper."

Another artillery explosion shattered the air, this time closer than any of the previous shells. At first, Whitmore thought the Post Office itself had been hit, but when he looked up he realized it was the *Freeman's Journal* building on Abbey Street, around the corner from the Metropole Hotel.

In the Post Office, Sean McDermott could not suppress a smile when he learned where that shell had landed, for the *Freeman's Journal*, more bitterly than any other Dublin newspaper, had opposed the movement for Irish independence. Earlier, when MacDermott had been told that the insurgents' armament shop was filling grenades with lead from the *Freeman's Journal* print shop, he had said, "It's the first time any of that type has ever been put to good use."

As evening arrived, the gunfire seemed to slacken, though it quickly erupted again whenever anyone dared show himself on O'Connell Street. Desmond Fitzgerald, having finished for the moment his commissary duties, came downstairs to talk to Plunkett, who lay on his cot behind the main counter, and to Pearse, who was standing nearby. The knowledge that Plunkett, despite his cheerfulness, was near death from tuberculosis, filled Fitzgerald with a special pity that puzzled him when he stopped to reflect that he, too, and everyone else in the Post Office was near death. Anyone who doubted it had only to take five or six steps outside the front door. Perhaps some would survive, but none could count on survival, and a few, like Pearse, could hardly escape the realization that they were as certain to die as Plunkett.

Fitzgerald could not look at Pearse's face without being moved. Its natural gravity now conveyed a sense of great tragedy, perhaps because Pearse was convinced, as he looked at all these men and girls around him, that they were likely to perish in a cause to which he had rallied them—a cause whose very worth must appear questionable to some of them at this moment. While they were offering their lives for the Irish people, they couldn't help knowing their sacrifice was unappreciated, as he himself knew from those who had gone out on errands and reported back that the people they encountered were in a mood to attack them. Aside from the Irish Republican Brotherhood, the Citizen Army, and a few members of the Hibernian Rifles, no group of Irishmen had endorsed the rebellion. Even the bulk of the Volunteers, under the influence of MacNeill, had repudiated it.

Fitzgerald kept wanting to ask why the rebellion had not been postponed when it became apparent that no outside help would be forthcoming. There was, of course, the so-called Castle Document, which had been publicized the week before. It indicated that the British government was planning to arrest all the known nationalist leaders before they could get a rebellion started. If the document was genuine, it might have given the leaders reason enough to plunge ahead for fear their plans might be thwarted completely by imprisonment. But some people seemed to think the Castle Document was a forgery, fabricated by Joe Plunkett and perhaps Sean MacDermott to persuade the moderate faction in the Volunteers against delay. If so, it had failed.

In the conversation between Pearse, Plunkett, and Fitzgerald, the one theme that recurred more than any other was the moral rectitude and theological justification of what they were doing. There was no attempt to deny responsibility for the death and destruction produced by the rebellion. The question was how that death and destruction would appear in the eyes of God. They were, after all, waging a war, and the Church had never proscribed war so long as it was fought in a worthy cause. Could anyone doubt that the freedom of Ireland was a worthy cause? But what about a war undertaken with so little hope of victory? Could not such a war be called suicidal, and therefore sinful? No. Sacrificial, perhaps, but not suicidal. The difference was significant. They were not killing themselves. Indeed, they were fighting for their lives. Yet they were willing to die, if need be, as a sacrifice to the cause of Irish freedom. Did not Christ sacrifice himself in much the same way, though for a higher cause? He proclaimed at the Last Supper his intention to offer his life for the redemption of all mankind. He told his apostles that his body would be delivered unto death for them and that his blood would be shed for the remission of the sins of man. Could it not be said that even the concept of redemption applied, in a limited way, to the rebellion? Surely the people of Ireland were in need of redemption after centuries of bondage—especially the people of modern Ireland, many of whom had fallen so far as to accept the shame of bondage. If some must die to achieve redemption, why should they fear death? Saint Paul said, "The sting of death is sin." But Christ, by taking away the sins of the world, had robbed death of its terror. By dying he destroyed death, and by rising from the dead he restored life. Was it not fitting, then, that this rebellion, the purpose of which was to restore life to Ireland, be launched at Eastertime? And if at first it might appear to result in failure, one should remember that the crucifixion of Christ made many people think he had failed. Yet if the resurrection of Ireland were to result from this rebellion, from the sacrifice of lives, would it not one day be regarded as a glorious success?

Sometimes, when Pearse or Plunkett made a particularly telling point in the discussion, Fitzgerald would ask that it be repeated and would press for exact, authoritative references to back it up, partly because he wanted to be able to requote it to others who might feel the burden of such questions upon their consciences, but partly also perhaps because he needed reassurances himself. And while all the arguments the three of them could marshal were painstakingly appraised, developed, and assembled into their bulwark of exculpation, the guns kept bursting sporadically outside and bullets spattered against the building's exterior walls, no more than twenty feet away.

Fergus O'Kelly and his men, after a hazardous journey that entailed many delays, had now managed to regain the Dublin Bread Company building, the Marconi radio school, and Hopkins and Hopkins, which they had evacuated in the early afternoon as a result of a wrongly delivered order from James Connolly. On their return to the wireless school, they resumed transmitting messages about the new Irish Republic at frequent intervals, wondering as they did so if anyone was receiving them. Unable to make their own receiving set work, they had no replies to show for all their messages. Because they still considered the messages worth sending, however, and because they knew the wireless school would not be operable much longer in the building that housed it, they decided to try to move it to the Post Office under cover of darkness and reassemble it there. A few of the men, carrying light sections of the apparatus, were able to run across O'Connell Street without being hit, but enemy snipers made the project of moving the heavy parts on a horse-drawn van impossible.

By this time, fires of untraceable origin were beginning to spread in abandoned buildings on Lower Abbey Street and O'Connell Street. The smoldering remains of Lawrence's toy shop at the corner of O'Connell and Cathedral Streets also burst again into flames, which a steady wind threatened to carry to the building adjoining it. Tonight there was no hope that the fire brigade might arrive to fight these fires. The recurring gun bursts were too dangerous.

The light from the flames on Lower Abbey Street enabled Fergus O'Kelly to see that British soldiers now commanded the entire sweep of that street from a barricade at Beresford Place. O'Kelly's peace of mind was further threatened when he noticed that the men in the Hibernian Bank building on the opposite corner of Abbey and O'Connell Streets were evacuating their post and either filtering down the back lanes toward Amiens Street or running the gauntlet of sniper fire across O'Connell Street toward the Post Office. Each successful crossing was greeted by cheers from windows on both sides of the street. One man ran across toward the Post Office carrying a mattress to shield himself from the bullets. About halfway across, he spun around and fell to the pavement with the mattress on top of him. The cheering stopped. He lay motionless for several minutes until finally the gunfire stopped. Then suddenly the mattress sprang up again with him behind it, and before the snipers resumed firing, he was under cover of the Post Office portico listening to the cheerful roar that now arose once more from insurgents on both sides of the street.

O'Connell Street lay quiet thereafter until about ten o'clock, when a drunk emerged from the shadows and began weaving his way toward the Post Office as he sang, repeatedly, a line of a song:

> *Two lovely black eyes,*
> *Two lovely black eyes . . .*

When he reached the Post Office, he stopped near a front window.

"Two lovely black eyes. Hurro! Three cheers for John Redmond!"

John Redmond was the leader of the Irish party in the British Parliament and a strong opponent of revolution; the three cheers for him were not returned. One of the men in the window, perhaps aroused from a nap, spoke up sharply to the drunk.

"Will you, for God's sake, man, shut up and go home!"

The drunk was offended by both the suggestion and the tone of voice. "What's that ye say? Come out here and talk that way, I dare yiz. I'll go home when I bloody well please. What right has the likes of ye to be interferin' with a dacent man?"

"Go home before you get shot."

"Get shot, will I? Faith and who'd be shootin' me? Come on out here and I'll bate the lot o' yiz."

Several men inside laughed.

"Oh, yiz needn't laugh. I'd make ye laugh if I had a hoult of ye! What do I care for the English! To hell with the English! I cud bate you and them together! So cud Dan O'Connell! The boul' Danny, he wouldn't be afraid of ye, nor the English nayther. Here, I'll sing ye a song if ye'll jist have some manners, please, and listen like Christians: 'God save Ireland sez the hayroes, God save Ireland sez they . . .'" And away he went, still singing as he turned the corner into Henry Street.

A few moments later another drunk appeared on O'Connell Street as if he had been waiting in the wings for the first one to make his exit. This one, looking prosperous and wearing a tall hat, came around the corner of Hopkins and Hopkins to show himself openly under the street lights at O'Connell Bridge. From both sides of the river shouts arose: "Go back! Go back!" The man stopped and looked around as if puzzled. He jumped nervously as a few bullets hit the pavement near him. After a short hesitation, he took a few steps toward the bridge, only to be stopped by a sudden, deadly impact. Twitching violently as he fell, he wriggled for a few moments on the pavement, his tall hat rolling crazily away from him. After one last surge of motion, he sprawled out absolutely still.

An officer at a window in the Post Office ordered four of his best riflemen to smash the arc lamps that had exposed the man. A few moments later O'Connell Street was in darkness except for the flashing eruptions of light from the fires on the opposite side.

The O'Rahilly and Desmond Fitzgerald, as they had done Monday and Tuesday, made late-night rounds of the upper floors of the building to see that the windows in all the rooms were properly manned. The men, looking out at the spreading fires across the street, spoke softly, as if they didn't want to exclude the roar of the flames. They obviously felt, as did O'Rahilly and Fitzgerald, that those flames signaled the approaching end of their adventure. For the first time, O'Rahilly and Fitzgerald were forced to take notice of a marked decline in morale.

When he visited the roof, O'Rahilly found another reason for concern. On the rooftops of buildings west of the Post Office he saw so much shadowy movement he decided he had better warn James Connolly of the possibility of a British night attack. He descended to the main floor only to discover that Connolly was asleep. In O'Rahilly's judgment the danger was sufficient to warrant waking him, so Connolly was aroused from his first nap in more than twenty-four hours.

O'Rahilly said, "The British are moving across the rooftops on Henry Street."

Connolly, not yet sufficiently awake to comprehend, stared up at him and said, "They are not." Then he turned and sank back to sleep.

He was not destined to remain asleep very long. A boy young enough to be in bed at this hour came running into the Post Office, preceded by the sound of his loud, piercing voice.

"Will ye give us some food!" he shouted. "We'll all be after starvin' to death if we don't get some food! The whoul neighborhood's not got a crust of bread! The whoul city, for sweet Jasus' sake! The shops is empty, ye can see that. How can anybody eat if there's no food?"

Connolly, though he had managed to resist O'Rahilly's effort to arouse him, had no such luck against the boy, whose voice was as effective and as persistent as a bugle. Sitting up, Connolly glared at the boy in bewilderment, then called him over to his cot. But perhaps because he was still sleepy, he didn't ask the obvious questions—what was the boy doing out so late, and who had suddenly appointed him to worry, in the middle of the night, about feeding the city. The likelihood was that the boy had awakened in panic at the dire rumors he had been hearing for the past two days and had jumped out of bed to come to the Post Office for some kind of reassurance.

Connolly smiled at the boy and patted his shoulder. "Who's been telling you things like that?" he asked. "You shouldn't be spreading such stories. Food may be a bit scarce, right enough, but nobody's about to starve. You can go home and tell that to whoever sent you. Tell your folks to keep their chins up. They've nothing to worry about. Now run along with you, so we can get some sleep."

The boy listened intently and after a few more questions left the Post Office, his peace of mind apparently restored as he disappeared into the night. As for getting more sleep, Connolly and most of the others on the main floor of the building were now out of the mood. There was a restless stirring, and even in the dim light the haggard, worried expressions showed on the tired faces. Connolly got up from his cot and made the rounds, comforting, exhorting, sometimes scolding, but even by moving among the men at this hour he showed his own concern about their dwindling spirits. Everyone had abandoned by this time the myth of possible victory. There was nothing left for these exhausted and frightened men to think about but the imminent assault against them and, for the survivors of the battle, the dire consequences of defeat.

Connolly looked into their faces, one after another. Then suddenly, without warning, he broke into a bellowing chorus of one of their favorite marching songs, a song that would one day become the Irish national anthem—"The Soldier's Song."

> *We'll sing a song, a soldier's song,*
> *With cheering, rousing chorus,*
> *As round our blazing fires we throng,*
> *The starry heavens o'er us.*
> *Impatient for the coming fight,*
> *And as we wait the morning's light,*
> *Here in the silence of the night*
> *We'll chant a soldier's song.*

The men listened to him dumbfounded at first. Then a few smiles began to appear and a few more voices began to rise until, within a minute or two, the main floor of the building was filled with the song:

> *Soldiers are we, whose lives are pledged to Ireland;*
> *Some have come from a land beyond the wave;*
> *Sworn to be free, no more our ancient sireland*
> *Shall shelter the despot or the slave.*
> *Tonight we man the bearna baoghail*
> *In Erin's cause, come woe or weal;*
> *'Mid cannon's roar and rifle's peal*
> *We'll chant a soldier's song.*

Michael Collins, who had proven himself one of the most effective soldiers in the building and who had been able to sleep even through the visit of the raucous-voiced boy, could not block out the roar of fifty voices. He opened his eyes and shook his head in disgust. Looking up at Connolly's secretary, Winifred Carney, he said, "If this is supposed to be a concert, they'll want the piano in the back room."

Patrick Pearse, who had scarcely slept since Monday, watched the scene without any noticeable change of expression. His face gloomy and his eyes looking weary, he turned to Desmond Ryan, one of his former pupils at St. Enda's college.

"When we are all wiped out," Pearse said, "people will condemn us and blame us for everything. But in a few years, they will see the meaning of what we tried to do."

IV. *Thursday, April 27*

Dᴜʀɪɴɢ the early hours of Thursday morning, the gunfire was so infrequent that the attention of the sleepless, waiting men in the Post Office was diverted to something almost as unpleasant—the putrid stench of the two rotting horse carcasses that had lain, since Monday's Lancer charge, on O'Connell Street, just north of Nelson's Pillar. Because the Post Office windows had been smashed, it was impossible to shut out the odor, so nauseating now it drove some of the men to the point of vomiting. The sickening stink was further intensified by the sun, which shone warmly through broken clouds. Men held their noses or shook their heads as if to throw off the scent. Few enjoyed their breakfasts, despite a marked improvement in the quality of the food.

The Cumann na mBan girls now had the commissary running as smoothly as a restaurant, thanks to the continuous and persistent industry of Peggy Downey and Louise Gavan Duffy, who had not slept since Monday. Miss Duffy's only rest came during short conversations with her superior officer, Desmond Fitzgerald. She made no secret of her disturbance at the situation in which they found themselves. She would be happier, she told him, if she could be certain the uprising had been justified. "But I can't get over the feeling," she said, "that our moral position is doubtful." Her feeling did not, however, affect her work. She and her staff now served better meals than most of the men were accustomed to eating at home, and on good china with excellent cutlery borrowed from nearby hotels and restaurants. The only complaints were against the portions, rationed carefully by Fitzgerald in compliance with Patrick Pearse's order. This morning, with the wind blowing in from the direction of the dead horses on O'Connell Street, few of the men quibbled about their portions.

The snipers on the roof, damp and chilly from the night air, looked up at the sun and absorbed its warmth as they stretched their limbs in a common morning ritual that, however, they were forced now to perform lying down rather than standing. Despite the lull in gunfire, they knew better than to show themselves to the increasing numbers of British snipers closing in on them.

Shortly after dawn, the lull ended. From the south, north, and east, machine guns opened up against the GPO. Patiently the men on the roof and on the Imperial Hotel roof across the street studied the directions of fire, seeking out the gun positions. Each time they found the range on a gun, however, it would be moved, then augmented by another, as British firepower multiplied from minute to minute.

On the main floor of the Post Office, someone gave birth to a new rumor. The British were about to launch a gas attack. The word spread as fast as gas, and by the time everyone had heard it twice, it had achieved general credence. Joseph Cripps, an assistant in the infirmary, was asked by one of the officers if he knew an antidote to gas; he was a druggist, so he did. The only possible defense under the circumstances, he said, would be a towel saturated with a hypo solution. He didn't recommend it. As soon as he had spoken, he wished he had kept his mouth shut, for he was immediately dispatched on the perilous and impractical mission of requisitioning hypo from neighborhood pharmacies. After returning from this errand, luckily without confronting any British or insurgent bullets, Cripps began mixing the solution by the bucketful and taking it around to the men at the windows. He was beginning to think the job was as endless as it was useless when, fortunately, he encountered another officer, Michael Collins, who brought the entire project to a quick conclusion.

Collins looked at the solution, smelled it distastefully, and said to Cripps, "What the hell good will that do?"

"None," said Cripps, and with a smile, he returned to the infirmary, where he was needed.

By midmorning, the din of gunfire was constant and ear-piercing. It was not loud enough, however, to drown out a shell burst at ten o'clock on Lower Abbey Street, around the corner from O'Connell Street. From the *Irish Times'* reserve print shop, where the shell struck, a few wisps of smoke rose, then slowly began increasing in volume. Finally, as men in dozens of nearby windows looked on expectantly, the entire building erupted into flame.

On the roof of the Post Office, Patrick Pearse's brother Willie, watching the huge tongues of flame rise above the Lower Abbey Street buildings, made the kind of bemusing, self-evident observation characteristic of him.

"That fire," he said, "won't be easily stopped."

Before the day ended, the fire was to prove his remark an understatement, but at the moment, most of the men in the GPO were less concerned about it than about the shell burst that started it. Again the word spread through the building that the long-awaited British attack was imminent, and again many of the men accepted the rumor as if it were an official notice from British headquarters. Even Connolly arose once more to the expectation of immediate onslaught. The infantry attack, he believed, would be straight across O'Connell Bridge and up the broad thoroughfare toward the Post Office. Though such a belief was an insult to the intelligence of the British commanders, it was not completely without foundation. The man-wasting frontal assault was an accepted strategy in the British military tradition. Just the previous day, Connolly had sent two girls to warn De Valera's men in the Mount Street area of a British advance from the harbor at Dun Laoghaire, and though he did not yet know the details, his warning had led to an engagement in which wave after wave of British soldiers were mowed down attempting to rush insurgent positions near the Mount Street Bridge.

Connolly's decision now was to prepare for the expected infantry advance up O'Connell Street by reinforcing the garrison at the Metropole Hotel, which protected the south side of the Post Office and which also commanded Middle and Lower Abbey Streets. Gathering a detail of twenty men, he marched them from the Post Office across the narrow, sheltered width of Prince's Street and turned them over to the Metropole Commander, Lieutenant Oscar Traynor. After a quick inspection of the men in the Metropole block of buildings, Connolly then strode out onto Middle Abbey Street, scornful of snipers' bullets, to assess the defensive prospects there.

"We need a barricade in front of Easons'," he said, pointing to a nearby bookstore, and within a few minutes, work had begun, with stacks of books included in the jumble of furniture and junk that extended out into the street. The work continued despite the sniper fire it attracted, but it was not destined to continue very long. In addition to the sniper fire, it soon attracted artillery fire, and after a shell opened a hole in the building a few feet from Connolly, even he became convinced it was too late to build barricades there.

The fire in Lower Abbey Street, across O'Connell Street to the east, was spreading so fast that Connolly turned away from the useless project he had just launched and stood aghast, watching the flames from the *Irish Times* print shop spread to the Ship Hotel, the Hyland wine shop, Henry's tobacco shop, and Keating's and Kelly's cycle shops. So ferocious were the flames now that they burst out into the street, igniting the junky barricade the insurgents had built Monday afternoon. In a matter of minutes, the barricade carried the fire all the way across the street, where Wynn's Hotel (in which the founders of the Irish Volunteers had first met, at the suggestion of The O'Rahilly three years before) was waiting to become fuel for it. Connolly shrugged helplessly, shook his head, and returned to the Post Office.

Meanwhile, the concern of Patrick Pearse and the other insurgent leaders over the lack of a chaplain had become increasingly acute as the tempo of British gunfire mounted. Finally, they hit upon a strategy to lure a priest to the Post Office. Choosing a girl in civilian dress, they sent her on a mission to the Pro-Cathedral, one block north and one block east of the GPO.

At about 10:30, Father John Flanagan, a curate at the Pro-Cathedral, was astonished to hear the hall doorbell ring. It was difficult to believe anyone could have traveled the streets in that area without being shot. At eight o'clock he had said mass, attended by frequent gun bursts from all directions, but no congregation. The streets were so unsafe the church had been closed the day before. Two of Father Flanagan's colleagues were at Jervis Street Hospital, a few blocks west of the Post Office, attending victims of the rebellion, and two were away on vacation, leaving only three priests on duty.

When Father Flanagan answered the door, he was confronted by a girl quite respectably dressed but soiled and rumpled.

"Father will you please come with me to the Post Office?" she begged. "We've a man dying there."

Father Flanagan, who had spent several hours in the Post Office hearing confessions Monday night, was annoyed at what seemed to him an unreasonable request that he return there, across O'Connell Street, under the perilous conditions that prevailed this morning. The route from the Post Office to the Jervis Street Hospital, where two priests were on duty, was comparatively protected. Why hadn't the insurgents taken the wounded man there?

The girl looked sheepish. She had no answer.

The priest shook his head in exasperation. He had very little sympathy for the rebellion, but if a man was dying and in need of the sacraments, there was no choice. Taking down his stovepipe hat (a customary headdress for priests in that day), he followed the girl, carefully, into the street.

They walked quickly along Thomas' Lane to Marlborough Street, in an easterly direction, away from the Post Office. As they headed up Marlborough toward Parnell Street, a bullet whizzed past, driving them to cover. Clinging to the walls and protected also, no doubt, **by** the fact that one was a girl and the other a priest, they made it safely to Parnell Street, then west to O'Connell Street, where they had to face British guns to the north and insurgent guns to the south. Nevertheless, the priest, matching the girl's bravery, followed her across, and though a few bullets hit the pavement behind them, as if to hurry them on their way, they reached the other side unscathed and continued on to Moore Street, where they turned south in the direction of the Post Office.

As they approached Henry Street, and it appeared they would complete the journey without serious incident. Father Flanagan was amazed to see a man in front of him whom he recognized. An old friend. Before the priest had time to ask him what he was doing on the street, a bullet ripped the man and he slumped to the pavement. As the girl guide stood by, nervously glancing in all directions, the priest knelt beside him, comforted him, and, determining that his condition was grave, anointed him where he lay.

When several people appeared in nearby doorways to watch, Father Flanagan called out, "Is there anyone who can help get this man to Jervis Street?"

Several young lads emerged from a shop with a hand cart, into which they lifted the man, and as they moved off with him toward the hospital, the priest and the girl resumed their journey toward the Post Office. Now, however, they suddenly found they had company. Joseph Cripps, out on one of his frequent trips to find more hospital supplies, had happened along, wearing his Red Cross armband, as Father Flanagan was anointing the wounded man.

"Where is it you're going, father?" he asked.

"To the Post Office."

"Ah, well, in that case you'll want to follow me. I know the safest way."

The priest eyed him carefully. "You're another of them, then, are you?"

"I am, father."

The priest shook his head. "You should be home with your family where you belong, a young lad like you. Whatever possesses you I don't know. Do you really believe a ragged little handful of you, with rifles and Red Cross armbands, can stand up to the British army?"

"No, father," Cripps said. "I'm afraid not."

The candidness of the answer stopped the priest's questions. In silence, he and the girl followed Cripps, on the run, across Henry Street into Randall's boot factory and up the stairs to the second floor. From there, Cripps led them through jagged holes in the connecting walls of one building after another until they suddenly found themselves in the Post Office.

Father Flanagan took off his tall hat, soiled now by plaster that had rained down on it, and asked to be taken to the dying man for whom he had been summoned. The girl looked embarrassed. Cripps, who knew nothing about the scheme to procure a chaplain, took him downstairs to the infirmary. Glancing from man to man as he walked along the row of cots, the priest could see quickly that no one here was near death.

"Where is the man I've been called for?" he demanded.

By this time, the infirmary was crowded with insurgent soldiers wearing mischievous smiles. They stood silent as Father Flanagan repeated his question, then one of them said, "Sure, you've been called here for all of us, father."

The priest, looking into their grinning faces, could not sustain his exasperation. Trying to suppress a smile, he said, "All right now, get out of here, the lot of you. Let me talk to these wounded men first."

By 11 A.M., the fires on both sides of Lower Abbey Street had reached O'Connell Street and had become a matter of major concern to the insurgent leaders, even though the flames were still a block away from the Post Office and on the other side of the wide thoroughfare. It occurred to the leaders now that an incendiary bomb might have started the blaze. If fire was to be one of the British weapons against them, how long would the Post Office side of the street remain unignited? And with the city fire brigade inactive, who could stop any fires that might break out? The British strategy, it seemed now, must be to put all O'Connell Street to the torch, then—while the insurgents were busy fighting the fires—launch their still expected infantry bayonet attack.

This supposition was strengthened by an action developing in Lower Abbey Street. With the barricade there burned away and insurgents driven out of their window positions by the flames, British foot soldiers were encouraged to begin an advance from Marlborough Street west toward O'Connell Street. Metropole garrison riflemen, in the windows of the Manfield boot factory at the northwest corner of Abbey and O'Connell Streets, caught glimpses of the advancing khaki behind billows of smoke and opened fire.

From south of the river, British machine guns attacked the Manfield building, and a three-cornered battle was under way.

The insurgents, peppered by this new flow of bullets, ducked their heads to window-sill level, and some of them swung their rifles south in the direction of the machine-gun fire. The placement of the machine guns, which had been difficult to pinpoint, was now obvious. At last it would be possible to apply some pressure against them, but before there was time to do so, a frustrating order was issued.

"Forget the machine guns! Fire at the infantry!"

It made sense, of course. The insurgents could hardly afford to knock out the distant machine guns at the cost of being overrun by the approaching foot soldiers. Reluctantly, they turned once more to Abbey Street, where the British infantry was edging up closer and closer behind the screen of smoke. The insurgent riflemen filled Abbey Street with a crisscross of bullets so intense it drove the British to the walls. But the insurgents were now firing so fast their rifles became too hot to touch. One after another, the guns began to jam.

A man at a corner window said, "Haven't we got anything to cool these bloody barrels?"

Another man said, "Nothing but the oil in those empty sardine cans over there."

A joking remark, but was it so outlandish? The man at the window said, "Bring me one of those cans."

Pouring the sardine oil onto his gun, he aimed out the window and pulled the trigger.

"Look! It works!" he shouted as the gun went off.

The rush for sardine oil began and the jammed guns were soon back in action, filling the street with such a school of bullets that the British troops did not emerge from their curtain of smoke to try a frontal assault. So many Abbey Street buildings now were either burning or completely burned out that the British found themselves facing the insurgent barrage with nothing but the smoke to cover them. Smoke does not stop bullets, so they finally retreated, after a brave battle against the virtually unseen insurgents in front of them, to the Marlborough Street barricade from which they had advanced.

This success in driving back the enemy on one flank did not, however, delude the insurgents into thinking they might prevail. By the time the battle subsided, the riflemen in the O'Connell-Abbey Street corner windows were choking on the smoky fumes from their own guns and on the plaster dust that had been blasted from the walls by the machine guns south of the river.

Meanwhile, the insurgents in the Hopkins and Hopkins–Dublin Bread Company block between the river and Abbey Street, hemmed in by the fires and threatened with isolation by the attempted British advance, were faced now with a new inconvenience. The British big guns across the Liffey began an artillery bombardment against them. Unable to fight these shattering blasts, the men hurried to the basement of the DBC building, where they huddled in corners, breathing smoke as they listened to the shells explode and the fires roar above them.

In the Post Office, Tom Clarke, convinced by the fires that the end was near, called for Desmond Fitzgerald and took him out into the covered courtyard at the rear of the building.

"First of all," Clarke said, "I want to inform you that you've been promoted."

Fitzgerald smiled. "Thank you, sir." Then it occurred to him that since he didn't know what rank he had held, he couldn't even guess what rank he had now attained, but it seemed pointless to ask Clarke, who probably didn't know either. The promotion announcement, which had been made as if it were a prelude to some new assignment, was perhaps just an idea that had suddenly occurred to Clarke.

Pointing out to Fitzgerald a heavy concrete opening into a dark, bunkerlike room, Clarke said solemnly: "I want you to mark this place well. When the end comes, it will be your responsibility to gather all the girls inside here and defend them to the last."

After pausing to give Fitzgerald time to absorb this order, Clarke continued: "This means if you are not killed beforehand, you will be taken by the enemy and probably executed."

Fitzgerald had assumed he would die in the uprising and was resigned to the thought of death, but Clarke's pronouncement about execution chilled him, because it brought to his mind a possible way of death that had always horrified him—hanging.

"What do you mean by 'executed'?" he asked uneasily. "Hanging or shooting?"

Clarke, who was as resigned to one as to the other, said casually, "I should think they'll shoot the men they take. But they may keep to the hanging. The English love hanging."

Fitzgerald, appalled by the word "hanging" almost as much as if it were the deed, longed for Clarke to revise his assumption. "But you can't say for certain?" he asked anxiously.

Clarke shrugged. "I should think it would be shooting, after a rising like this, right in the middle of a war."

Fitzgerald felt somewhat relieved. He so dreaded hanging that the possibility of being shot rather pleased him, and he clutched at Clarke's remark in favor of shooting as if Clarke's saying it would make it so. He still wished, though, that Clarke could have been more certain.

"Now, do you understand your orders?" Clarke said.

"Yes, sir."

"And you accept them?"

Fitzgerald nodded. "Yes, sir." But he was far from happy. He hoped he would be shot defending the girls, thus depriving the British of the option of hanging him.

In the course of his rounds, Father Flanagan encountered all the insurgent leaders, but he never did determine which of them had evolved the scheme to lure him to the Post Office. Pearse seemed delighted to have him there. It was Pearse who had asked him to come Monday night and hear confessions. But wasn't Pearse too serious a man to have come up with such a trick? MacDermott was the one with mischief in his eyes. It was most likely he whom the priest could "thank" for his presence in this God-forsaken purgatory. But MacDermott's light-hearted friendliness was so disarming Father Flanagan soon decided it didn't matter who had lured him there. He belonged there because he was needed. After attending the wounded, he went upstairs to where the prisoners were kept; several of them were Catholic, and one of them, he had been told, was in desperate need of him. Finding the man in a state of deep fright, he talked to him at length in an effort to soothe him. But the poor fellow's mind had been affected by the events of the last three days. The priest decided there was nothing more he could do, and after administering a blessing, he moved on, making the rounds of the building. As he met more and more of the insurgents, he gradually found his attitude toward them changing. They put up such a brave front for him, they appeared to be as gay and debonair an army as ever took up arms. Nevertheless, they did not deceive him. Behind their laughter was a fear that few of them could conceal.

Even Connolly had now dropped the pretense that he expected victory. This became apparent about noon when a man found his way to the Prince's Street gate to plead with the guards there, Volunteers Joe Good and Sean Gallogly, for a chance to join the rebellion. While Gallogly went to ask Connolly whether they should admit the man, Good covered him with his rifle.

"You can trust me," the man said to Good. "You needn't be afraid of me."

"While I'm at this end of the gun," Good told him, "you're the one to be afraid."

When Gallogly returned, Connolly was with him. After listening to the man talk about his eagerness to help, Connolly shook his head sadly and said, as if it would be foolish for anyone at such a late hour to join such a hopeless cause, "No, you'd better go home. There's nothing you can do to help here."

A few of the men in the Post Office were beginning finally to show the effects of the constantly increasing pressure and lack of sleep. One Volunteer, in an overwrought condition, began running through the building, waving his gun and uttering outlandish threats. Patrick Pearse, hearing about the man, hurried to him and by force of will imposed discipline upon him. But the man's disturbance was too deep to be eliminated by a few firm words. After talking to him for several minutes, Pearse decided he would have to be confined until his anxiety diminished.

A short time later, another man, dropping his rifle and waving his hands excitedly, ran out the front door of the Post Office into bullet-swept O'Connell Street. He scarcely had time to hear the shouts of the men in the building pleading with him to come back. Before he was more than twenty feet down the street, a bullet hit him, spun him around, and knocked him down. There was silence inside as men at the windows watched him writhe on the pavement and listened to him call out in pain.

Two hospital men rushed to the door with a Red Cross flag and, after waving it in front of them for a minute or so, emerged carefully into the street. The gunfire abated. They reached the man, grabbed him by the arms, and dragged him into the shelter of Prince's Street. The gunfire resumed.

The Dublin Bread Company–Hopkins and Hopkins garrison in the block just north of the river was now isolated from the Post Office by the fire, which had turned the corner at Abbey Street and was moving steadily, from building to building, up the east side of O'Connell Street. The men in the Imperial Hotel garrison, directly across the street from the Post Office, could see the flames gradually approaching whenever they dared glance out a window to the south. Their communication with the Post Office was now cut off by the collapse of the twine "cable" on which they had been sending slips of paper back and forth. It was pointless to try to shout messages across the street over the racket of the gunfire, so they simply carried on as before, under the command of Brennan Whitmore, returning British barrages from north, south, and east with sporadic rifle bursts.

On the Post Office roof and at the south corner windows riflemen saluted the enemy with intermittent gun bursts to let him know they were still there. Elsewhere in the building, everyone tried to go about his business as if it were just another day, but the fire down the street was such a physical, dramatic, and incontestable sign of approaching disaster no one could avoid occasional glances out the windows at it. The flames, still on the opposite side and almost a block away, were leaping twice as high as the buildings feeding them, and the heat was beginning to warm the Post Office even though the breeze wafting it northward was slow and gentle. The gunfire either had diminished or had become more difficult to hear as the roar of flames, the hiss of steam, the creaking of steel joists, and the crackle of burning wood filled the air.

O'Rahilly, who was no longer confining himself to the upper floors of the Post Office, became so conscious of the deepening gloom of the men on the ground floor that he began to sing—songs like "Rory of the Gael," "O, God Rest You, Robert Emmet," and another he himself had written, "Thou Art Not Conquered Yet, Dear Land":

> *Though knaves may scheme and slaves may crawl*
> > *To win their master's smile,*
> *And though thy best and bravest fall,*
> > *Undone by Saxon guile;*
> *Yet some there be, still true to thee,*
> > *Who never shall forget*
> *That though in chains and slavery*
> > *Thou art not conquered yet!*

Most of the men joined in the singing, since it seemed expected of them, but there was not much gusto or gaiety in their voices.

About 2 P.M., the GPO was rocked by a pair of shell bursts close enough to stop the singing. British big guns, apparently

aiming at the Post Office, had again hit the *Freeman's Journal*
building, the rear of which was not more than twenty yards
away in Prince's Street. This signaled a general increase of
enemy fire behind the Post Office to the west, on the one flank
that had hitherto been fairly well protected by the narrowness of
the streets and the danger they would present to invading British
soldiers. Connolly, afraid the British might now enter these
streets and learn what he already knew—that they were unoc-
cupied by insurgents—decided he had better prepare for the
worst by setting up a few new outposts. Because he was either
eager to get out where there was action or convinced that no one
else would select the right locations, he himself led a company
into Henry Street, disregarding the danger of British snipers, and
dropped the men off in twos and threes at one building after
another as far west as Liffey Street.

A shell, apparently aimed at the Post Office, bounced and burst
on the roof of the Metropole Hotel, just across Prince's Street.
Rifleman Charles Saurin, on duty in one of the top-floor rooms of
the hotel, was suddenly inundated with plaster dust, chimney
soot, and the fumes from the explosion above him. As he staggered into the hall, trying to cough some air into his lungs, another shell hit the roof, and though, like the first one, it miraculously failed to come through before bursting, it still had enough
kick in its explosion to put a huge crack in the corridor wall.
Beginning now to wonder if the shells were chasing him, Saurin
sprinted down the hall to get away from the part of the building
that had suddenly become so popular with the British artillery-
men, but as he was about to pass an open door, a stream of
machine-gun bullets, having entered a window and passed
through an entire room without encountering anything solid,
crossed his path. Saurin stopped short, watched the bullets reduce
the corridor wall in front of him to plaster dust, then, glancing
over his shoulder at the dirty clouds behind him raised by the
two shell bursts, sat down with a shrug of resignation to wait for
a lull.

When the smoke cleared and the machine-gun fire abated,
Lieutenant Oscar Traynor ordered Saurin and all but one of the

other men at the top of the building to come down to the comparative safety of the lower floors. The man he left at the top was a London Irishman, who had no interest in descending to a level where his view of the action would be restricted. Traynor, after arguing with the man about the danger involved in remaining, decided it might be useful to leave someone on the roof as a fire watch. The man stayed, sitting on a parapet from which he could see the raging fire across the street and, through field glasses, the booming British artillery guns across the river.

In the Post Office, someone saw an armored car approaching from the west along Henry Street. So many men crowded around the windows on that side to look out at it that the building would have sunk if it had been a boat. And if the armored car had been equipped with a machine gun or two, the insurgent headquarters would have been decimated. As it developed, this armored-car incident, the second of the week, was a standoff. None of the insurgent bullets fired at the thick metal plating inflicted any damage; at the same time, the unseen men in the vehicle had so little firepower they could inflict no damage on the Post Office. Eventually the armored car retired and was soon forgotten by the insurgents, whose anxious minds became occupied once more by the nerve-straining wait for the final battle.

As the afternoon progressed, the cannonading intensified and the flames on the east side of O'Connell Street continued to spread. They were now consuming the entire short block to the north of Abbey Street as far as Sackville Place. They had also spread south from Abbey Street to the river, a block away, and were eating the houses on Eden Quay. From one building after another fire-frightened people emerged, running east away from O'Connell Street toward the Custom House, with bundles of belongings in their arms. The gunfire from across the river suddenly ceased; a British soldier appeared from the east to knock on doors and make sure all the doomed buildings were evacuated. Another soldier arrived with a megaphone and raised a shout that had to compete with only the roar of the fire now that the guns were silent.

"Come out! Come out!" he called.

More and more people emerged, to be steered toward the Custom House. Then, as the two soldiers followed the refugees and reached the safety of the nearest British barricade, the big guns from Trinity College boomed again and the first shell landed a short distance from the Post Office.

The British now brought into action another artillery piece, which they installed north of the Post Office near Parnell Square. Its first lob overshot the Post Office and crashed through a dormer window on the top floor of the Metropole Hotel, from which Lieutenant Traynor had fortunately evacuated his men. Succeeding shells from the north came closer and closer to the intended target.

The explosions and machine-gun fire, increasing from all directions, made the men on the Post Office roof acutely aware that they had only one exit in case of disaster and prompted them to begin chopping a hole near the parapet through which to descend if hard pressed. As the shells continued to explode near the building, one man was wounded, then another and another, until Lieutenant Michael Boland, who was in command, began to think the British were using shrapnel. A closer examination of the wounds, only one of which was serious, convinced him they were caused by bullets. But whatever comfort this might have brought was quickly banished by the force of a shell that struck the north portico of the Post Office, shattering part of the ballustrade. Though it left virtually undamaged the statue representing Fidelity, just a few feet away, it neatly eliminated the pole from which one of the Republican flags had flown.

This explosion rocked the building and everyone inside it. The O'Rahilly was so worried about the prisoners, of whom there were now sixteen, that he removed them to an interior room on the second floor where they would be safest.

"I give you my word," he said to them, "that you will escape with your lives. Have no fear of that." He spoke with such determination many of their faces brightened visibly, as if they were getting this word from a man completely capable of fulfilling it.

There was no doubt that, if possible, O'Rahilly intended to

fulfill it. After leaving the prisoners relatively secure, he gathered their guards together and addressed them soberly, almost sternly. "Let every man remember this," he said. "As custodians of the prisoners you must never forget the honor of your country. Whatever happens to the rest of us, the prisoners must be our first concern."

The great fire had now advanced so much closer and had become so enormous and intense that even the extraordinary width of O'Connell Street no longer protected the unwindowed Post Office from its scorching heat. Billowing clouds of dark smoke carried with them sparks and bits of burning debris as an accelerating wind pushed the inferno northward. On the Post Office roof, the coughing, squinting riflemen carried their three wounded comrades to the stairway exit, from which they were removed to the infirmary below. In this process, two more men were wounded. Within the building, the heat was so searing and the air so smoky that the fire-watching pastime had lost its appeal. Men sat on the floor at the rear of the building, looking glum, waiting for new catastrophes.

Morale was such a critical factor that Patrick Pearse had been working since the previous night on a speech to the men. At three o'clock, the speech was finished and polished. James Connolly, after posting sentries at the doors, lined up all the available troops in the main room on the ground floor. When everyone was in place, Pearse approached, Connolly stepped back a pace, and Pearse, in his slow, deliberate but forceful voice, began to speak.

The forces of the Irish Republic, which was proclaimed in Dublin on Easter Monday, have been in possession of the central part of the capital since 12 noon on that day. Up to yesterday afternoon, headquarters was in touch with all the main outlying positions, and despite furious and almost continuous assaults by the British forces all those positions were then still being held, and the Commandants in charge were confident of their ability to hold them for a long time.

During the course of yesterday afternoon and evening, the enemy succeeded in cutting our communications with our other positions in the city, and Headquarters is today isolated.

The enemy has burnt down whole blocks of houses, apparently with the object of giving themselves a clear field for the play of artillery and field guns against us. We have been bombarded during the evening and night with shrapnel and machine gun fire, but without material damage to our position, which is of great strength.

We are busy completing arrangements for the final defense of Headquarters, and are determined to hold it while the buildings last.

I desire now, lest I may not have an opportunity later, to pay homage to the gallantry of the soldiers of Irish freedom who have during the past four days been writing with fire and steel the most glorious chapter in the later history of Ireland. Justice can never be done to their heroism, to their discipline, to their gay and unconquerable spirit in the midst of peril and death.

Let me, who have led them into this, speak in my own name, and in my fellow commandants' names, and in the name of Ireland present and to come, their praise, and ask those who come after them to remember them.

For four days they have fought and toiled, almost without cessation, almost without sleep, and in the intervals of fighting they have sung songs of the freedom of Ireland. No man has complained, no man has asked "Why?" Each individual has spent himself, happy to pour out his strength for Ireland and for freedom. If they do not win this fight, they will at least deserve to win it. But win it they will although they may win it in death. Already they have done a great thing. They have redeemed Dublin from many shames, and made her name splendid among the names of cities. They have held out for four days against the might of the British Empire. They have established Ireland's right to be called a Republic, and they have established this government's right to sit at the peace table at the end of the European war.

Aside from that concluding fantasy, the speech sounded more like an apology to posterity than a pep talk to the troops. Phrases like "final defense of Headquarters" and "although they may win it in death" (a concept Pearse cherished) could not have been reassuring to anyone who listened carefully, yet many of the men were uplifted by it, perhaps because it offered them something that would at least pass for information about their plight. After a spontaneous cheer, they went back to their posts with renewed belief in what they were doing.

Some people in the Post Office, however, understood too well the implications of what Pearse had said. One of the girls in the kitchen, her worry showing on her face, went to Desmond Fitzgerald.

"The fires are terrifying," she said. "I'm in a state of utter depression. What do you think is going to happen?"

Fitzgerald shrugged. "There's no doubt about what's going to happen," he said. "The only question is how much longer we can last."

"And do you think every one of these young fellows will be shot?"

Fitzgerald knew what was on her mind. She was engaged to be married to one of the men, and though her own danger was almost as great as his, her concern was chiefly for him. Fitzgerald longed to tell her God was watching over them and everything would turn out well in the end, but she was an intelligent girl. It would be pointless to try to fill her with false hope. "I'm afraid we'll all be shot," he said, wondering as he said it if it would actually happen that way or if they would be hanged instead. His dread of hanging was so intense he had not yet been able to put from his mind Tom Clarke's casual remark about it that morning.

"I wouldn't mind for myself," the girl said, "but it seems terrible that all these young men are going to be sacrificed." She put a hand to her eyes. "And they don't even realize it." She turned quickly to walk away.

It occurred to Fitzgerald that it was no longer justifiable to keep all these girls in the Post Office. The leaders of the rebellion, and the girls themselves, had already established the important ideological point that women, being equal to men, were entitled to and ought to fight alongside them. It seemed too hard a thing to ask that they also die alongside them. When he tried out the idea on Louise Gavan Duffy and Peggy Downey, who worked under him in the commissary, both agreed it was time for the girls to leave. All the girls, that is, except themselves. Fitzgerald told them he would speak to Pearse about keeping them.

Across O'Connell Street from the Post Office the fire was moving steadily northward in the direction of the Imperial Hotel, but most of the men in the hotel had only a general notion of its progress because if they were to stick their heads out of the window to look they would be inviting machine-gun fire. The reflection of the flames in the windows of the Metropole Hotel just south of the Post Office was enough, however, to impress them with the magnitude of what was approaching them.

Five men suddenly emerged from the burning buildings and dashed into the street, toward the GPO. Despite the bullets kicking up pavement around them, the first four reached the shelter of the Post Office portico without mishap. The fifth tripped and fell over the trolley wire that had been extended across the street Tuesday in an effort to hold back the crowds but was now dangling loosely. For a half-minute, which seemed like a half-hour, the man lay there, breathing heavily, grimacing in pain, as British snipers framed him with their bullets. Then, just as it was beginning to look as if he must be badly hurt, he got to his feet and limped the rest of the way to safety.

In the main hall of the Post Office, James Connolly called fifty men to attention in front of him. He was furious. He had sent out a company to occupy the *Irish Independent* newspaper building at the corner of Middle Abbey and Liffey Streets, west of the Post Office, but the company had returned. The gunfire, the men said, was so heavy they couldn't get there. In Connolly's view they had lacked courage. He was determined to occupy the *Independent* offices because he still feared a British attack from the west.

"I want thirty men who are not afraid to go out on the street," he said.

The fifty men standing in front of him were all afraid to go out on the street, but since most of them were even more afraid to admit to him that they were afraid, he soon had his thirty. When they were assembled, he chose one of them, a young Volunteer named John McLoughlin, to lead them. McLoughlin had impressed Connolly earlier in the week while he was acting as a courier between the Post Office, the Four Courts, and the Mendicity Institution. His reports of what he had seen on the streets had proven reliable and his suggestions had been intelligent.

After dismissing the other men, Connolly led McLoughlin and company into the courtyard at the rear of the building and gathered them at the Prince's Street gate.

"Follow me!" he shouted, and the thirty men, bending forward to minimize themselves as targets, trotted behind him out the gate. But before they had gone more than a few yards, Connolly stopped short, piling them up in a bunch at his heels. He had decided that first of all, they should build a barricade right here in Prince's Street. After announcing this new plan, he sent men back into the Post Office and into the Metropole Hotel to find suitable materials.

Among the items used in the construction of this Prince's Street barricade was O'Rahilly's Ford, which he had driven through the Irish countryside the previous weekend in his campaign to prevent the rebellion. As the men piled machinery, furniture, barrels, junk, and stacks of paper around the car, Connolly hurried them along, supervised their work, warned them to stay under cover as well as possible while he himself stomped back and forth in the open, blatantly exposed to any snipers who might find him within range. He acted like a man who wanted to be hit, wanted to become a martyr to the Irish cause. On Monday, just before marching off from Liberty Hall to the GPO, he had said to an old friend, sotto voce so the men would not overhear, "We're going out to be slaughtered." And when the friend had asked, "Is there no hope at all?" he had said, "None whatever." He acted now as if he were determined, at least for himself, to fulfill that prediction.

In the midst of issuing an order to the barricade builders, he abruptly stopped short, just after the bark of a rifle two or three blocks away. Had the men not been busy, they might have noticed him wince, but before there was time for them to realize anything was amiss, he resumed his command in the same firm voice he had begun it. For a few minutes he stood where he was, making sure the barricade was built the way he wanted it. Then, telling them he would be back directly, he went into the Post Office at his normal, quick stride.

Entering the hospital section, he approached Jim Ryan, who was in charge.

"Is there a private place where we can talk?" Connolly asked.

They went behind a green, folding screen, where he took off his coat and displayed a flesh wound in his arm. As soon as Ryan had dressed the wound, he put on his coat and prepared to leave. Before going, however, he issued an order.

"Not a word about this to anyone. I don't want garbled reports floating around. I don't want people to think I've actually been hurt."

Returning to the men in Prince's Street, he inspected their barricade and, when he was satisfied with it, assembled them once more for their primary mission. Leading them himself, he hurried them through an alley to Middle Abbey Street, where the gunfire was heavy even before they arrived. Connolly was not deterred. He moved out of the alley onto the footpath to survey the situation; then quickly dividing his company into two groups, he ordered twenty of them to occupy the *Independent* offices at the Liffey Street corner and the other ten to occupy the Lucas lamp and bicycle shop directly opposite. As the men trotted down the footpath, clinging to the buildings for whatever protection they might offer, Connolly himself stood out in the open, sending them on their way with words of encouragement. Only when he was satisfied that they had made it to their destinations did he start back toward the Post Office.

He had taken no more than a step or two in the direction of the alley when a bullet hit the pavement beside him, skipped up, and shattered his left ankle. Connolly went down as if someone had knocked his legs out from under him. For a moment he was aware of nothing but the paralyzing pain. Then he was tempted to shout for help until he realized that shouting would only attract more British bullets. Despite his agony, he had to get himself back to the Post Office. A glance at his ankle indicated there was nothing left of it but a jumble of bone fragments. On his hands and one knee, he dragged himself out of the street into the alley. Almost passing out from the pain and the nausea it produced, he inched his way along the alley to Prince's Street, where he fell flat in the gutter, unable to move any further.

Fortunately, he was now back in his own territory. One of his men saw him lying there, and he was soon carried into the Post Office. By the time he was lifted onto a hospital table, his pain was so severe he was soaked with perspiration.

Lieutenant Mahoney, the captured British army doctor who was standing by, observed the rate at which Connolly was losing blood and immediately applied a tourniquet, suggesting as he did so that one of the assistants, Dan McLoughlin, fashion a splint from a piece of wood. Mahoney could see that the bullet had smashed the bone just above Connolly's ankle.

At this point, Jim Ryan, conscious of his responsibility as chief of the hospital, stepped in to take charge of the case. Mahoney watched silently while McLoughlin, who had attended medical school for ten years without approaching a degree, administered a weak solution of chloroform and set about applying the splint. There was nothing to hold the torn ankle in place, and the bones were protruding through the flesh. And the chloroform had not put the patient to sleep. Mahoney could contain himself only for a few minutes.

"For God's sake, have you nothing stronger than chloroform?" he asked.

McLoughlin remained calm. "That'll do the job all right," he said.

Mahoney shook his head. "It would take a whole lake of that stuff to put him under."

After a rather lively discussion, Ryan sent a young spectator to get some stronger chloroform and anesthetic ether. As Ryan administered it, Mahoney stepped in once more, released the tourniquet, extracted the bone fragments from Connolly's leg, ligatured the blood vessels, and applied a new splint with a foot piece attached.

During this excruciating process, despite the stronger anesthetic, Connolly still remained conscious. Mahoney called for Joseph Cripps, the hospital assistant who had already made countless excursions outside to procure supplies.

"We must get hold of some morphine," Mahoney said. "This man is in terrible pain."

Patrick Pearse, who was standing by, wrote on a slip of paper an authorization for Cripps to procure morphine wherever he might find it. The neighborhood pharmacies had all been left unattended three days before, so Cripps did not know why he would need such an authorization, but he took it anyway. Once more he went through a window onto Henry Street. This time he attracted a bullet the moment he exposed himself, but fortunately it hit only a finger. Bandaging it with his handkerchief, he hurried along on another round of the now-familiar shops, running a zigzag course to avoid meeting any more bullets. The only morphine he could find was mixed with distilled water and would have to be injected, but when he returned with it, Mahoney didn't stop to quibble. He quickly administered a significant dose, and Connolly at last got some relief from his pain.

When relative quiet returned to the hospital, Desmond Fitzgerald came in to talk to Mahoney. "You're not to go back to the other prisoners tonight," he said. "You'll stay right here."

Fitzgerald ordered a cot brought in for him immediately, but it was a long time before Mahoney got a chance to use it. There were now sixteen wounded men on hand. Though none was injured as seriously as Connolly, all needed attention. And Connolly's pain was such that he kept waking in spite of the morphine. On one of these occasions he called Mahoney to him and said, "You know, you're the best thing we've captured this week."

There was no question now of withholding from the men the news of Connolly's injury. Morale in the Post Office dropped as the word went from mouth to mouth. Connolly's unshakable authority had been like a shield to them. It was he who had ordered them about, scolded them when they did things wrong, cheered them when they showed proper courage, buoyed them up when their spirits lagged. Without him they felt suddenly exposed to the enemy. Despite his gruffness, they had come to love him.

Volunteer Eamonn Dore, hearing about his wound, went into

the hospital, stood beside his bed, and began to cry. Then quickly he pulled himself together because he realized he'd better not show any funk in front of Connolly. He might catch hell for it.

Because Pearse was temperamentally unsuited for the rough-and-tumble of field command and Plunkett was so ill he seldom arose from his cot, authority now fell between Tom Clarke and Sean MacDermott, neither of whom made any pretense of military ability (though MacDermott had bought and studied a United States army drill manual in anticipation of the uprising), and The O'Rahilly, who had been one of the foremost opponents of their rebellion.

The first problem confronting them was a new barricade the British were beginning to build at the top of Moore Street near the Rotunda Hospital. Moore Street ran south to Henry Street, coming to an end near the side door of the Post Office, so this barricade completed would allow the British to pump a continuous flow of bullets across Henry Street, further constricting the insurgents. The new commanders met the threat by sending a squad of riflemen into the Coliseum theater, which abutted the Post Office on Henry Street, and faced Moore Street. These riflemen launched such a lively traffic in bullets up Moore Street toward the barricade builders that for a time it looked as if they might discourage the project. But the British chose this moment to figure out a worthy use for their armored car, which had until then been so useless. They put it to work depositing sandbags for the barricade. The work was soon completed and the insurgents gradually slackened their futile rifle fire. They had to accept the fact that one more street was virtually closed to them.

At dusk, someone in the Post Office, apparently alarmed by the artillery shells that kept dropping into the Metropole Hotel, sent an order to Lieutenant Oscar Traynor to evacuate the position. Traynor gathered his men together and they scurried across Prince's Street, through the side gate into the Post Office courtyard. They had been in the Post Office only a few minutes, standing around, wondering what to do next, when Pearse spotted them. What were they doing there? Why would anyone

have ordered them to evacuate the Metropole? It wasn't even on
fire. It was simply absorbing a few shells. To give it up so easily
would be to admit defeat, and Pearse was not ready to admit
defeat. Within another few minutes, they were back at their old
stand in the Metropole, shuddering at each new shell burst as
they watched the fires rise on the other side of O'Connell
Street.

The spectacle was now so magnificent it could make them
forget from moment to moment that it was also the most frightening they had ever seen. When Hoyte's oil and chemical stores
at the south end of the Imperial block erupted into flame, men
dropped whatever they were doing to watch the spouting rockets, the star bursts, the jets of every color shooting out in every
direction.

Brennan Whitmore, at the Imperial Hotel, stared in sinking
melancholy as the Hoyte establishment, struck by an incendiary
bomb, began to smoke, then exploded like a huge bundle of fireworks. He and his men watched the flames sweep toward them
through the gray-black clouds and wondered how long it would
take this final catastrophe to reach them. Young Sean MacEntee,
seated near a window, gazed as if hypnotized at the reflections of
the fires in hundreds of panes of glass and in every piece of metal
or polished stone on the Post Office side of the street. Fascinated
by the inferno's awful beauty, he continued to stare at it and
even admire it until finally, overcome by weariness, he closed his
smoke-reddened eyes and dropped off to sleep.

The hospital section of the Post Office was now the busiest
part of the building. Even the morphine could not contain Connolly's pain, and he was a cause of concern to Ryan and Mahoney. As they hovered over him, doing what they could, Pearse,
Clarke, MacDermott, and everyone else who could gain admit-
tance kept dropping in to wish him well or get his advice about
something. Men who lacked sufficient excuse to get inside stood
at the infirmary door hoping to get a glimpse of their fallen
leader or to hear some news about his condition.

In the midst of this commotion, a new patient was brought
down from upstairs. One of the men had such an uncommon case

of diarrhea his superior officer decided he needed some kind of treatment. But Joseph Cripps, who undertook to care for the man, found himself confronted with an amazing handicap. His patient spoke no English—only Spanish. No one seemed to know where he had come from or how he had gotten into the building, but he had apparently been there all week, crouched at a window, firing a rifle at anything that looked British. Unable to understand Spanish, Cripps called on Father Flanagan to help him figure out what might be causing the man's present distress. Finally, by communicating in a mixture of Church Latin and simple Spanish, the priest learned what had happened. The man had seen a pail of the hypo solution Cripps delivered earlier in the day, when the gas attack scare arose. Thinking the solution was nothing but water with a peculiar taste, he had drunk enough of it to loosen the bowels of a horse. When Cripps realized what had happened, he did what any good Irish doctor would do. He gave the man a strong dose of that most Irish of medicines, whisky, and sent him off to the toilet.

Because the fires moving south from Abbey Street had not yet reached Hopkins and Hopkins jewelry store at the quays, the British apparently decided to hasten matters there. Insurgents in Hopkins and Hopkins were still spraying the south bank of the river with their pestiferous shotgun pellets. The solution to that problem was now obvious. Within a few minutes, the building absorbed a generous selection of incendiary bombs, and the three insurgents inside began rushing back and forth with buckets of water, trying to douse them. It was an unrewarding project. The incendiaries kept coming faster than the water. Within fifteen minutes, the building was a bouquet of clustering fires; within a half-hour, they had fused into one big flame and the three insurgents were finally forced to leave their post as it burned around them.

Led by Seamus Robinson, they raced along the back alleys toward Amiens Street, but they needn't have hoped they would be able, this time, to circle around and get to the Post Office as they had done the day before. Ducking into a side street that led north, they stopped short at the sight of khaki a few yards ahead.

Without breaking stride, they reversed their direction, pulled back out of the street and continued east before the surprised British had time to open fire. But in every street or alley they tried now, the three men faced the same reception. The British were everywhere. The air filled up with British voices shouting alerts and all hope of escape ended. The three men could expect nothing but death as they ran into a narrow alley and found it to be a dead end.

Stopping, out of breath, they waited helplessly, listened to the approach of hobnailed boots, caught glimpses in the dark of the metal gleam of British rifles. It was all over now. At any moment, the first gun would fire and dozens of bullets would riddle them as they stood against the dead-end wall.

But as the British soldiers closed in, a pleasant surprise began to dawn upon the three men. The guns did not bark at them. The faces staring at them in the dim light were not even angry. They had luckily fallen into a company of new recruits who had just arrived in Dublin and weren't yet mad at anyone.

One of them said, "A scruffy lot, aren't they?"

Another laughed nervously. Moving forward, they grabbed the guns from the cornered insurgents, and the Hopkins and Hopkins men ended their part in the rebellion with more than they had reason to hope for—their lives.

The British were also closing in tighter and tighter from the northern end of O'Connell Street. Their snipers were now on the roof of the Gresham Hotel, from which they directed steady fire at the Henry Street corner of the Post Office, neutralizing the men at the windows there.

By ten o'clock, the Imperial Hotel and the whole block of buildings around it were filling up with flames contributed by the fire in Hoyte's stores.

Brennan Whitmore, having no other way to communicate with the Post Office, went to the front door and shouted across the street.

"What are the orders?"

Above the roar of the flames around him he could scarcely hear himself. The hope of being heard across the street was so

futile he decided to stop shouting for fear his troops might think
he had lost his mind. He realized he was on his own with eighty
desperate men awaiting his command. His garrison, which he had
established with ten men, had increased eight-fold as the fires
squeezed into it the refugees from other untenable positions.
Now his position was untenable. The flames were consuming the
south side of the building, driving men to the north side, where
they had to turn their backs to protect their faces from the
blistering heat. There was no choice but to evacuate, yet there
was no place left to go. Once again he wondered why the leaders
had not devised a plan for fleeing into the hills. Since it was the
only hope, he decided to try it.

Calling the eighty men to the North Earl Street door, Whitmore sent them running, single file, across to the same tobacco
shop through which some of them had made their way to the
Imperial. From the tobacco shop, which they all reached safely,
they passed on to Cathedral Street.

As he gathered them there, in comparative safety, he began to
think he might make it to the country after all. "This is what
headquarters ought to be doing," he said to Gerald Crofts, one of
his aides. But then, looking at his assembled company, he noticed
a problem that had not occurred to him before. The group included four Cumann na mBan girls, who couldn't possibly travel
fast enough to keep up with the men.

Crofts had a suggestion. "Why don't we leave them in the Pro-
Cathedral presbytery?"

To Whitmore it seemed an inspiration. As they passed the Pro-
Cathedral he stepped up and knocked until a priest came to the
door. The priest was not happy to see them.

"I suppose you want sanctuary," he said.

Whitmore said, "Not for ourselves, father. Only for these four
girls."

It was the first the girls had heard of the plan and their reaction
almost doomed it. They were no more eager to stay than the
priest was to take them. But Whitmore could not afford at the
moment to carry on a prolonged discussion of the options. He
won the argument with the priest by keeping his foot in the

door, and he won the argument with the girls by ordering his men to shove them, forcibly, inside. After a short, unhappy struggle, his point of view prevailed, the presbytery door slammed behind the girls, and the seventy-five or so soot-blackened men went running along Marlborough Street, clinging to the walls.

As they made a right turn into one narrow street and a left turn into another, their progress was so unimpeded Whitmore began to wonder where the British had gone. But when he tried to cross the next street opening, he found out. A bullet hit his leg and he went down. As he lay there, another gun fired and another man fell near him. Suddenly it was as if these two rifle shots had awakened the whole British army. Machine-gun fire filled the street, bounding off the walls and pavement. Engulfed by darkness, harassed by bullets, and unable even to see their fallen leader, the men became confused, stumbled into each other, muttered oaths, ran back and forth looking for shelter, then broke into smaller groups and began to scatter.

Whitmore, hearing voices from a doorway, dragged himself to it and found nine men there. But neither he nor any of them could guess where they were. In their desperate need of shelter, they scouted the immediate area hoping to find a warehouse or a shop they could have to themselves. The best they could find was a tenement house. Helping Whitmore and the other wounded man, they made their way to it carefully and silently to avoid stirring up the British machine guns again. They had no trouble getting inside. It was never difficult to enter a Dublin tenement; few of them had locks and some of them didn't even have doors. Whitmore and his men were impeded in this one only by the swarms of women and children who filled the front hall. Like most Dublin slum houses, it was so crowded people seemed to spill out of the rooms. And the people were so unwashed, the building so permeated with toilet and cooking odors, that it was almost preferable to stay outside and face the British guns. However, the desperate insurgents threaded their way in among the raucous, hostile shawlies, the barefooted little boys in ragged pants, the barefooted little girls in flimsy cotton dresses. Whitmore, on the arm of one of his men, dragged himself from room to room, looking for one that might be empty.

A man with an angry expression on his face appeared in a doorway. "Get outta here, ye bloody rebels!" he shouted. "Yiz got no right breakin' into a respectable house. Wait till the soldiers come. They'll bate yer bloody heads off, they will. Get out! Get out!"

Whitmore looked at him coldly. "My dear man, you can go to hell."

The man glanced at the insurgents' guns then receded into his room. Whitmore's troops continued down the hall until they found a relatively empty room, where he ordered them to place the other wounded man on the only bed and to spread themselves out on the floor with their backs to the walls.

"Wake me up before daylight," he said, then rolling under the bed, he dropped off to sleep despite the swarm of biting fleas that quickly found him.

Of the eighty men who had followed Whitmore from the Imperial Hotel, about half had run in the same general direction when the British machine-gun barrage scattered them. These men stumbled onto each other in a dark alley a hundred yards away and formed a new group. They were at a disadvantage because they had lost their officers and because many of them, having come from England, knew little about Dublin. One of them, however, Paudeen O'Keefe, not only knew the area but also knew how to take command of men. He led them down a long passageway into Cathedral Lane, then, after two more turns, into Marlborough Street, where they aroused the British machine guns again. Back they went, as fast as they could run in the dark, through Cathedral Lane to the passageway from which they had started. But now they had lost another ten or fifteen men, including O'Keefe. Another new leader, J. J. McElligott, took over and decided to make a dash for the Post Office. If he made it, he would have one of the doors opened, and at a given signal—two rifle shots in quick succession—the others were to follow.

McElligott disappeared into the darkness and after a reasonable length of time, two shots did ring out, whereupon the others had to decide whether they would follow. To reach the Post Office they would have to cross O'Connell Street in the bright light of the fires that engulfed it. Four of them, including Sean MacEntee, decided that couldn't be much more dangerous than any of the other courses open to them. Stumbling through a series of alleys to the burned-out shell of Lawrence's toy shop at the corner of O'Connell and Cathedral Streets, they waited in the shadows for a break in the gunfire. As soon as it stopped, one of the men dashed across, reaching the other side easily. MacEntee was so pleasantly surprised he followed immediately. Just before he reached Nelson's Pillar, halfway across, the guns took notice of him and he had to dance the rest of the way as lead kept skipping off the pavement near his feet. Diving into the shelter of Henry Street, he looked back anxiously for the two men following him.

Despite a rat-a-tat of rifle and machine-gun fire, they came on together, zigzagging like drunkards. After a quick dart into the shadow of the pillar, they ran out again into the light of the huge fires illuminating the street and, though one of them stumbled slightly, finally arrived to be welcomed by MacEntee in Henry Street.

Their troubles, however, were not quite over. The Post Office door on Henry Street was closed, contrary to their expectation, and because they were in almost as much danger on the street from the bullets of their friends as from those of the enemy, they had to attract attention quickly, but not too much of it. They tried a few knocks on the door without response, then they called at the windows to no apparent avail. The fire noise from across the street drowned them out. They decided to try the front door despite the dangers of O'Connell Street and were crawling around the corner when someone appeared at a window and they were helped inside to what they considered safety.

No one else in the Post Office at that moment would have described it as a safe place to be. Some of the men, on the verge of heat prostration from the holocaust across the street, were pouring water on themselves and seeking shielded places to stretch out in the rear of the building. Others were hosing the window casements to make sure the flammable materials stacked up around them did not catch fire. The hot, smoky air produced a chorus of choking coughs. Only Joseph Plunkett showed any sign of high spirit or excitement. Arising from the cot on which he had lain most of the week, he gathered energy into his wasted body from some hidden source and went rushing from man to man, smiling, shaking hands, telling them he was proud of them, trying, in his own way, to boost their sagging morale.

Turning to the fire, he gazed dreamily at the rampant flames shooting more than a hundred feet into the air and said, as if in exultation: "This is the first time it's happened since Moscow, you know. The first time a capital has burned since 1814." Nobody reacted. Some of the men who heard him turned away as if they were concerned about his sanity.

The arrival of the handful of refugees from the North Earl Street–Imperial Hotel garrison, the harrowing story of their misadventures after their evacuation, and the realization that most of the men who fled the fires in the Imperial were still trapped in the darkness east of O'Connell Street convinced Pearse, Clarke, and MacDermott that they must soon decide how to get their "army" out of the Post Office when it finally burst into flames.

The increasing heat was making instant steam of the water poured on the window casements. The men handling the hoses were scalded and scorched at the same time. The moment called for some kind of plan, but the best suggestion anyone could offer was that they put a pick-and-shovel squad to work burrowing a tunnel under Henry Street. The suggestion was adopted despite the evidence that if they were all to reach the other side of Henry Street safely, they would then find themselves in a block of buildings even more difficult to defend than the Post Office, and they would hardly have escaped their present predicament since they would still be within the British cordons. The squad of diggers went to work eagerly, and their labor was its own justification inasmuch as they had no more promising way to pass the anxious time, but their high hopes for the project gradually faded as the enormity of the task became apparent. They soon realized the rebellion would have to last a long time before they could get any good out of the Henry Street tunnel.

Pearse, Plunkett, and Desmond Fitzgerald, having little else to do, engaged in another of their discussions about the situation into which they had put themselves. Only Plunkett was cheerful. Pearse remained somber. Fitzgerald was depressed. He still found himself agonizing over the fate of the girls in the building.

"It's ridiculous to keep them here any longer," he said. "Especially the girls in the kitchen. We don't need them."

Though Pearse agreed, there remained the problem of how to get the girls out safely. None of the three had a ready solution. If no way could be found for the men to escape, it seemed pointless even to discuss the possibility of the girls getting through the British lines.

"What's going to happen to all these men?" Fitzgerald said reflectively. He gazed down at the exhausted troops sprawled on the floor.

Since he was not expecting an answer, he was startled to hear Pearse say: "They'll all be shot, I expect."

Plunkett nodded in agreement. They seemed remarkably calm for two men who were envisioning the deaths of several hundred of their followers and who were also admitting for the first time the absolute inevitability of their defeat. But it was neither their calmness nor their admission that struck Fitzgerald most forcibly. Pearse's words filled his mind once more with the absurd phobia that had been nagging him since his macabre conversation with Tom Clarke that morning.

"Are you sure they won't hang us?" he asked.

Pearse thought it over a moment. "They could hang us," he said, "but I think they'll shoot us."

Plunkett said, "What difference does it make?"

Fitzgerald didn't tell them that to him it made all the difference. He knew his preference for shooting rather than hanging was laughable, yet he couldn't shake it.

Upstairs, The O'Rahilly stood gazing at the fires on the other side of O'Connell Street. Beside him was a young man named James O'Byrne. "Do you know why they're burning all those buildings?" O'Rahilly asked.

O'Byrne said, "To have them out of the way, I suppose, so they can get a good bang at us."

"That's not the reason," O'Rahilly said. "It's to show you and me exactly what they think of poor old Ireland."

James Connolly's shattered ankle was still so intensely painful he had to be given successive injections of morphine. As each injection wore off he would awaken from fitful sleep and grip the sides of the bed. With sweat standing out on his face he glanced at Harry Walpole, a Citizen Army man who had been his orderly and "bodyguard" since the day in January when he returned from his "kidnapping" by MacDermott, Clarke, and Pearse. Walpole stepped closer to the bed, thinking his chief might want something, but Connolly only shook his head from side to side.

"Oh God!" he cried, "did ever a man suffer more for his country?"

Patrick Pearse, making late rounds of the building to encourage the men, encountered a former student of his, Desmond Ryan. They exchanged a few words, then Pearse fell silent. Ryan, knowing him well enough to find nothing unusual in this, waited for him to resume. An eruption of gunfire brought Pearse out of his revery.

"Isn't O'Rahilly a great man," he said, "Coming in here with us despite the way he felt about the rising?"

Ryan nodded, waited again.

Pearse gazed out toward the enormous fires still raging across the street. The walls of one of the buildings cracked, wavered, then crashed with a roar, sending patches of smoldering brick and debris down onto the pavement. The city he loved was crumbling around him, as was the revolution to which he had committed his life, but he did not look like a man facing catastrophe. His dream still showed in his face as his mind went back to the great Irish rebels of the past—Lord Edward Fitzgerald, Theobald Wolf Tone, Robert Emmet.

Turning again to Ryan, he said: "Emmet's insurrection was nothing compared to this, you know. They will talk of Dublin in the future as one of the splendid cities, as they speak today of Paris. Dublin's name will be glorious forever."

v. *Friday, April 28*

D AWN Friday found The O'Rahilly sitting on his cot, writing
another of his daily notes to his wife and children. During the first three days of the uprising, he had been able to get his notes out of the Post Office by messenger. Since then he had continued to write them only in the hope that they would be found on his body when he died. Expecting each note to be his last, he wrote his love for the family he was sure he would never again see, and he wrote about the rebellion, but he no longer wrote about it as if it were a hopeless thing. Four days in the presence of Pearse, Connolly, MacDermott, Clarke, and Plunkett had convinced him that though their insurrection would be an apparent failure, the Irish people would eventually arise as a result of it and gain independence. It was a measure of the force of Patrick Pearse's convictions that O'Rahilly had now come around to this viewpoint despite his initial certainty that the uprising was a stroke of madness. He had even developed civil relations with the other leaders, and when Connolly had been injured the previous day, he had stepped in, as had Sean MacDermott, to assume a greater share of command responsibility.

In the hours before dawn Friday, he had ordered all surplus grenades and explosives removed from the roof and the top floor in anticipation of the bombardment he was sure morning would bring. For the two previous days the British had been dropping shells on all sides of the Post Office as if they couldn't quite find the range. No one in the building understood why a target so large had been hit only twice, and both times superficially. O'Rahilly did not expect such good fortune to last. Despite an outward calm that was a marvel to everyone who saw him, he was awaiting a cataclysm.

During the night, machine-gun and rifle fire had continued sporadically. In the middle of O'Connell Bridge lay the body of an old man killed several hours before. An armored car, illuminated by the fires in O'Connell Street, had approached the bridge from the south bank of the Liffey, as if about to cross into insurgent territory, but had then retreated. A stampede of horses, turned loose into Middle Abbey Street from a burning stable west of the Post Office, had started rumors of another British cavalry charge. And a lull in the gunfire about daybreak had started rumors of a truce that would be followed by arbitration. Many of the insurgents firmly believed one of Pearse's most wishful thoughts—that having fought for more than three days, they had earned recognition under international law as belligerents in the European war and would therefore be entitled to representation at the peace table when it ended.

The fires were beginning to abate now on the other side of O'Connell Street, leaving two blocks of twisted, smoldering steel skeletons and jagged brick walls. As the flames continued to eat up the remaining combustible material, more walls collapsed, deepening the piles of brick and debris that already covered the street. The whole roasting mess still produced enough heat to take off the morning chill.

In the slum house just to the northeast of the fire area where Brennan Whitmore and his men had taken refuge the night before, they were awakened by a swarm of British soldiers bursting into the room. Whitmore, under the bed and still befuddled by sleep, reacted instinctively. He whipped out his revolver and fired at the first khaki uniform he saw.

The British soldiers, too astonished to return the fire, stood together in the middle of the room, staring down in amazement at the grimy-looking insurgents sprawled out along the walls. The lieutenant in charge was the first person to react to Whitmore's bullet; it had gone through his sleeve, ruining his uniform and arousing his anger.

"Who fired that gun?" he demanded.

No one spoke.

"Unless you tell me who fired that gun, you'll all be shot."

The silence continued until the lieutenant became so furious he ordered his sergeant to take them into the street and search them. Whitmore, needless to say, left his revolver under the bed. When they were searched, they were all found to be unarmed, a circumstance that further enraged the lieutenant, because he knew at least one of them must have a gun. The bullet that just missed him could not have fired itself.

Pointing to a brick wall across the street, he said, "All right, sergeant, line them up over there and get on with it. I want every last one of them shot."

A crowd of tenement dwellers who had gathered to watch the fun burst into a spontaneous cheer.

Someone shouted: "That's it! Give it to 'em!"

"Kill 'em!"

The idea appealed to the whole crowd. A woman shouted: "Shoot the bloody Shinners!" And a dozen others took up the chorus. The lieutenant seemed pleased with their sentiments.

The sergeant whispered to Whitmore, "'E's off 'is head." But the sergeant did not reject the command.

"March!" he ordered.

The prisoners stood staring at him, so bemused by what was happening they couldn't react to it.

"March!" he repeated.

One of them took a step forward. The others followed. Meekly they straggled across the street toward the brick wall, their exhaustion preserving them from the full comprehension that with each step, they were acquiescing in their own deaths.

Fortunately for them, a British captain chanced upon the scene, looked at them, then at the lieutenant.

"Where are you taking those men?" he asked.

"Across the street to have them shot," the lieutenant said, holding up his sleeve to show the bullet hole in it. "See what one of them did?"

The captain stared at him a moment in disbelief, then turned to the sergeant. "Take them to the Custom House," he ordered.

The sergeant, as he marched them away, glanced toward Whitmore and winked. "You're a lucky lot of bastards," he said.

Whitmore, limping and still in pain from the wound he had received the night before, stared back at him dumbly. Suddenly his stomach began to churn, his hands trembled, and beads of sweat sprouted on his forehead. It had dawned on him at last, how close they had come to execution.

The gun bursts were so infrequent in the early-morning hours that the men in the Post Office, accustomed now to continual firing, became uneasy about the lull. The British, they decided, must be planning something horrendous for them, but they had no way to counter it, so they went about their daily chores, keeping their fears mostly to themselves as they waited for something to happen. Nurses carried trays of food from the kitchen to their patients in the infirmary. Father Flanagan heard confessions in one corner of the mail-sorting room. At the front end of the building, squads of men were piling up debris-filled mailbags and coalbags to create a breastwork in case the British stormed the door.

James Connolly, after an agonizing night, was now comfortable enough to demand that he be transferred to a bed with castors so he could be moved out among the men. Hospital officer Jim Ryan and Lieutenant Mahoney both argued that he should stay put and get some rest, but he brushed aside their objections and the men at their stations in the main hall were soon treated to the sight of a bed rolling past them with Connolly propped up in it, cheering them on like a spectator at a sporting event.

As he passed young Sean MacEntee, standing at attention, Connolly recalled having sent him north Monday to help muster the men there. Ordering that his bed be halted, he asked MacEntee how successful he had been. MacEntee had nothing encouraging to report. He had found the men in Louth, then lost them after several misadventures. The men at Tara had failed to muster. At no place had he observed any effective action against the enemy.

Connolly was visibly disappointed, yet as soon as his bed had been wheeled to a spot from which he could survey the whole room, he called for Winifred Carney and began dictating to her a stirring and imaginative communiqué about the wondrous progress of the rebellion. This done, he settled back against the pillows, lit a cigarette, and accepted a book offered by one of the men. When Harry Walpole, his orderly, arrived on the scene, he looked up from the book and smiled.

"What do you think of this?" he said. "A morning in bed, a good book to read, and an insurrection, all at the same time. It's revolution deluxe."

But when The O'Rahilly came downstairs to visit him, it became apparent that Connolly was not as strong as he pretended.

"Would you do me a favor," he said. "I've written a message to the men. Would you read it to them?"

O'Rahilly gathered the men together in the main hall and in a loud, clear voice, began to read:

> Army of the Irish Republic
> Headquarters (Dublin Command)
>
> 28 April, 1916

To Soldiers:
This is the fifth day of the establishment of the Irish Republic, and the flag of our country still floats from the most important buildings in Dublin, and is gallantly protected by the officers and Irish soldiers in arms throughout the country. Not a day passes without seeing fresh postings of Irish soldiers eager to do battle for the old cause. Despite the utmost vigilance of the enemy, we have been able to get information telling us how the manhood of Ireland, inspired by our splendid action, are gathering to offer up their lives, if necessary, in the same holy cause. We are hemmed in, because the enemy feels that in this building is to be found the heart and inspiration of our great movement.

Let us remind you what you have done. For the first time in seven hundred years the flag of a free Ireland floats triumphantly in Dublin city. The British army, whose exploits we are forever having dinned into our ears, which boasts of having stormed the Dardanelles and the German lines on the Marne, behind their artillery and machine guns, are afraid to advance to the attack or storm any positions held by our forces. The slaughter they suffered in the first few days has totally unnerved them, and they dare not attempt again an infantry attack on our positions.

Our Commandants around us are holding their own.

Commandant Daly's splendid exploit in capturing Linen Hall Barracks we all know. You must know also that the whole population, both clergy and laity, of this district are united in his praises.

Commandant MacDonagh is established in an impregnable position, reaching from the walls of Dublin Castle to Redmond's Hill and from Bishop Street to Stephen's Green. (In Stephen's Green Commandant Mallin holds the College of Surgeons, one side of the square, a portion of the other side, and dominates the whole Green and all its entrances and exits.)

Commandant De Valera stretches in a position from the Gas Works to Westland Row, holding Boland's Bakery, Boland's Mill, Dublin South Eastern Railway Works, and dominating Merrion Square.

Commandant Kent holds the South Dublin Union and Guinness's Buildings to Marrowbone Lane, and controls James's Street and district. On two occasions the enemy effected a lodgement and were driven out with great loss.

The men of North County Dublin are in the field, have occupied all the police barracks in the district, destroyed all the telegraph system on the Great Northern Railway up to Dundalk, and are operating against the trains of the Midland and Great Western.

Dundalk has sent 200 men to march on Dublin, and in other parts of the North our forces are active and growing.

In Galway, Captain Mellowes, fresh after his escape from an Irish prison, is in the field with his men. Wexford and Wicklow are strong, and Cork and Kerry are acquitting themselves creditably. (We have every confidence that our allies in Germany and kinsmen in America are straining every nerve to hasten matters on our behalf.)

As you know, I was wounded twice yesterday, and am unable to move about, but have got my bed moved into the firing line and, with the assistance of your officers, will be as useful to you as ever.

Courage, boys, we are winning, and in the hour of our victory let us not forget the splendid women who have everywhere stood by us and cheered us on. Never had a man or woman a grander cause; never was a cause more grandly served.

> *James Connolly*
> Commandant-General
> Dublin Division

This cheerful flow of words did not mean Connolly still believed that people were rising in the country to support the cause or that the British were afraid to attack insurgent positions. He was simply using the communiqué in an accepted military tradition, as a palliative for the men. And the men, though they knew there was no help on the way, were willing to believe anything he said because they needed the comfort he offered.

In the main hall of the Post Office, just inside the front entrance, three lines of breastworks had now been built by piling up bags full of sand and debris. The purpose of these barricades was to stop the British if they were to storm the building. Though no one could possibly believe the British would be stopped by such flimsy obstacles once they got that far, it was another myth the men willingly accepted, and it kept a number of them busy. The bag barricades were swamped with water so the British would be unable to burn them if and when they did encounter them. And Connolly watched all this with approval, though he was now convinced the British had no intention of sending in their infantry. Why should they, when it was so much easier to send fire?

In midmorning, the first fire arrived. An incendiary bomb landed on the roof of the Post Office near the southeast corner. The men on the roof were expecting it, and they had no trouble putting it out, but as they did so, they couldn't help wondering how well they would do if such bombs began landing in clusters. Having reduced this one to harmless smoke, they stared out toward British gun positions south of the Liffey, expecting the next one at any moment. Again the British seemed to be teasing them. Minutes then hours passed without any follow-up to the first incendiary.

Connolly, the commandant general of the Dublin division, had produced what might be a last message to the men, and it was fitting that Patrick Pearse, as commander in chief and president of the Republic, do likewise—and quickly, for there might be very little leisure time left. He went into a small room off the main hall where, with his brother Willie standing silently a few feet away to avoid disturbing him, he began to write in his slightly back-handed, round-lettered style. But he was so exhausted, having slept not at all for a week and hardly at all for two weeks, that he could think of very little new to say. The message he produced was nearly the same as the one he had delivered to the men the previous afternoon, though with a different ending. After outlining the military situation far less optimistically than Connolly had done, he paid homage to the gallantry of the men "lest I may not have an opportunity later" and paid special tribute to Connolly, who "lies wounded but is still the guiding brain of our resistance."

His conclusion had none of Connolly's fanciful optimism. He was now so resigned to inevitable defeat that he ended on a valedictory note that included, besides a wishful reference to what might have been, a final expression of magnanimity toward those who had disappointed him:

If we accomplish no more than we have accomplished, I am satisfied. I am satisfied that we have saved Ireland's honor. I am satisfied that we should have accomplished more, that we should have accomplished the task of enthroning as well as proclaiming the Irish Republic as a Sovereign State, had our arrangements for a simultaneous Rising of the whole country, with a combined plan as sound as the Dublin plan has proved to be, been allowed to go through on Easter Sunday. Of the fatal countermanding order which prevented those plans being carried out, I shall not speak further. Both Eoin MacNeill and we have acted in the best interests of Ireland.

For my part, as to anything I have done in this, I am not

afraid to face the judgement of God, or the judgement of posterity.

> (Signed) *P. H. Pearse*
> Commandant General
> Commander in Chief, the Army of the
> Irish Republic and President of the
> Provisional Government

Even his prose style, still moving but less graceful than usual, showed the depths of his exhaustion.

He delivered his message to a group of men who crowded around him in the main hall, their faces tense, sober, mournful. After his last words, he looked from one to another of them, awaiting a reaction. There was none. Slowly, deliberately, he folded his paper and walked away. He found a place to lie down and tried to take a nap; sleep did not come.

The men he had just addressed stood still for some minutes after he left them. The guns outside were ominously silent, and no one seemed to want to move. Finally someone spoke. Then there was a babble of voices and someone laughed. The tension broken, the men returned to their duties, and the gunfire soon resumed.

The gunfire intensified from all directions as the British, having burned out the opposition from the east side of O'Connell Street, were able to close the ring even tighter around the insurgent headquarters. But the riflemen in the Post Office, in the Metropole Hotel, and in Manfred's shop at the Abbey Street corner still kept them back behind the rubble of the charred buildings. Though the artillery shells had not yet found the range of the Post Office, so many of them were dropping on the Metropole that the men there began wishing they would.

The bombardment concerned the prisoners in the Post Office even more than it did the insurgents, for the prisoners, besides being restricted in their movement, were also quartered on the second floor, where they were vulnerable to the expected bombs. Fortunately, The O'Rahilly was also concerned about them. He ordered them fed early, then taken to the cellar. The move did not comfort them. The possibility of the building collapsing on them in the cellar was as distasteful as the possibility of being killed by their own artillery on the second floor.

O'Rahilly tried to reassure them.

"I give you my word," he said, "that you will escape with your lives."

Locked in the dark, damp cellar, listening to shells explode above them, they were not convinced.

Shortly before noon, Pearse and Connolly decided it was time to evacuate the women in the Post Office. After passing the order for all the girls to assemble, they discussed the difficulty of getting them through the British lines. They did not anticipate another difficulty almost as great—the reluctance of the girls to leave.

Three young ladies from the kitchen, Louise Gavan Duffy, Peggy Downey, and Mae Murray appeared in front of Pearse like the three Furies and swarmed all over him, insisting they be allowed to stay. Pearse, whose poise and comfort fled him when he had to deal with women, quickly bowed to their demands.

Then someone mentioned that it would be impossible to let the nursing girls go, because there were sixteen wounded men who needed care.

Finally, twenty girls were lined up in the main hall. When Connolly suggested that his secretary, Winifred Carney, join them, she looked at him as if he were going dotty. Did he think she would even entertain the idea of leaving him at a time like this?

Pearse stepped up to the twenty girls, none of whom had yet been told they were leaving, and addressed a short speech to them:

When the history of this week is written, the highest honors will be afforded to all of you, whose bravery, heroism and devotion in the face of danger have surpassed even that of the women of Limerick in the days of Sarsfield [one of southern Ireland's few heroes of the Battle of the Boyne in 1690]. You have taken part in the greatest armed attempt at liberation by Ireland since 1798. You have obeyed the order to come here. Now I ask you to obey a more difficult order—the order to leave. Remember, it is equally binding upon you. It may not be easy for you to escape from here safely. There is a possibility that some of you may be shot after you leave this building. But you showed your readiness for that when you came here. Now go, and God be with you.

It took a while for the girls to comprehend this abrupt and unexpected farewell address. When they did, some of them broke into tears. Others appeared about to break into revolt.

"No!" they shouted.

"We won't go!"

"We stay as long as the men stay!"

Desmond Fitzgerald, who was standing by, knew Pearse's limitations in handling women. Sensing danger, he quickly turned the entire group toward the Henry Street door and ordered them to march. But not quickly enough. Sean MacDermott, who had come upon the scene, countermanded the order.

"I don't think they should be made to go," he said to Pearse. "They could be killed out there. They should be told they're free to go if they wish."

The girls, hearing him, roared out their agreement.

"If the men stay, we stay!"

"What about women's rights. You said we were equal!"

Pearse, surrounded by them now, visibly wavered.

Fitzgerald raised his voice above the racket. "These girls have received their orders," he shouted. "If they stay here, they'll eventually be shot."

His words encouraged Pearse, who quickly seconded them. Regaining command, he repeated his order until the girls, unable to sway him, gradually subsided. Fitzgerald once again ordered them to march. This time they moved, reluctantly, to the door.

Under the slim protection of a Red Cross flag, they stepped out into Henry Street and with tearful farewells on their lips, walked westward. Before they had gone two blocks, they were taken into custody by British soldiers.

Louise Gavan Duffy, Peggy Downey, and Mae Murray hurried back upstairs to get the noon meal ready for the men. They were now short-handed and they had lost time in the controversy over whether they could stay. They also had another problem. It was Friday and they were without fish. They quickly arrived at a sensible solution. We serve meat, they decided, and so they did, but not without evoking comments and uncertainties about it.

One of the British soldier prisoners who helped wait on tables, a Catholic boy named Tommy Murphy, took a look at a platter of chicken and said, "Father Flanagan will never eat that."

Desmond Fitzgerald said, "Take it to him and see."

Every eye in the dining room turned as Tommy Murphy carried the platter of chicken to the table at which the priest was sitting. Murphy set down the platter and stepped back. Father Flanagan eyed it for a moment, then picked up his fork and speared the nearest piece. The room blossomed with satisfied smiles and everyone pitched into the chicken.

Among the men at the table with Father Flanagan were Tom Clarke and Eamonn Dore. After they finished eating, Dore turned to Clarke and said, "What will you do if we win this fight, sir?"

Clarke shook his head wistfully. "We won't win this time."

"But what if we did win?"

Clarke said, "I'd get a little cottage someplace with a garden and grow flowers."

At about one o'clock, the artillery bombardment increased. The British had installed another eighteen-pounder at the top of Moore Street, near the Rotunda Hospital, and its shells, lobbed over the intervening blocks of buildings, began landing near the Post Office. The riflemen on the roof winced at each explosion. One of them, unable to see any targets for his rifle, put it down in front of him and took out his rosary beads. Another man, seeing him, took out his beads, then another and another. Soon, a half dozen men were huddled together in a protected corner, one of them calling out, time after time, "Hail Mary, full of grace, the Lord is with Thee, blessed art Thou amongst women and blessed is the fruit of Thy womb, Jesus"; and the others chanting in response, "Holy Mary, Mother of God, pray for us sinners now and at the hour of our death, Amen."

Though the explosives on the top floor of the building had

been taken to the cellar several hours before, the other floors had magazines full of bombs, grenades, and gelignite. If an artillery shell were luckily to hit the right spot, the British would have done for them the job of eliminating the insurgents. O'Rahilly decided it was time to carry all explosives to the cellar, and the laborious, dangerous job was now begun.

Patrick Pearse was so near total exhaustion he went to Jim Ryan in the hospital and asked for something that might help him get an hour's sleep. When Ryan suggested a narcotic solution, Pearse balked because he wanted to be able to awaken immediately if needed. Ryan talked him into taking a weak solution and Pearse stretched out on one of the beds, but he was not destined to sleep. Before the narcotics had time to take effect, the shout of "Fire!" began echoing through the building and Pearse was on his feet once more, though with his self-control further impaired, because Ryan's potion was now beginning to get to him.

It was shortly after 3 P.M. when Volunteer Joseph Sweeney, on the roof of the Post Office, heard a shell coming his way and dived for cover. When he raised his head again, he saw a cluster of flames erupting near the front portico. An incendiary bomb had half-penetrated the roof before exploding to distribute its several packages of fire.

Despite danger from British snipers, men grabbed the extinguishers that had been brought to them in anticipation and attacked the fires so quickly that for a time they appeared to be gaining control. But there were too many clusters. Each time they defeated one, another would appear.

Hoses, already connected, were pushed up to the roof from the top floor.

"Water!" someone shouted.

"Turn them on!"

But when the hoses were turned on, they produced more profanity than water. Most of them were so old and rotten the water spurted through leaks and was lost before it reached the nozzles. Had the hoses been in good condition, however, it would have made little difference, for there was hardly enough water pressure even for the few usable ones. It was insufficient to cope with the growing fires.

Pearse and Plunkett came running to the scene. They could do nothing. Plunkett, quickly overcome by the smoke, had to be helped downstairs again. The O'Rahilly arrived and assumed command, to no avail. Due to the leaky hoses, there was now more water on the top floor than on the roof, where it was needed. And the British, having decided finally that the Post Office must go, began lobbing more incendiary shells, one after another, onto the roof and through the windows of the building at all levels, thus ending the light talk about their apparent difficulty in finding the range. Soon there were so many fires that O'Rahilly's men, no longer hopeful of putting them out, concentrated on keeping them away from the elevator shaft. If the flames were to go down the shaft to the cellar and reach the explosives now stored there, the rebellion would end with a climax more sudden and spectacular than anything Dublin had ever seen.

Downstairs, the men reacted with surprising calm and resignation to the fires above them. Riflemen stuck to their window positions, still alert against the fading possibility of a British charge. A large squad, under the direction of Sean MacDermott, hastily removed all unneeded combustible materials from the building. Another squad tested the ground-floor hoses and discarded the rotten ones. Connolly had his bed moved into the glass-covered court, from which he could see the dancing flames on the roof. Pearse paced back and forth, head down, as if he had decided to ignore what he could not prevent.

Joseph Plunkett, having recovered from his near-suffocation by smoke, marched through the building with furious energy, exhorting the men to greater efforts. With his bandaged throat, his carefully pleated uniform, his bangled wrist and ringed fingers, his dangling saber and pistol, he was a curious, unreal, even comical figure, yet few laughed or even smiled at him except when he made outlandish remarks like, "One of the enemy's barracks is on fire." The men so much admired his courage they accepted his eccentricities.

Fires on the two upper floors of the building, from incendiary shells coming through the windows, were beginning to grow and to put greater demands on the limited water pressure. Sounds of crackling wood, roaring flames, running feet, shouting voices filled the air. The heat on the upper floors became intense. Long tongues of fire curled and leaped around the glass canopy that covered the central court. Burning pieces blown from the roof fell down on all sides. The men on the roof, trying to protect the elevator shaft from the flames, were driven back closer and closer to it until O'Rahilly realized the project was hopeless. He ordered everyone off the roof and went downstairs himself to devise a way of protecting the shaft from below.

Some time later, while he was directing a play of hoses into the shaft, he learned that there were still men on the roof. Running up a ladder through the almost insufferable smoke, he found a small squad, surrounded by flames but fighting back at them with hoses and extinguishers.

"Come down!" he shouted. "I ordered you down!"

A dissenting chorus greeted him.

"Leave us alone!"

"We're getting ahead of it!"

"Do something about the water pressure!"

O'Rahilly was unmoved. "You heard what I said. Down you go." As he hurried over to them, all but one, despite their grumbling, obeyed him. One man continued playing a hose on the fire, ignoring his order.

O'Rahilly argued with the man for a few moments, then taking out his revolver, pointed it at his head. "I told you to go down," he said, "and you're going down."

Finally the man dropped the hose and preceded O'Rahilly down the ladder into the building.

Floor by floor, O'Rahilly, Michael Collins, and a large detail of men held the fire at bay for as long as possible, putting barriers of sand across the doorways and flooding the floors with water. As each floor became untenable, they descended to the next.

When O'Rahilly reached the ground floor, he found almost total confusion. There were now so many fires throughout the

building that it was impossible to deal with all of them. Men ran
from one to another with little sense of which were most dangerous and which could be ignored. When flames appeared in the
elevator shaft, no one seemed to know what to do about them.
Even Pearse had lost his composure. He and Plunkett, their faces
flushed, stood shouting at each other. Connolly lay helpless on his
bed. MacDermott and Clarke were in another part of the
building. O'Rahilly stepped between Pearse and Plunkett, calmed
both of them, then took over direction of the fire battle, ordering
immediate concentration on the flames in the elevator shaft. Every
hose that could reach it began pouring water up into it.

About six o'clock, Pearse, MacDermott, Clarke, Plunkett, and
O'Rahilly got together at Connolly's bed and decided the time
had come to work out an evacuation plan. Since the sewers
offered an obvious possibility, they sent two men to explore
them, but the men returned, looking dirty and smelling foul, to
report that the filth they encountered was impenetrable. There
was no way out except through the streets, and unless the fires in
the Post Office slowed down, the whole garrison might be forced
into the streets before dusk, without even the protection of darkness.

One remote possibility presented itself. On Parnell Street, a
long block north, stood a large stone building, the Williams and
Wood soap and candy factory, which might serve as a new base
of operations if they could break through the British lines and
reach it. Someone would have to lead an advance party up Moore
Street, in the face of British guns, to capture it. The O'Rahilly
said he would do so when the time came. Then he went back to
his battle against the fires.

Beams were crashing on the upper floors now as the entire
front of the building appeared to be aflame. Near the front, the
ceiling of the ground floor had ignited and burning fragments
were dropping from it. The heat was intense throughout the
building. But more serious than the heat was the fact that live
sparks and burning particles were now falling down the elevator
shaft into the cellar. O'Rahilly decided all the explosives in the
cellar magazine would have to be moved to the rear of the build-

ing. When he called for volunteers, twenty men stepped forward. Under the command of Diarmud Lynch, they made their way carefully down the stairs by lantern light as O'Rahilly himself manned one of the hoses pouring water into the shaft.

Though the magazine was very near the already burning elevator shaft, Lynch had the presence of mind to take some important precautions before he let the men handle any explosives. With lantern in hand, he worked out a circuitous route around three wings of the building to the very rear, by way of a cavernous passage under O'Connell Street at the front, then right, back along the south wall to the place most remote from the fires. On that route, at frequent intervals, he placed men with lanterns. And after an almost superfluous warning about the danger of the task, the need for extreme care, he put the rest of his squad to work snatching armloads of dynamite from the approaching flames.

The basement was dark, even with the lanterns lit, and the floor was littered with debris, so each armload offered a trip to eternity if dropped. Everyone bore this danger in mind, but another arose that could not have been foreseen. Volunteer John McLoughlin had just taken a heavy load of gelignite in his arms when the O'Rahilly, playing water down the elevator shaft from the ground floor above, momentarily lost control of his hose. McLoughlin was hit in the chest by a stream of water heavy enough to knock him to the floor. But fortunately it knocked him backward so his body cushioned the fall of the gelignite; after a few choice Irish epithets, he was on his feet again and off along the perilous route with his dripping load.

On the ground floor, the heat was so intense that Pearse didn't have to worry about gathering the men together so they would hear his evacuation order when it came. They had all crowded into the large sorting rooms and the covered court near the rear, where they could at least avoid roasting. But even here the fires were growing on all sides of them and above them so they seemed to be in a cavern hollowed out of the flames. Sheets of fire would sweep across the covered roof, cracking and shattering sections of glass, sending down shards and sometimes molten drops. The fires were so enormous now that Pearse realized they would not be able to hold off evacuation until dark. He sent word that the men in the Metropole and all other outposts should return to the Post Office. Then he ordered the men on hand to divide into two ranks and stand by for instructions.

O'Rahilly, despite the heat and the flames around him, continued to play a stream of water into the elevator shaft. But the water pressure had become pitifully low, and eventually the flow stopped. He shouted down to Diarmud Lynch, "How are you doing?"

"Almost finished!"

"You'd better be. There's no more water to hold back the fire. Bring up the men. Hurry!"

While Lynch went to do so, O'Rahilly heard for the first time a jumble of hoarse, desperate cries from another part of the cellar.

"Help!"

"We can't breathe!"

"Let us out of here!"

"We'll burn to death!"

It was the prisoners, whom he had not been able to hear while his hose was running. He shouted for Lynch to go tell Connolly about them and make sure they were moved. Then he himself hurried off to see about something else that was worrying him. His sister's son, a youngster named Richard Humphreys, was one of the Volunteers in the Post Office. He was there partly because of hero worship for his uncle, whom he had first seen several years before as a romantic figure returning from a sojourn in America. O'Rahilly's energy, his cleverness with mechanical things, his enthusiasms, especially for Ireland, had dazzled young Richard and still did. He loved his uncle and O'Rahilly, knowing it, wished to make sure the boy would be as safe as possible. He sought him out and told him the Post Office would soon be evacuated.

"I want you to report to Desmond Fitzgerald," he said. "Do what he tells you." Then, with a smile and a pat on the shoulder, he left the boy and went looking for Pearse. If they expected him to lead an assault force to Williams and Wood, it was about time to make some plans.

Fitzgerald and his kitchen crew were busy distributing to the men, as per instructions from Pearse, all the food they could carry. Hams, cakes, bread, tea, bacon, cabbages, sugar, flour were piled upon the already overloaded men. In Pearse's view, they still might need several days' rations. He had also given Fitzgerald his specific assignment for the coming evacuation. Instead of standing guard over the remaining women in a concrete bunker until death, as Clarke had told him to do, he was to help lead the women and the wounded to Jervis Street Hospital if he could manage to get them there.

"You must do your best," Pearse had said, "but I think it will be in the hands of the enemy."

Fitzgerald had swallowed hard, trying to decide whether this new assignment was any better than the one Clarke had given him. Pearse had then looked at him solemnly and said, "Incidentally, you've done an excellent job and you are hereby promoted."

Pearse didn't know that Tom Clarke had done the same thing the day before. Pearse didn't even know what rank Fitzgerald held. But then, neither had Clarke, and neither did Fitzgerald himself. Whatever it might be, he didn't expect to hold it long.

Connolly, in his bed near the Henry Street door, listened to Diarmud Lynch's report about the prisoners and pondered what to do with them. If he released them now they would get back to the British with too much information about the condition of the insurgents and the preparations to evacuate the Post Office. They would have to be held a little longer. It would be inhuman, though, to leave them in the cellar. "Bring them upstairs and put them someplace in the rear," he said, "but keep a guard on them." Lynch hurried to comply.

To facilitate the escape of the wounded and the women, a squad of men broke holes through a succession of buildings along Henry Street as far as the Coliseum theater. The farther the party could get from the Post Office before emerging into the street, the better their chances of reaching the hospital. Pearse and Plunkett gathered the rest of the men in the yard by the great side gate and made sure each man had a ration of food. The fires continued. On the upper floors, abandoned small-arms ammunition was exploding like strings of fire crackers, and abandoned grenades kept going off with heavy thuds. Floor sections were crashing down, raising clouds of dust to mingle with the smoke and flame. Into this atmosphere came the men of the Metropole Hotel garrison, dashing across Prince's Street and through the gate to add more congestion to the already crowded courtyard.

Plunkett, after helping gather the men, sought out Winifred Carney; he wanted her to do him a favor. In his breast pocket was a sealed envelope containing a short note to Grace Gifford and a will bequeathing her his entire estate, which was considerable. Although he was certain he would never again see his fiancée, he thought Miss Carney might. The insurgent women were not likely to be shot.

"Would you do something for me?" he asked her.

By this time she would have been happy to do almost anything for him. Whatever she might think of his style of life, she could no longer question his courage, loyalty, or determination. She gazed sadly at his bandaged throat and his pale features and realized that even if the British did not execute him, he could scarcely live more than another few days.

He gave her the envelope addressed to Grace Gifford, then took off his filigreed bangle and put it on her wrist and placed one of his large antique rings in her hand.

"Will you see to it that Grace gets these things?" he asked.

Winifred Carney nodded. Plunkett thanked her and walked away.

All the wounded men except Connolly were now prepared for evacuation. When Lieutenant Mahoney approached to get Connolly ready, he waved him away.

"I'm not going out with the wounded," Connolly said. "My place is with my men."

Both Mahoney and Jim Ryan argued with him to no avail. After giving him several reasons why he should be in a hospital,

Mahoney shrugged in resignation and turned his attention to the sixteen wounded men who would be going.

Desmond Fitzgerald, Father Flanagan, and Mahoney were to lead the party, which also included the hospital attendants bearing stretchers and twelve of the fifteen women left in the Post Office. Three women were to remain—Winifred Carney, who still refused to leave Connolly; and two nurses, Elizabeth O'Farrell and Julia Grenan, who were needed to take care of him and any other men that might be wounded in flight.

As the twelve girls gathered around the stretchers awaiting the order to go, men began coming to them with messages, prayerbooks, rosaries, pictures—whatever remembrances they might have for their people at home.

Tom Clarke walked over to Leslie Price, a girl he knew well because of her Cumman na mBan activities, and said to her, "If you see my wife, tell her the men fought to the . . ." He tried to finish the sentence, then shook his head, turned, and walked away.

At the height of the confusion around the girls, Pearse called for order. The roar of voices subsided and the men formed once more into two ranks. Pearse, looking even more grave than usual, asked if each man had his ration. Then he went down the lines, picking out one man after another and drawing them aside. Because the chosen were apparently marked for some special duty, every man stood on edge, wondering if he would be taken, and those who were passed over didn't know whether to feel slighted or relieved. After Pearse had selected thirty men, he formed them into a special squad apart from the main body, then addressed to them a few special remarks.

"As you must know, we are preparing to evacuate headquarters," he said. "But you men will not leave with the rest of us. You will move out as an advance guard under the command of The O'Rahilly. Your task will be to secure the Williams and Wood factory on Parnell Street and hold it until we arrive. The assignment is difficult, but you have proven yourselves as soldiers. I am confident you will succeed."

Then he turned, raised his voice for everyone to hear, and

repeated the general plan. "I want all of you," he said in conclusion, "to be ready to go out and face the machine guns as if you were on parade."

The men, who had listened silently, remained silent for a minute after Pearse finished. Then one voice sang out: "Soldiers are we . . ." A moment later, more than 300 voices, singing "The Soldiers' Song," rose up in answer to the roaring flames and exploding bullets.

Still singing, the men moved to the Henry Street exit, where they waited again for the officers to give them marching orders. As they waited, their ranks became gradually less orderly, then broke down completely, until the men were milling around each other, asking questions, exchanging rumors. In the confusion, one of the hair-triggered shotguns went off, spraying out a cartridgeful of pellets. Charles Saurin of the Metropole garrison was hit in the palm of the hand, but not seriously injured. Andy Furlong was hit in the leg, and so was a man next to him, an English-Irishman with a cockney accent.

Swaying against Saurin's left shoulder, the man said, "Can't you stand away and let a fellow lie down?"

As Saurin and several others stretched him out on a pile of mail sacks, Lieutenant Oscar Traynor arrived and asked how badly he was hurt.

The man looked up with an expression of dignity and resignation. "I'm dying, comrade," he said.

Desmond Fitzgerald, who came to investigate, decided the man was in a less serious condition than he thought himself to be. After administering first aid, Fitzgerald had the two wounded men put on stretchers and transferred to his party.

Pearse watched all this, his face tense with worry, then raised his voice in an order. "Unload your guns, everyone, and hold your muzzles up." There was so much noise no one seemed to hear him at first. He kept shouting the order until they did.

The O'Rahilly, with only a few minutes left before departing on his perilous mission, thought again of the prisoners, to whom he had promised safe passage. He had them all brought forward and placed, still under guard, near the Henry Street door, from which they could dash for freedom when Pearse gave the word. Then he shook hands with each of them in turn and said, "Good-bye, I may never see you again, but good luck to you."

Having completed that duty, O'Rahilly sought out Desmond Fitzgerald and Father Flanagan, who were busy with the wounded. After telling Father Flanagan the best way to get to Jervis Street Hospital, he knelt and asked for last absolution and blessing. When the priest granted it, O'Rahilly stood and the two men shook hands.

"Father, we shall never meet again in this world," O'Rahilly said.

He went over to Desmond Fitzgerald and the two old friends gazed at each other for a long moment before impulsively clasping each other's hands.

O'Rahilly said, "Good-bye, Desmond. This is the end now for certain. I never dreamed it would last so long." He paused and broke into a wide smile as he thought of a joking remark on which to go out. "The only thing that grieves me is that so many of these lads are Irish speakers," he said, referring to his own long campaign in favor of the Irish language. "But never mind. When it comes to the end I'll say, 'English speakers to the fore, Irish speakers to the rear, charge!'" And as he turned to go he added, "But fancy missing this then catching cold running for a tram."

At the Henry Street door, where O'Rahilly's squad awaited him, he inspected the men carefully and ordered them to fix bayonets. Then, taking out his own Mauser pistol, he turned to Patrick Pearse, who repeated their mission and wished them well. O'Rahilly stepped in front of them, smiling, and made just one simple statement.

"It will be either a glorious victory," he said, "or a glorious death."

As the men filed out of the Post Office, he lined them up in a single rank against the sheltering wall and, taking his place at the head of the rank, called out, "Left turn, quick march." Clinging to the wall, they started off along Henry Street to the T-shaped corner where it meets the lower end of Moore Street.

Inside the Post Office, as dusk settled, Desmond Fitzgerald's party of women and wounded began the hopeful journey toward Jervis Street Hospital by climbing through a hole chopped in the rear wall of the building. The infirmary assistants carried the wounded on stretchers. The others, including the girls, carried first-aid equipment and bedding as they made their way westward through holes in building after building toward the Coliseum theater. When they came to the end of the series of holes, they had to climb a ladder, one by one, the stretcher-bearers with wounded men on their backs, and continue along a series of roof-tops. Joseph Cripps worried about the stitches in a man he was carrying because he had sewn up the man himself. As they moved farther from the burning Post Office, they could feel the chill in the air. Looking back, they could see the clusters of in-cendiary shells still dropping and bursting into little patches of flame. Fitzgerald, who had left his coat in the fire-heated Post Office, wished now he had brought it, especially when he recalled that there were some pound notes in it. After a sudden, ridiculous impulse to go back for it, he laughed at himself and cautiously moved on, leading the party across the rooftops. When they reached the theater, they were able to crawl through a window into its restaurant-bar.

As soon as the wounded had been laid out on the rich, thick carpet, the stretcher-bearers tried to lower the theater's fireproof stage curtain in the hope of making the place safer until dark, when they would be moving on again. They were unable to operate the curtain, however, because it was electric, and though the British had failed, amazingly, to turn off the water in the Post Office area, they had turned off the power.

In the restaurant, Jim Ryan lightened the mood of the moment by volunteering to tend bar.

"All right, gents, the drinks are on the house. What'll yiz have?"

But while everyone laughed, the prohibition against drinking in this rebellion was so strong that no one dared take him seriously. Father Flanagan was gratified to notice that though the insurgent forces had been in and out of the Coliseum all week, not one bottle of liquor appeared to have been touched.

While the party waited for enough darkness to offer some

protection in the streets, word came that Lieutenant Mahoney was needed back in the Post Office. Though he was still a prisoner, it did not occur to anyone that he should be escorted there under guard, so he climbed out the window alone, across the rooftops, down the ladder, and through the holes in one wall after another, back to the burning building he had so recently escaped.

The main body of men was still there, also awaiting darkness, and so were the other prisoners, standing nervously by the door. Mahoney had been recalled, as he soon learned, because one of the men had fallen over Commandant Connolly's foot and smashed the cradle splint on his shattered ankle. Mahoney repaired the damage while Connolly clenched his teeth to avoid crying out in pain. After finishing his medical chore, Mahoney stood up and surveyed the scene.

Pearse was circulating among the men, apparently calm, as were all of them. His orders were firm but not loud, and he showed no sign of panic or even fear as he made sure every man was ready for the ordeal ahead. Mahoney, watching Pearse, came to a sudden conclusion, one that had not occurred to him before: this man was, indeed, a gifted leader, supremely fitted to command.

There was no further need for him in the Post Office, so Mahoney once again stepped through the hole in the rear wall of the Post Office and made his roundabout way back to the Coliseum.

O'Rahilly's thirty-man assault party, sticking close to the buildings for protection, arrived at an insurgent barricade near the Moore Street corner. As silently as possible they moved one end of it aside and slowly filed through it. Just before they reached the corner, O'Rahilly stopped them and divided them into two squads. One was to go up the right side of Moore Street while O'Rahilly led the other up the left side. As the men stepped furtively around the corner into Moore Street, clinging to the walls on either side, they were conscious of a deep stillness all around them. But before they had gone ten yards the British, from behind their own barricades at the top of the street, cut loose with every gun they had.

Patrick Pearse, in the Post Office, decided it was now almost as dark as it was going to get. He went to the prisoners, shook their hands, apologized for the inconveniences they had suffered, and told them they were free now to make a break for the British lines. Led by the lieutenant who had spent the days of his captivity first in a drunken stupor, then in a nervous frenzy, they ran out the door across Henry Street into Henry Place (a street just slightly wider than an alley) and followed it to the left, which took them toward Moore Street, where O'Rahilly's assault squadron had inspired a storm of British bullets. Quickly doubling back, the now-freed but frightened British soldiers, boxed in by the gunfire of their comrades, jumped over a low wall and found themselves in another alley that seemed to lead nowhere. Here, the lieutenant collapsed. One of his enlisted men carried him into a cellar, where they all took refuge.

Moore Street was so thick with bullets that O'Rahilly and his men had to press themselves against the sides of the buildings and inch their way forward, taking cover where they could find it, sometimes in doorways six inches deep. Several, unable to find cover, fell victims of the first strong British volleys. The others continued the advance.

O'Rahilly paused in a narrow doorway as he neared Sampson Lane. He could look back on both sides of the street and see men writhing on the pavement. Behind him, on his side, men were still pressing forward, exposed to the withering fire as they followed his lead. There was no way to shelter them in this doorway. He would have to move on.

Taking a deep breath, he came out of the doorway and ran toward Sampson Lane. He had almost reached the corner when he was stopped short by the thudding impact of bullets hitting his midsection. Gasping in pain, he went down on one knee, then pitched forward on his face. But he did not lose consciousness. After the shock subsided, he realized he had to find cover, for bullets were still dancing all around him. Inch by inch, clutching his wounded belly, he dragged himself into Sampson Lane, where he fell against the sheltering wall of the corner building.

Lying on the damp pavement with the Post Office fire casting enough indirect light to let him watch the blood ooze from his body, O'Rahilly decided his week-long expectation of death was now an almost immediate certainty, and he longed to say at least a few final words to his family before he died. He searched in his pocket for a piece of paper and found a letter from one of his little boys, Aodhgan. On the back of it he wrote a note to his wife and children, assuring them again of his love, and asking them to try to understand the beliefs and feelings that had brought him to this end. Having finished the note, he folded it, put it into his breast pocket, and turned his head to peer around the corner, up the fire-lit street toward the British barricade from which the bullets were coming.

At 8:40 P.M., Patrick Pearse, standing near the doorway of the burning Post Office with drawn sword, explained again to his men that their objective was the Williams and Wood factory on Parnell Street and told them how to get there. Volunteer John McLoughlin, who had somehow missed the earlier announcements of their destination and who had spent the first three days of the week on the streets, carrying messages to the eastern outposts, stared in surprise and horror at his commander in chief.

"We can't go there, sir," he said. "The British have been in control of that whole area since Wednesday."

It was not exactly news to Pearse. The British controlled almost every area in the city, but he wasn't hoping to take over an area. He would be satisfied at this point to seize just one solid building. He called out the long-awaited evacuation order, and the men, so frightened of the flames behind them that they gave small thought to the bullets in front of them, began dashing out across Henry Street into Henry Place. British snipers on rooftops to the west soon saw what was happening and opened fire. Joseph Plunkett, Sean MacDermott, and Pearse himself went into the street, spurring the men on, buoying up their courage in the face of the gunfire. Pearse stood in the street, indifferent to the bullets as he supervised the operation. Connolly was carried across on a stretcher, as fast as his bearers could run with such a heavy burden. Close beside him on one side ran a young lad who had decided that with his own body he would shield his commandant from further injury. Just as close beside him on the other side ran

Winifred Carney, who was equally willing to die protecting him. All three of them and the stretcher-bearers reached Henry Place safely. Behind them, guided across the street by Pearse himself, came Elizabeth O'Farrell and Julia Grenan, the two nurses who had remained with the main body. And behind them, carrying an apothecary's basket full of dressings, disinfectants, and stimulants, came Jim Ryan, who, after escorting the wounded as far as the Coliseum theater, had returned to accompany the main body out of the Post Office.

Pearse, after leading the two girls across the street, went back to the Post Office. When all the men were out, he and Tom Clarke made what seemed to be the final trip into Henry Place, where the rear guard was awaiting its orders. Pearse paused and looked once more at the splendid, flame-stricken building they had held for a week. Was it possible anyone might still be inside it? He had not made the rounds before leaving. Impulsively he ran back across the street and disappeared into that furnace he had just escaped. The men in Henry Place stood waiting through several minutes of increasing concern before he rejoined them, his eyes swollen by a concentrated dose of heat and smoke.

The vanguard of the insurgents had run into desperate trouble as they rounded the Henry Place corner and turned north into Moore Lane, an alley parallel to Moore Street. Clusters of British machine guns opened up at them from behind a barricade at the top of Moore Lane and from the roof of the Rotunda Hospital at the corner of Parnell and O'Connell Streets. Men were falling in agony and scattering in confusion when John McLoughlin, brandishing a sword and assuming command, lined them up and marched them back, with their wounded, toward Henry Place. It was not quick enough for some of them. The end of the column caught such heavy fire several more fell; others bolted for cover over walls, through windows, and into barns. So many bullets were hitting the stone wall of the warehouse facing the lane that a cloud of white dust grew out of it.

Joseph Plunkett, arriving on the scene as the battered column retreated from Moore Lane, assessed the difficulty and ordered a van dragged across the mouth of the lane. Behind this bullet catcher the men were able to continue their flight in the direction of Moore Street. What they would do when and if they reached Moore Street no one had yet decided. O'Rahilly's squadron had stirred up enough gunfire to make it impassable. Yet Plunkett, showing his own courage, stood in the open shouting, "Don't be afraid! Don't be cowards! On! On! On!"

In the Coliseum theater, Desmond Fitzgerald and Father Flanagan, concerned at the increasing volume of gunfire around them, discussed the possibility of flying a Red Cross flag from the roof of the building. The idea was soon abandoned because the rain of fire bombs and shrapnel was now so intense no one could go safely onto the roof. Just below them in Henry Street an armored car appeared through the dense smoke and began sending rifle bullets up Moore Street to mingle with the machine-gun bullets coming down the street. Occasionally, O'Rahilly's men appeared through the smoke, crouching in doorways, taking advantage of every inch of cover they could find.

Fitzgerald and Father Flanagan, aware that the Coliseum would soon be as fiery as the Post Office, searched for a safe exit from the building while the wounded and the women waited, anxiously but quietly. The exits were all padlocked except, fortunately, the one that seemed to offer the best chance of escape—a rear door leading to a gate into Prince's Street, where the gunfire had now subsided. With a pick ax, one of the men broke the lock on the gate. Waving a Red Cross flag, the party filed out into the narrow street, across a burning barricade, through a passageway, and finally into Middle Abbey Street, where a few insurgent stragglers, holed up in a house, were exchanging fire with the British behind a barricade near the Jervis Street Hospital.

The appearance of the Red Cross flag, which was actually a Red Cross nurse's apron on a pole, stopped the gunfire. The soiled, straggling party of girls and wounded men, with a priest and a British medical officer at the fore, moved slowly along the footpath toward Jervis Street in the fierce glare from burning buildings.

At Liffey Street, a British voice from behind a barricade ordered them to halt, and for five fearful minutes they awaited the next command.

Finally, the same voice called out: "The bearer of the flag and one more advance for a parley."

Father Flanagan turned to Lieutenant Mahoney, who quickly shed his coat, exposing his khaki British officer's uniform. They stepped deliberately forward until they were about twenty paces from the barricade and could see the muzzles of the guns pointed at them.

"Halt!" The two men stopped.

"Who are you and where do you think you're going?"

Mahoney said, "Lieutenant John Mahoney, Indian Army Medical Service. A prisoner of the insurgents since Tuesday."

The man behind the barricade seemed unconvinced of Mahoney's identity. Father Flanagan spoke. "We have a party of wounded. We want to get them into the hospital."

"You can't pass this barricade."

"We wouldn't have to pass the barricade," Father Flanagan pointed out. "We could go in the side door."

A monocled major appeared and carried on a protracted conversation, none of it audible, with the man in charge of the barricade. The man in charge then said to the priest, "What's your name?"

"Father John Flanagan."

A few minutes later, two young men, both of whom looked Irish, were brought out the front door of the hospital and up to the barricade.

An officer said to them, "Have you ever seen that man before?"

Father Flanagan recognized both of them as medical students who worked in the hospital, and fortunately they recognized him.

"That's Father Flanagan," one of them said, and the other nodded.

The party was then passed through the military lines into the hospital to be received by the nuns and nurses. Father Flanagan, a familiar figure at the hospital, was welcomed like a returning hero. And Lieutenant Mahoney, free at last, went to report to the military authorities about his days as a prisoner of the insurgents. Hospital attendants took charge of the wounded while Desmond Fitzgerald and the stretcher-bearers stood by, waiting to be put under arrest. They were surprised that they hadn't been seized immediately, but, of course, their arrival had created so much confusion everyone was too busy to deal with them. So they continued to wait.

They were beginning to think they had been forgotten completely when an officer took notice of them and they turned to him, expecting the order that would send them off to a military prison. They were not prepared for what he said:

"All right, now, all you other people get out of here. Go back to where you came from."

They looked at each other, then again at the officer, thinking they had heard him wrong. Was he actually letting them go? One of them turned to walk away, as if testing his words. The others followed, uncertainly, and it began to dawn on them that they were free. But their elation did not last long, for they found themselves walking back into no man's land, where the gunfire was resuming. They would have to seek shelter until the fighting stopped, then try to reach their homes through the side streets and back alleys. Fitzgerald picked up a cap he saw in the gutter, put it on his head and tried to look like someone who might live in the neighborhood. Then, like the other men, he ducked into a building and waited for the right moment to break for home.

In Sampson Lane, The O'Rahilly, clutching his wounds, gathered his strength for another advance against the British barricade at the top of Moore Street. A few of his men had now caught up to him. Only by rushing the barricade could they hope to take the pressure off their comrades pinned down in the Moore Street doorways.

Bringing himself to his feet, O'Rahilly grasped his Mauser and, ordering a new assault, stepped out into Moore Street, firing at the barricade as he ran toward it. Supported by a handful of followers, he pressed his charge, answering the machine-gun fire with pistol shot. To take attention from the men behind him, he zigzagged his way across the street as he advanced, but while he moved along untouched, as if he were picking his way between bullets, his men began to fall, one after another.

He had almost reached the corner of Sackville Lane, a short half-block from the barricade, when his luck expired. A bullet pierced the note he had just written his family and entered his chest. Once again he pitched forward to the pavement, but once again he gathered his strength and, with an ultimate effort, flung himself into Sackville Lane, where the corner building kept any more bullets from reaching him. The attempt by his assault squadron to reach the Williams and Wood factory was at an end. Of the thirty men who left the Post Office with him, most were now lying on the pavement, either dead or wounded. The others made their way into alleys, houses, or barns where they could only wait for whatever might happen next.

In the alleys, yards, and stables between Moore Street and Moore Lane, the main body of insurgents scurried for cover as more British machine guns began to spray the area. Jim Ryan and four or five others worked their way into a bottle store, then climbed through other stores and over several roofs until they descended into a small courtyard. Racing through machine-gun fire across the courtyard, they vaulted a low wall and found themselves in a crowded yard at the rear of Cogan's grocery shop, which was on the corner of Henry Lane and Moore Street.

There were so many men milling about in this yard Ryan decided he had, at last, been reunited with the main body. Among these men were about a dozen who had been wounded, some seriously, in the flight from the Post Office. They needed immediate attention, but when Ryan saw them, he realized he had lost the basket of medical supplies he had brought for emergencies. He could do nothing for them here in the dark, on the cold ground. He would have to get them into a house.

The yard belonged to a small cottage that adjoined Cogan's shop. One of the able-bodied men went to the cottage door, tried it, and found it locked. He decided to open it by shooting the lock.

Inside the cottage were Mr. and Mrs. Thomas McKane, their

ten children, and Mrs. McKane's brother, Joe Gorman. For two days they had all been confined to the crowded house by the intermittent gunfire. McKane, with a pair of his children in his arms, heard someone try the lock at the back door and went to investigate, threading his way between several of his other children, including his sixteen-year-old daughter, Bridget, in the back room.

Just as McKane reached the door, the insurgent soldier fired his gun into it to break the lock. The bullet passed through the door, through McKane's shoulder and into Bridget's head.

Mrs. McKane, hearing the shot, rushed into the room crying, "Oh God, where's Daddy?"

Her husband was on the floor, blood pouring from his shoulder as he still clutched the two uninjured children. Bridget had swooned onto a bed-chair with a huge hole in the right side of her head.

The insurgent soldiers, now that the lock was broken, swarmed into the room, carrying their wounded.

Jim Ryan entered the scene to find a houseful of crying, terrified children with an anguished mother distractedly trying to aid her wounded husband and daughter. A quick examination told Ryan that Bridget was dead. He consoled her mother, then turned to McKane himself, whose injury was serious but not necessarily fatal.

"Linen," Ryan said to the woman, thinking of his wounded comrades as well as McKane. "Bring me all the linen you can spare."

"My husband is dying!" Mrs. McKane cried. "I must get a priest." But even as she spoke, she was gathering up all the linen she had in the house.

"Your husband will be all right," Ryan assured her. Brushing four or five children and a few of his own men out of the way, he got McKane up onto a bed and began dressing his wound. He had no antiseptics, so the job was simple: all he could do was bandage.

"My husband is dying!" Mrs. McKane repeated. "I'm going

out for a priest." She picked up her black shawl and started for the door.

One of the Volunteers stood in her way. "Woman, you must be daft. You can't go out there. It's pourin' bullets."

The door opened as more insurgents arrived, including Sean MacDermott and Joseph Plunkett. MacDermott's eye fell immediately on the shattered head of the dead girl.

"Who did that?" he demanded.

The room fell silent, confirming his supposition that one of the insurgents had shot the girl.

He stepped up to Mrs. McKane, his face gathering wrath. Through clenched teeth he said, "I want you to point out to me the man who did that."

Mrs. McKane looked around the room at the sad, anxious faces of the dishevelled troops, then shook her head. "Ah, it was only an accident," she said. Glancing toward her daughter's body, she began to cry, then turned away. "My husband is dying! I must get a priest."

This time when she rushed toward the door, no one had the presence of mind to stop her.

Disregarding the bullets, her shawl wrapped tightly around her, she stepped boldly into Moore Lane, which was still illuminated by the Post Office fire. The British behind the barricade at the top of the lane silenced their guns when they saw her, and as she walked toward them a British voice called out: "Get back to hell out of here, you silly fool!"

"I'll do nothin' of the kind," she shouted. "My husband is next to death. I'm lookin' for the clairgy!"

They waited impatiently until she passed.

In an alley to the west of Moore Street, twelve men, the remnant of O'Rahilly's assault squadron, tried to detemine another route to their assigned destination, the Williams and Wood factory.

"I know a lane," one of them said, "that opens onto a street that leads to the rear of the place."

This remark might have sounded vague to anyone unaccustomed to Irish directions, but it sounded promising enough to these twelve men. Sean MacEntee, who was among them, lined them up single file and, without hesitation, they set out in search of the desired street. When they found it, they marched into it cautiously. Though they could still hear gunfire two or three blocks away, it was silent here. They began to think they had a safe passage ahead. Then a sudden gun burst taught them otherwise. Five men cried out and fell wounded as the street filled with bullets. MacEntee called quickly for a retreat and the seven healthy men dragged the five casualties into a lane.

There was no more talk about other routes to Williams and Wood. They found a brick stable, picked a lock to get inside, and made straw beds for the wounded. One man, actually just a boy, had a foot mangled by a bullet. Two others had arms broken; another, wounds in his arm and chest. One of the twelve was carrying a first-aid kit, so he was able, at least, to bandage all the wounds while his able-bodied comrades fortified the windows against a possible British assault. MacEntee took stock of their provisions, which consisted of a few biscuits and some chocolate, plus a handful of jelly squares that someone found in the stable. The wounded men needed water but there was none to be found. MacEntee mounted a watch at the windows and the twelve settled down to wait for morning.

Connolly arrived at the McKane cottage, carried on a stretcher accompanied by Winifred Carney and Elizabeth O'Farrell and Julia Grenan. When he saw the room full of wounded men and the dead body of the McKane girl, he reacted in a surprising way for a man who had never been devoted to the outward signs of religion and had often differed with the Church.

"We need a priest," he said. "If only there were some way to get one."

When he was told the woman of the house had gone out after one, he sighed with satisfaction. "Now if only I could have a cup of tea," he said. "I would dearly love a cup of tea."

There was no tea, but one of the men had some Bovril, the British beef tea, which Winifred Carney hastened to prepare for him.

The back door opened and Mrs. McKane came bursting into

the room showing no damage from her hazardous trip. To every-one's amazement, she had with her a priest, a Father McInerney, whom she had found on the street near the Rotunda Hospital.

The priest stood for a moment in the center of the little room, gaping in disbelief at the bleeding men crowded together on the floor all around him. Overcome by the sight, he suddenly burst into tears. But when he noticed that the room had gone silent and everyone was watching him, he quickly wiped his eyes, went down on one knee, said a prayer for all of them, then began going from man to man, administering the last sacraments.

Connolly called Mrs. McKane over to him and reached out to take her hand. "You're a brave woman," he said.

Outside, at the corner of Henry Place and Moore Street, Volunteers Sean Nunan and Frank Kelly, who belonged to a squad trying to build a barricade, suddenly heard a man's agonized voice from across the street.

"Water! Water!"

The cry came from Sampson Lane, into which some of O'Rahilly's men had retreated. Nunan, turning to his command-ing officer, Lieutenant George Plunkett, said, "That must be one of our boys."

Plunkett, stepping forward, said to Kelly, "Give me your water bottle and keep me covered, but don't fire unless you must."

Skirting the pitiful fragment of barricade they had so far man-aged to build, Plunkett dashed across the street and, though he attracted a volley of British bullets, reached shelter in the narrow alley, which was lighted only by reflection from the Post Office flames. Continuing cries for help led him to a man, obviously wounded, lying on the pavement. It was not until Plunkett bent over the man that he noticed the khaki uniform and realized he had come upon a British soldier. But instead of wondering how a British soldier had managed to get so deeply into no man's land, Plunkett became furious at himself for having risked his life to save an enemy. The man did need saving, though. No doubt about that. So Plunkett, after pouring a volley of oaths upon him, hoisted him onto his shoulder and carried him, on the run, out into the street, wondering which of them the British bullets would find first.

The guns from the top of the street cut loose at them the moment they appeared. But after a few quick bursts, when the nature of Plunkett's burden became obvious, the British ceased firing, though in the dim light they could not have discerned that they were thus sparing one of their own men.

Plunkett, reaching the other side, dumped the man upon Nunan and Kelly. "Would you look what I've found," he said. "Here, take him. I'm going back after his rifle." And with more luck than good sense, he made another dash across the street, picked up the rifle, and returned with it before the British realized how his mission had changed.

The wounded British soldier was carried into the McKane cottage, where he got the same treatment as all the wounded insurgents—he was laid out on the floor, washed, bandaged with sheeting, covered with a blanket, and soothed with comforting words. One of the insurgents near him, who had been shot through the lung, was coughing blood and appeared so near death that Jim Ryan hovered over him, trying desperately to think of something useful to do for him.

"What's your name?" Ryan said to him, but the man said nothing. "For God's sake, can't you please say your name?" Ryan repeated.

Finally, with difficulty, the man gasped, "O'Loughlin."

Ryan hurriedly scribbled the name on a piece of paper, which he handed to Mrs. McKane.

"If the poor fellow is still alive when we go," he said, "would you give him a sip of water whenever he asks for it. And when he dies, will you try to get in touch with his people?"

Mrs. McKane, who was extremely untypical of Dublin slum dwellers in that she harbored a touch of sympathy for the Republican cause, accepted the charge willingly.

When Patrick Pearse and the rear guard of the Republican "army" finally reached the McKane cottage, he was stunned at the sight of all the wounded men. Seeing the dead girl he went to her mother and said, "My God, I'm sorry this happened. What can we do?"

Mrs. McKane shook her head. "There's nothing can be done," she said.

Around Connolly's stretcher, Pearse, MacDermott, Clarke, and Plunkett gathered to decide their next move. Someone said, "Where do we go from here? We're surrounded."

One of the McKane daughters, Mary, who looked about twenty-five years old, said, "Why don't you knock holes in the houses and move on up the street?"

Perhaps it occurred to her as the easiest way to get rid of them. The house was now so crowded with people that one more arrival might be enough to burst the walls. In any case, what she suggested was the obvious thing to do, and as soon as they could clear enough space for a man to swing a pick, they began attacking the common wall between this house and the house next door. It was none too soon, for stragglers were still finding their way to the McKane cottage and there was simply no room for them. As soon as the hole in the wall reached man size, the troops began crawling through it into the house next door. In house after house they repeated their hole knocking, up Moore Street almost halfway to the corner of Sackville Lane, where, though they didn't know it, O'Rahilly lay dying.

In an hour, the remains of the headquarters garrison had established a new garrison, with only one minor mishap. A man crawling through a hole between two of the houses accidentally prodded the man in front of him with his bayonet. But the resulting yelp of discomfort was soon quieted, and to avoid a recurrence, the offending bayonet point was scabbarded in a ham that someone had brought from the Post Office.

Pearse, after setting up a headquarters of sorts in Cogan's grocery shop at the front of the McKane cottage, assigned John McLoughlin to post sentries in all the houses and to fortify them against a posible assault. Connolly, whose ankle still throbbed with pain, settled down for the night with the help of Winifred Carney. Nurses Elizabeth O'Farrell and Julia Grenan went from one wounded man to another, offering whatever comfort they could.

And everyone without special assignments sought out empty beds, chairs, or corners where they could sleep without disturbing, any more than they had already done, the terrified residents of the houses they were occupying.

Sean MacDermott found in one of the houses a feather bed, which he invited Jim Ryan to share with him. But by the time they had removed their boots and coats, MacDermott was called to inspect the emergency defenses and Ryan was called to attend Connolly, whose pain increased when he no longer had the excitement of the Post Office evacuation to occupy his mind.

Even Pearse tried to get some sleep. He and his brother Willie stretched out on a table in a second-floor corner room above Cogan's shop. He lay there for more than an hour, listening to the sounds of gunfire and artillery throughout the city. Then he got up, went downstairs, and began crawling through the holes from house to house, making sure the men were reasonably comfortable. There was little talk among them now. A few were whispering to each other. Some were snoring. And from darkened corners came the repeated chant of "Hail Mary" as many of them said the rosary. Pearse turned and made his way back toward Cogan's shop.

O'Rahilly, lying against the wall of a house at the corner of Sackville Lane, unaware that his comrades in arms were so close to him, felt a terrible thirst as his several wounds continued to sap his strength. About midnight, he began crying out for water. Though none of his own men heard him, a woman in a nearby cottage did. Clutching a cup, she tried several times to go into the street and reach him, but each time she was driven back by the gunfire that erupted when she emerged from her doorway. Clutching the cup in her trembling hands, she made one final effort, stepping boldly into the street and hurrying toward his prostrate form. But before she was close to him, she stumbled in the dark and the water spilled from her cup. In anger and frustration she shouted at the British barricade from which the gunfire came: "May God forgive you that you wouldn't let me give a drink to a dying man."

VI. *Saturday and Sunday, April 29, 30*

For nurses Elizabeth O'Farrell and Julia Grenan, the night was long, fearsome, foreboding—and it offered no rest. They had on their hands seventeen men wounded in the retreat from the Post Office; the previously wounded James Connolly; the rescued British soldier, whose condition was serious; and Thomas McKane, the householder who had been shot accidentally when the insurgents invaded his tiny cottage. Though most of the insurgent troops had moved on through the holes in the walls to other houses up Moore Street, some remained in the McKane house, standing guard against attack. There were also, under foot, the nine surviving McKane children, bewildered by five days of gunfire, horrified by the sight of their sister's death, too frightened to sleep despite their mother's attempts to comfort them. On a bed against one wall in the back room was the covered body of their sister Bridget, who had been killed by the same bullet that wounded their father. One could hardly expect these children to stop crying so the wounded men might sleep. The young Misses O'Farrell and Grenan, still smiling and looking pretty despite their soiled uniforms, moved indiscriminately among the men and the children, adjusting bandages, wiping the perspiration from foreheads, offering water or Bovril, applying soft hands or soft words wherever they were needed. They had often to do their best with soft words where strong medicine was needed. They were now almost completely destitute of medical provisions. Even warm water was in short supply, and so many of Mrs. McKane's reserve sheets had been used there weren't enough left with which to replace the blood-soaked bandages of the more severely wounded. As the two nurses went from man to man, trying to avoid treading on legs or hands, they smiled to conceal their own fears; they talked to muffle the sounds of machine guns and hand grenades and the roar of the flames that still fed on the Post Office a block and a half away.

At three o'clock Saturday morning came a sound that could not be muffled. The fires in the Post Office had finally reached the gunpowder and gelignite stores that O'Rahilly's men had removed to the rear of the cellar. The resulting explosion rocked the area for blocks around and awakened those few insurgents in Moore Street who had, thanks to their exhaustion, found fitful sleep. One of the wounded men on the floor of the McKane cottage opened his eyes and groaned. Elizabeth O'Farrell bent toward him and put a hand on his forehead. The ground under the house trembled as the shock waves of the explosion passed; then, for a short time, as if in homage to the stupendous blast, the British guns fell silent and the city seemed to sleep. Soon, however, the guns again began to bark; Misses O'Farrell and Grenan resumed moving from man to man in the semidarkness of candlelight. And once more the besieged insurgents tried to settle down —except for Patrick Pearse, who continued to crawl through the wall holes, making his rounds, showing the men his doleful face in the belief it would buoy their spirits.

Dawn came up sunny and by Dublin standards warm, promising a day that would be ideal for walking the strand at Sandymount or strolling through St. Stephen's Green or cycling around the bay to the Hill of Howth. The insurgent troops aroused each other, stood up, stretched, peeked carefully out the windows, wondered about breakfast, and resumed their work of burrowing from house to house up the east side of Moore Street.

When they broke through to the last building, which was Kelly's market on the corner of Sackville Lane, they encountered the entire Kelly family of twelve (with the exception of one son who had joined the British forces because his father, catching him smoking, had given him a crack on the jaw) plus about twenty neighborhood children who had been playing in the Kelly yard the previous evening at the time the Moore Street fighting began. To those thirty or so people already in the house, the insurgents added as many men as they could find space for, because the corner was too important strategically to leave undefended.

When the men posted at the windows looked out into the street they saw The O'Rahilly sprawled on the pavement, obviously dead now, his green officer's uniform spattered with blood, his felt hat and his revolver a few feet from his body. Near him were the bodies of two of his men.

In Cogan's shop, adjoining the McKane cottage, Elizabeth O'Farrell, Julia Grenan, and Winifred Carney, none of whom had rested at all that night, went to work scraping together a breakfast for the approximately 250 men and uncounted civilians on whom the insurgents were now imposing. Fortunately, Mrs. McKane was helpful. The McKanes were known in the neighborhood as prodigious potato eaters. On an ordinary day, Mrs. McKane would put three stone—forty-two pounds—in the pot. Today she kept the pot boiling until her potato supply was exhausted. Augmenting the potatoes was a random variety of foods the men had carried with them from the Post Office the previous day—hams, bacon, cakes, canned goods, Bovril, candy. Patrick Pearse found in one of the houses a sack of wheat meal, which he brought to the four women in the hope they might make bread or cake with it. They accepted the sack politely without bothering to tell him they had none of the other provisions necessary to make use of it. They continued cooking until everyone was fed.

Then they sat down to rest a few minutes and to wonder where they would find enough food for the noon meal.

After breakfast Pearse and MacDermott decided that the most secure place for their headquarters was in the middle rather than one end of the block they occupied, so the entire party began a move, through the holes in the walls, up to Hanlon's fish market at 16 Moore Street. Because some of the holes were through downstairs walls and others (where the ground-floor walls were too thick) through upstairs walls, the move was tedious; for the more seriously wounded, who were jostled against the narrow apertures as they were lifted through, it was agonizing. For Connolly it was especially painful, because his shattered ankle had now turned gangrenous, and in order to get him through the narrow holes, his bearers had to transfer him from his mattress to a sling of blankets, which offered his leg no protective padding. Hanlon's fish market was chosen as the new headquarters partly because it would be inhumane to take him any farther than necessary.

Connolly was placed in a back room at Hanlon's, which, however, he had to share with four other wounded men, including the injured British soldier whom Joseph Plunkett's brother George had rescued from the street the previous night. Pearse (followed by his brother Willie), Plunkett, MacDermott, and Clarke filed into the room and gathered around Connolly's bed to begin a council of war, disregarding the fact that an enemy soldier was within earshot.

The British soldier himself reminded them of his presence when he looked up at Elizabeth O'Farrell, Julia Grenan, and Winifred Carney, who were trying to make him comfortable in a bed against the wall, and said to them, "Do you think Mr. Pearse would speak to me?"

A puzzling request, but Pearse, when it was relayed to him, said, "Certainly," and walked over to the man's bed.

The soldier said, "Would you please lift me a little higher?"

As Pearse bent to lift him, the man put his arms around his neck. When he had moved the man a few inches toward the top of the bed, Pearse stood up and the two looked into each other's eyes for a moment. Was the man Irish and in sympathy with the rebellion, or had he asked for Pearse's help simply because he didn't think the women were strong enough to lift him? Pearse could see he was badly wounded. His eyes were slightly glazed. He looked feverish and his breath came hard. He said nothing. Pearse said nothing. Turning away, Pearse went back to Connolly's bedside and the council of war resumed as if the British soldier were not there.

The conversation between the five leaders had scarcely begun, however, when it faltered. No one could offer even a poor answer to the question that filled all minds: how were they to escape the trap in which they now found themselves? Joseph Plunkett, whose military imagination was so unrestrained he had once told a German general how the war in Europe should be conducted, had no clever solutions to the present dilemma. And Connolly, the only other member of the provisional government with military pretensions, was in such pain he couldn't give the problem his full attention. Pearse decided to call in a few subordinate officers for consultation.

One of them, John McLoughlin, pointed out that as soon as the weakness of their position became apparent to the British the whole of Moore Street would be set afire and they would all provide sport for the British guns as they ran from the flames. "We've got to get out of here," he said, "and wherever we go, we've got to go quickly."

One of the other officers said, "What about storming the barricade at the top of the street?"

McLoughlin said, "Impossible." He had been in Parnell Street above the barricade on several runs as a courier during the early part of the week, and even as long ago as Wednesday he had seen enough British troops there to handle all the insurgents in Moore Street. "The only hope," he said, "is to go west along Henry Street and link up with the boys in the Four Courts."

"But who's going to cover us," someone asked, "long enough to get us into Henry Street?"

"It'll take a diversionary charge against the barricades," Mc-

Loughlin said. "About twenty men with bombs, guns, bayonets, everything they can carry."

Pearse, who had been listening quietly, turned to McLoughlin and asked, "How many lives would we lose?"

McLoughlin said, "Well, we'd lose those twenty. And we'd lose more on the way to the Four Courts because the British are strong in Denmark Street. But we're all doomed if we stay here."

Pearse, with a deep frown covering his face, listened carefully. They would almost certainly lose those twenty. It was inescapable. When he sent O'Rahilly out with thirty men the day before, there was a good chance they might break through. Perhaps some of them had broken through. He had no way of knowing. But twenty men committed to storming that barricade at the top of Moore Street today could not hope to survive. He would be assigning them to certain death. The responsibilities of sending men into battle were infinitely more oppressive than a person could ever imagine before he found himself doing it. McLoughlin's plan would force upon him the coldest, most absolute, most frightening decision he had yet been called upon to make. Yet it was the only practical plan anyone had proposed. Pearse closed his eyes, put his hand over his face, and tried in vain to think of some other way. Then he opened his eyes and glanced from Clarke to MacDermott to Plunkett to Connolly. In none of their faces did he find the suggestion of an alternative idea. Approaching Connolly's bed he brought them all in close, and the five men began a whispered conference while everyone else in the room fell silent, straining to hear. Finally, Pearse looked up and turned to McLoughlin.

"All right," he said. "See if you can find twenty volunteers." Would God forgive him for taking such a decision onto himself? Thoughts of God were weighing more heavily on him by the moment now.

McLoughlin nodded, saluted, and withdrew to begin crawling from house to house, looking for men who could see themselves as barricade stormers.

In O'Connell Street, the morning sun shone into the roofless, floorless shell of the burned-out General Post Office, but the shell itself, blackened by flames, pitted by bullets, surrounded by piles of debris, stood intact, a square, stone citadel with tattered fragments of the rebel flags still hanging crazily from its twisted standards. Smoke issued from some of its many chimneys—smoke from the fires still smoldering in the building's hot bowels.

Across narrow Prince's Street, machine-gun slugs spattered against the Metropole Hotel, which had withstood the bombardment of the day before but which incendiary bombs had now ignited. The vigor with which the British were attacking it, still from afar, indicated they did not yet know it was empty. They were apparently not yet convinced that the insurgents had evacuated all their O'Connell Street positions. The Metropole burned slowly, lazily; there were only gentle breezes to fan the flames, which were also eating their leisurely way into the Manfield building at the corner and Eason's book store west of it on Middle Abbey Street.

On the opposite side of O'Connell Street, from Eden Quay to North Earl Street, nothing remained standing except the burned-out shell of the Dublin Bread Company building, the Imperial Hotel, and a few more structures whose brick walls had survived the flames. Only fragments remained of the other buildings along the street. Near the quay, the statue of Daniel O'Connell, one ear punctured by a stray bullet, stood facing the undamaged south bank of the Liffey, as if the "Liberator" of the nineteenth century couldn't bear to turn his head and survey the destruction wrought all around him in the cause he had always cherished but for which he had never taken up arms.

At the upper end of O'Connell Street, beneath the monument to Charles Stewart Parnell, another nineteenth-century champion of Irish independence, stood a herd of about thirty insurgent prisoners, most of them ragged, soiled, a few of them bandaged, who had been rounded up during the night, in the eastern and northern parts of the city. They were surrounded by a cordon of British soldiers with menacing bayonets pointed inward toward them. There were no other human beings in sight along the entire length of the now desolate street.

In Moore Street, Jim Ryan became increasingly concerned

about the condition of the wounded. A rumor was circulating among the men that they would be expected to fight their way through the British lines and join another insurgent force in north County Dublin. Though no one had explained where this other insurgent force might be coming from, Ryan gave some credence to the rumor. They couldn't stay where they were. Their leaders must be planning to lead them someplace, and north County Dublin was no less likely a direction than any other. But would the wounded be able to make such a trip? Connolly, for instance, couldn't be moved again. Though he refused to complain, his leg was becoming more gangrenous by the hour. Unless they got some proper medical care soon, all these wounded men would be vulnerable to complications. Ryan went to Sean MacDermott and asked if there were any hope of removing the injured.

MacDermott, after breaking into his usual smile at Ryan's approach, sobered and shook his head. "I doubt it," he said.

They walked into one of the rooms where Ryan's patients were on the floor, wrapped in blankets. In a voice he kept low to prevent being overheard, Ryan said, "Look at these fellows, would you. One of them shot through the lung. What chance does he have if we don't get him to a hospital? What chance do any of them have with no medicine, no disinfectant, nothing but bloody bandages on their wounds and a glass of water now and again when those poor nurses have time. For God's sake, do you not think I should go out under a Red Cross flag and try to parley with the British?"

MacDermott looked at his young friend then broke into a rueful smile. "You're as innocent as you are brave," he said, turning to walk away, "but I'll see what I can do."

As the morning progressed, Patrick Pearse continued his endless rounds through the Moore Street houses his men held. In his somber face there was still a hard-jawed look of determination that convinced many of the men their struggle was not yet hopeless. Even Pearse himself had moments when he was still convinced of it. Returning to the McKane cottage at the corner of Moore and Henry Place, he thanked Mrs. McKane for her hospitality and told her again how sorry he was that her daughter had been killed and her husband shot.

"Ah sure, it couldn't be helped," she said.

Pearse, ill at ease as he always was with women, didn't know what else to say to her, but neither did he know how to make a graceful exit. There was an awkward silence.

Mrs. McKane looked up at him with pity, knowing what he would have to face in the next few hours. Despite the tragedy the insurgents had brought upon her, she still retained her sympathy for them and their cause. "What about yerself?" she said to Pearse. "It'll take the grace o' God to get you out of the spot yer in."

"Don't worry about us," he said. "We'll fight our way out." Then, turning to the oldest McKane boy, Tommy, who happened to be standing by, he said, "Why don't you take a rifle, lad, and come along with us?"

It was a thoughtless, unfortunate remark and Pearse realized it as soon as he saw the amazement, then the flash of anger on Mrs. McKane's face.

"With my daughter gone and my husband layin' there wounded," she said, "haven't we got enough troubles in this house? Now you want to take my boy away from me?"

Pearse held up his hand to stop her. "I understand," he said. "I'm sorry." As quickly as possible he retired from her house and continued on his somber rounds.

The twelve men from O'Rahilly's attack squadron who were now holed up in a stable to the west of Moore Street found themselves in almost total bewilderment as they faced the day. They didn't know exactly where they were. Though they heard gunfire in the vicinity, they could see no sign from the stable windows of either friend or enemy. They were unaware that the main insurgent force was also holed up, less than a block away from them in Moore Street. They had only enough food—a few biscuits and some chocolate—for a token breakfast. And they had no water left. The five wounded men among them, feverish and parched, had used up their entire supply during the night and were now begging through dry, cracked lips for more to drink.

Sean MacEntee, who had become the unofficial leader of the group, decided water was the primary need. He sent out two of the able-bodied men in quest of it and put the others to work chopping holes through the stable's brick walls into adjoining buildings. He could only hope that in one direction or another they might find an escape route toward the Williams and Wood factory, which had been their original destination. He was aware, however, that they might also be digging their way back toward Moore Street, where the British guns would still be waiting for them.

John McLoughlin, having found with surprising ease the twenty men he needed for the diversionary attack against the British barricade, lined them up in the yard behind Kelly's market at the corner of Sackville Lane. Some of the men were British Irishmen who had come from London and Liverpool to fight for the Irish cause, and it was understandable that they should volunteer for such a suicidal mission: they were certain they would be executed if they were captured and returned to England. The rest of the men had volunteered simply because, as McLoughlin had made them see, someone had to do it. A few of them even thought they could storm the barricade and survive.

Leaving the men in the yard, McLoughlin, with Sean MacDermott, went out into Sackville Lane to assess the situation. The lane was protected by buildings from British fire, so they could move about in relative safety. The first thing they came upon was the dead body of the O'Rahilly.

MacDermott stopped and clenched his hands as he looked down into the upturned face, becoming purple now and with specks of blood upon it. How could he ever have doubted that this man would have the courage to fight? Tears came to MacDermott's eyes and he stepped away, following McLoughlin to the corner. They peered out carefully at the British barricade scarcely twenty yards up the street. From its ugly network of interwoven furniture and trash, a hundred rifles pointed toward them. It was not surprising that O'Rahilly's body was so thoroughly riddled by bullets. The twenty men planning to storm that barricade today could expect no other fate.

Patrick Pearse, in 16 Moore Street, his "headquarters," heard a commotion and looked out the window to see what was causing it. Three civilians, waving white flags and shouting something incomprehensible, were trying to run across the street from a building that had caught fire on the other side.

Pearse shouted, "Don't shoot!" to any of his own riflemen who could hear him. Then he held his breath hoping the British would give the same order. But the three civilians had burst into view so quickly, and they were running so fast the men behind the British barricade reacted to their movement rather than their flags. A shower of bullets came down the street and all three fell to the pavement. Another volley riddled the three bodies. Two of the men raised themselves a few inches, then, with agony on their faces, slumped down, obviously dead.

The British guns fell silent, perhaps because the men behind the barricade had become aware, though too late, of the white flags now lying beside the three still-bleeding bodies. Pearse gazed out at the bodies, saw one of them quiver as the blood spurted from it. He winced and looked away, toward a wall, at which he stared for almost a minute. When he turned from the wall, his face, though no less pained, bore a decisive expression, as if he had suddenly made up his mind about something important.

Raising his hand for silence, he said, "Listen! I want everyone to hear this. There is to be no more firing until further notice. That's an order. Now pass it along."

As the word was repeated through the wall holes from house to house, Pearse sat down, head in hands, shaken deeply by what he had seen. Eventually he looked up and said to a man who was watching him: "Go find John McLoughlin and bring him to me."

When McLoughlin arrived, MacDermott was with him. Pearse looked at the two men in silence, then turned to McLoughlin.

"This plan of yours," he said, "it will mean the deaths of the twenty men who storm the barricade. Will it not also mean the deaths of a great many civilians? The houses around here are crowded with people."

McLoughlin nodded. "I'm afraid it will."

Pearse paced the floor, filled with anguish. He glanced at Mac-Dermott, who was now just as tormented, having seen the guns the diversionary squad would have to face at the barricade. Pearse walked up to McLoughlin and said. "I've issued a cease-fire order. I want you to see that it remains in force for the next hour." Taking MacDermott by the arm, he turned and walked with him into Connolly's room.

In the stable west of Moore Street where the remnants of O'Rahilly's squadron had taken refuge, Sean MacEntee welcomed back the two scouts he had sent out in search of water and information. Though they had found water, in a nearby yard, they had encountered neither enemies nor friends. And to add to their bewilderment, the air had become suddenly quiet with a stillness even more frightening than gunfire. MacEntee gave water to the five wounded men and exhorted the others to hurry the job of fortifying the building. A silence like this could mean only one thing—an attack must be imminent.

At the top of O'Connell Street, the thirty insurgent prisoners who had been rounded up near the Parnell Monument were marched away toward the north. Though the insurgent guns in the Post Office block had been silent since the night before, British soldiers remained safely concealed behind their barricades. After the prisoners departed, there were no people in sight. Next to the Post Office, the Metropole Hotel continued to smoke though it was almost completely burned out and most of its walls had collapsed. The dead street waited silently.

Pearse and MacDermott stood over James Connolly's bed, bending toward him, their faces white and unsmiling. The three men spoke in whispers for fifteen minutes, after which MacDermott, complying with a word from Pearse, walked over to nurse Elizabeth O'Farrell, who was attending one of the wounded men laid out on the floor.

MacDermott said to her in a tired voice, "Do you think you could find us a white flag?"

Looking into his large, sorrowful eyes, she knew immediately what his request meant. Before any tears had time to form in her own eyes, she turned and went into the next room to look for a piece of sheeting.

MacDermott, becoming impatient, climbed through a wall hole into the next house where one of the officers, Captain Michael O'Reilly, was shaving.

MacDermott said, "Doesn't anyone around here have something we can use as a white flag?"

O'Reilly reached into his breast pocket and produced a large white handkerchief that hadn't been laundered for a week. Without examining it too closely, MacDermott took it and tied it to a stick. He returned through the wall to number 16, where he found Pearse giving hurried instructions to Miss O'Farrell. She listened carefully and nodded, after which MacDermott took her by the hand and led her back into the adjoining house, number 15. O'Reilly, who was standing by, went and opened the front door, stuck out the flag and waved it. A volley of bullets made him pull the flag back inside. He looked around at MacDermott, then at Miss O'Farrell, who gulped nervously. MacDermott's face was passive. O'Reilly turned to the door once more and stuck out the flag a second time. He waved it gently gack and forth without drawing any fire. MacDermott, still holding Miss O'Farrell's arm, led her forward.

"God be with you," he said, and taking the flag from O'Reilly, handed it to her.

It was forty-five minutes past noon when the young, pretty girl, waving the flag in front of her, stepped out into Moore Street. She walked north, slowly and deliberately, toward the British barricade, hesitating only as she passed The O'Rahilly's body on the pavement near the corner of Sackville Lane. As she approached the barrier, her eyes fixed in fear upon the gun barrels pointing toward her, a voice called, "Come this way," and a soldier's head popped up. He directed her to a section of the barricade where the junk was piled rather neatly and two or three men helped her over it. Firmly on the ground once more, she looked around to find herself surrounded by khaki uniforms.

"I want to see the commanding general," she said.

There was a snicker from one of the soldiers, perhaps at the suggestion that a general would be in attendance behind a barricade like this. They took her to the officer in charge, a proper-looking colonel who smiled as she entered his makeshift office.

"I've been sent here by Commandant Patrick Pearse. He wants to treat with your commanding general."

The colonel was examining her. She was amazingly tidy for one who had gone through a week of battle wearing the same outfit. "How many girls do you have down there?" he asked.

The question startled her. She might have expected him to ask how many men they had. The girls were no threat to the British.

"Two besides myself," she said.

"Well, take my advice. Go back down there and bring them out of it."

His implication was not lost on her. He apparently wanted her to know that the whole block of Moore Street houses was about to be destroyed and she had better save her friends while it was still possible. But could they be planning to shell and burn all those houses? What about the hundreds of civilians inside them? Before she had time to mention them, he was leading her back toward the barricade. Then he stopped to think about what he was doing.

"You had better wait," he said. "I suppose this will have to be reported." And he sent a junior officer with her around the corner to a house on Parnell Street, where she was kept standing outside. After a short while, another colonel appeared in the doorway, surveyed her coldly, and waited for her to speak.

"The Commandant of the Irish Republican Army," she said, "wishes to treat with the Commandant of the British forces in Ireland."

The colonel did not conceal his contempt. "The Irish Republican Army? The Sinn Feiners, you mean."

Elizabeth O'Farrell was not intimidated. "The Irish Republican Army they call themselves, and I think that a very good name."

The colonel said, "Will Pearse be able to be moved on a stretcher?"

"Commandant Pearse doesn't need a stretcher."

"Pearse does need a stretcher, Madam."

The colonel was so sure of himself on the point she didn't bother to tell him he was thinking of the wrong man, that it was Connolly who would need a stretcher. She wondered how they knew that one of the leaders had been wounded. They must already have captured some of the men who had fled the Post Office.

The colonel, having satisfied himself that she was peddling false information, declined to continue the conversation with her. To another officer he said, "Take that Red Cross patch off her uniform. Bring her over there and search her. She's a spy."

The officer, having cut the Red Cross badges both from her arm and from her apron, took her to the hall of the National Bank at the corner of Parnell Street and Cavendish Row, where he began to search her as ordered. He did the job with polite consideration, dispelling her fears of rude hands upon her. He found two pairs of scissors and some candy, bread, and cakes. Having decided she was not very dangerous, he took her outside and marched her to a building on Parnell Street that the British had commandeered for the emergency. The building was Tom Clarke's tobacco shop.

At 15 Moore Street, Elizabeth O'Farrell's friend Julia Grenan, having watched her walk out waving the white flag, turned to Sean MacDermott and said, "Do you think they'll shoot her?"

A broad smile replaced the serious frown on MacDermott's face and he reassured her with his usual charm. "Ah, not at all. She'll be back here before you know it."

Patting her arm he turned and went through the wall to number 16. But she was not comforted. She, too, had seen the three civilians shot out from under their white flags. She couldn't hold back her tears as she paced the floor.

A few minutes later she was called into number 16. Connolly wanted to see her. As she approached his bed, wiping her eyes, he looked up and smiled.

"Don't be crying for your friend," he said. "They won't shoot her. They may blindfold her and take her to their commandant, so she may be away some time, but they won't shoot her."

Julia Grenan noticed that as he spoke, his smile faded and his face filled up with sadness. However much he might wish to reassure her, he could not overcome his own grief long enough to do so.

Surrender rumors were now spreading among the men in the Moore Street houses. Though some of them had been anticipating it—they had realized since dawn that they were hopelessly surrounded—many of them were still unwilling to accept it. There was talk in every house, especially among the English-Irish, of refusing to surrender, of going out en masse to storm the barricades and fight to the end.

Tom Clarke went among the men neither confirming nor denying the rumor, but thanking all of them for the courage they had shown. Returning to number 16, he spotted John McLoughlin, who had just finished disbanding his volunteer assault force. Clarke beckoned McLaughlin to him and the two men sat down at a table as Winifred Carney poured tea for them.

"You may as well know," Clarke said to the young man, "we've decided to ask for terms. A messenger is out now, treating with the military." When he saw the look of astonishment on McLoughlin's face, he added unhappily, "Maybe you were right. Maybe we should go on, fight it out to the end. We may all be killed anyway, but . . ."

When Clarke stopped talking there was no other sound to be heard except the continuing groan of one of the wounded men.

Patrick Pearse sat in a room with his brother Willie, awaiting Elizabeth O'Farrell's return. The two men said little to each other. The closeness of their relationship had never depended on conversation. Willie was constantly on hand to offer Patrick support and reassurance in all his dreams, his ambitions, his projects. And Patrick had always been to Willie what every boy wants his older brother to be—a genuine hero. Today he would be called upon to be more a hero than ever before. But he was ready.

In Tom Clarke's tobacco shop, Elizabeth O'Farrell, a prisoner now, raised her eyes as a tall, slender, handsome brigadier general appeared in the doorway. He was followed by a major, also tall, slender, and impeccably dressed, and by the colonel who had called her a spy. The general introduced himself politely—he was Brigadier General W. H. M. Lowe, commander of the Dublin forces—and asked her what she wanted. After she repeated to him her message from Pearse, he took a few moments to consider it.

When he turned to her he said, "I have a motor car outside. I shall take you to the barricade at the top of Moore Street. You will return to Mr. Pearse and tell him that General Lowe will not treat at all until he surrenders unconditionally. You will tell him also that you must be back here in a half-hour, and that in the meantime, hostilities must go on."

He then turned to the colonel and instructed him to put all this on paper. When it was done, he read it and signed it:

From
   Commander of Dublin Forces
To
   P. H. Pearse   29 April/16
                             1:40 P.M.

A woman has come in and tells me you wish to negotiate with me. I am prepared to meet you in BRITAIN ST. (Parnell Street) at the north end of MOORE ST. provided that you surrender unconditionally. You will proceed up MOORE ST. accompanied only by the woman who brings you this note— Under a white flag.

                            W. H. M. Lowe
                            B. Genl

When Elizabeth O'Farrell returned with this note to the insurgent headquarters at 16 Moore Street, Pearse, Connolly, MacDermott, and Clarke went into secret conference immediately. About twenty minutes later, Pearse handed her a folded note and she took it, without reading it, back up Moore Street, over the barricade, to the automobile in which General Lowe was waiting.

His face was severe. "Young lady," he said, "I told you a half-hour. You have exceeded it by one minute."

Though puzzled by such a fuss over one minute, she glanced at her own watch and found that she disagreed with him. "I'm on time by my watch," she said.

One of the officers in attendance looked at her watch, nodded, and set his own watch by it. Nothing more was said about the matter. The general had established his authority and indicated how precise the rules were to be. He took the folded note, opened it, and read it. Signed by Pearse, it stated simply that he requested no terms for himself, but that he wished to know what the terms would be insofar as his men were concerned.

After reading this, General Lowe looked up, scowling, and said, "Go tell Mr. Pearse that I will not treat at all unless he surrenders unconditionally. Tell him also that when he comes here, Mr. Connolly must follow on a stretcher." In a softer voice, he added, "I must apologize to you, miss, for an earlier misunderstanding. Apparently it is Connolly that was wounded, not Pearse."

As Elizabeth O'Farrell prepared for another journey over the barricade, the general had one more word for her.

"Unless Mr. Pearse and yourself are back here in a half-hour," he said, "Hostilities will resume."

As she crossed the barricade this time, she bore in mind how precisely he measured minutes. But she needn't have been concerned, because when she delivered this last message to Pearse, Connolly, MacDermott, Clarke, and Plunkett, they did not indulge in long deliberation. Their request for terms had been merely a hopeful formality. They had no power left with which to bargain.

At the final meeting between the five present members of the "provisional government" of Ireland, Pearse shook the hands of his co-revolutionaries, bade them farewell, and praised them for what they had accomplished. Though he would gladly offer his own life in an effort to save theirs, he could not doubt that all five would be executed. But they could all die in the certainty that the world would one day see their defeat and their deaths as a glorious victory for Ireland. No one would ever forget Easter Week 1916. Because of what had happened in the last six days, Ireland would soon be free.

When this meeting ended, Pearse walked into the living room of the house, which was crowded with downhearted men, all of whom knew, without having to be told, what was about to happen. In the middle of the room stood Elizabeth O'Farrell, her much-traveled white flag still clutched in one hand. She glanced apprehensively at her watch. It was almost 2:25 P.M. Beside her stood Winifred Carney and Julia Grenan.

Pearse looked around the room, from man to man, and in his look there was as much love as sadness. He hesitated, as if about to speak, but perhaps because he could not bring himself to utter the words he would have to say, he said nothing. Slowly he moved toward the front door, taking Elizabeth O'Farrell by the arm. There were tears in the eyes of most of the men. Julia Grenan ran after her friend Elizabeth and caught her at the door.

"Here, take this," Julia said, and pressed a string of rosary beads into her hand.

As soon as Pearse and his escort had left the house, Winifred Carney rushed into the room where Connolly lay and threw herself on her knees at his bedside.

"Is there no other way?" she pleaded.

Connolly answered slowly. "I cannot bear to see all these brave boys burn to death," he said. "There is no other way."

Patrick Pearse stepped into Moore Street, looking as presentable as possible in his soiled uniform. His boots, though unshined, were wiped. His long green overcoat and his military felt hat were carefully brushed. He walked erectly, proudly, and so quickly that Elizabeth O'Farrell had to hasten her steps to keep up with him. Even in defeat he was such an impressive figure that as he approached Kelly's market at the corner of Sackville Lane, Mrs. Kelly, looking out the window, said to her daughter Brigid, "That's a damn fine figure of a man."

Just past Kelly's, at the Sackville Lane intersection, Pearse saw for the first time the body of The O'Rahilly. He hesitated. Many times, publicly and privately, he had pronounced his willingness to die in battle if his death would help free Ireland. His fellow revolutionary leaders had all made the same pronouncement. Yet the only one of them who had actually died in battle was this man whom the others had considered afraid to fight. When one had survived the battle and was en route to surrender, it was unbearable to look upon the body of a man who had died so bravely. The deaths were not finished, however. Pearse was secure in his certainty of that. What he knew of the British military system convinced him that he and others would soon be joining O'Rahilly in the dust. A firing squad would correct the oversights of the battle. And by the time the last man fell before it, the people of Ireland would finally be aroused. The fight for Irish freedom was not ending here today. It was merely beginning. He hastened his step toward the British barricade.

It was 2:30 P.M. when Pearse, having been helped across the barricade with Elizabeth O'Farrell, was brought face to face with General Lowe and two of his aides on the sidewalk at the corner of Moore and Parnell Streets. Pearse came smartly to attention and identified himself.

The general, after surveying him, said to an aide, "Bring that officer who was held in the Post Office."

A few minutes later, Lieutenant King of the Royal Irish Fusiliers, one of the British prisoners released from the Post Office the day before, stepped forward. After staring at Pearse long enough to try the patience of his superiors, the lieutenant said to him, "Were you in the Post Office?"

Pearse said, "I was."

King said, "I didn't see you there."

Pearse had quickly grown tired of all this. Did they think he was about to deny his identity, deny the most glorious chapter of his life? Disregarding the lieutenant, he detached his sword, and holding it ceremoniously, in both hands, palms upward, he offered it to General Lowe.

The general took it, looked at it, and handed it to an aide. "My only concession," he said to Pearse, "is that I will allow the other commandants to surrender. I understand you have Countess Markiewicz down there."

Countess Markiewicz was actually with the insurgent forces in St. Stephen's Green. Pearse said, "No, she isn't with me."

General Lowe said, "Oh, I know she's down there."

Pearse exploded in anger. "Don't accuse me of speaking an untruth."

General Lowe paused before answering. "I beg your pardon, Mr. Pearse, but I know she is in the area."

Pearse, slightly mollified, said, "Well, she is not with me, sir."

The general glanced toward Elizabeth O'Farrell, who was standing to the side, then looked again at Pearse. "Am I to understand that your surrender will include all insurgent forces?"

"That is correct."

"Then I suggest we detain this young lady long enough for her to take your surrender order around to the other rebel commandants."

Pearse turned to Elizabeth O'Farrell. "Will you agree to this?" She nodded. "Yes, if you wish it."

"I do wish it," he said.

He stepped toward her and shook her hand. Two officers came up beside him, took him by the arm, and placed him in the second of two cars at the curb. General Lowe entered the first car, and the two cars sped away toward the Parnell Monument, an armed guard on the running boards of the car containing Pearse. Elizabeth O'Farrell lowered her head as the two cars disappeared from sight.

An officer standing near her reflected the common British belief that the entire rebellion had been nothing but a German plot. "It would be interesting to know," he said, "how many marks that fellow has in his pocket."

Another officer, a lieutenant, escorted her back to Tom Clarke's tobacco shop and gave her a cup of tea.

At 16 Moore Street, James Connolly called for Jim Ryan, who was doing his best, without medicine, to comfort the wounded men under his care. Connolly said to him, "I want you to get me ready for a journey to the Castle."

Since the Castle was the seat of British government in Ireland, Ryan knew what this meant. While Julia Grenan and Winifred Carney took care of Connolly's personal needs, redressing his wound, washing him, combing his hair, making his uniform as presentable as possible, Ryan procured a stretcher and appointed four men to carry it.

After helping place Connolly on the stretcher (exercising every care to favor his painfully shattered ankle), Ryan leaned toward him and said in a low voice, "Have you any idea, sir, what terms we can expect?"

Connolly put out a hand toward him. "Don't worry," he said. "Those of us who signed the Republican proclamation will be shot. But the rest of you will be set free."

The four bearers picked up his stretcher and, under a white flag, carried him out into Moore Street. To minimize his discomfort, they carried him at a slow, almost funereal pace toward the top of the street, while his men watched sadly from the windows of the houses they passed. When they reached the barricade, a section of it was set aside and they carried him through it. The barricade section was quickly put back in place, and James Connolly disappeared from sight.

An hour later, shortly after four o'clock, General Lowe himself returned to Clarke's tobacco shop, where Elizabeth O'Farrell was under guard, and presented to her Pearse's written surrender order, which Connolly had now also endorsed and which she was to carry to each of the other insurgent garrisons around the city. The general had with him a sheaf of typewritten copies. The document read as follows:

> In order to prevent the further slaughter of Dublin citizens, and in the hope of saving the lives of our followers now surrounded and hopelessly outnumbered, the members of the Provisional Government present at Headquarters have agreed to an unconditional surrender, and the Commandants of the various districts in the City and Country will order their commands to lay down arms.

> P. H. Pearse
> 29th April 1916
> 3:45 P.M.

> I agree to these conditions for the men only under my own command in the Moore Street District and for the men in the Stephen's Green Command.

> James Connolly
> April 29/16

When she read the note, General Lowe said, "The first thing I want you to do, young lady, is take that to your friends down there in Moore Street. And here, I want you also to take these surrender instructions. Make sure they read them carefully."

He handed her another note, which deepened her depression as she read it:

Carrying a white flag, proceed down Moore Street, turn into Moore Lane and Henry Place, out into Henry Street, and around the Pillar to the right hand side of O'Connell Street, march up to within a hundred yards of the military drawn up at the Parnell statue, halt, advance five paces and lay down arms.

As she prepared to go, he handed her a second set of orders, which she was to take to Edward Daly, the commandant of the insurgents at the Four Courts. Then an officer escorted her to the barricade, and once again she walked down Moore Street under her soiled handkerchief banner.

As the official word of surrender circulated from house to house in Moore Street, it created mutinous turmoil among many of the insurgent troops. The English-Irish, of whom there were between fifty and a hundred, faced immediately now the prospect of being returned to London, to be either shot as traitors or conscripted to fight for England in France, which was only slightly, if at all, preferable. If they were to die anyway, why shouldn't they die here, fighting for Ireland. In growing clusters they gathered to decide what to do.

Tom Clarke, hearing their voices rise, went among them and tried to calm them:

I'm fifty-nine years old, and haven't I spent my whole life in the struggle for Irish freedom? For fifteen years I rotted in British prisons. But there'll be no more prisons for me this time. They'll be quick to eliminate the need. I'm well aware of that. So if I'm satisfied that surrender is the only course open to us, why shouldn't you be just as satisfied? Don't worry about them killing you. They'll only kill those of us who signed the Republican proclamation. And you needn't fight to the death to feel you've accomplished something here this week. You've already done more than anyone could have hoped. Because of men like you, Ireland's future is secure. When the people of Ireland hear the full story of Easter Week, they'll rise up en masse, and this poor bedevilled country will soon be free.

Though Clarke's arguments were impressive, the men were not ready for them. They listened politely because they respected him, but as soon as he was out of sight, they began making plans.

Joseph Plunkett, hearing the talk, arose from his sick bed to reason with the men. Despite his increasing weakness, he was still able to erupt occasionally into short, excessive bursts of energy. He argued with passion, but to no avail. They had made up their minds.

Michael Collins, a man whose persuasive powers no one could doubt, stepped in and took up the argument. He pleaded, he entreated, he pointed out to them that "if you fight on, you'll do nothing but seal the death warrants for all of our leaders."

"Sure, they'll all be shot anyway," said one of the men.

In desperation, Collins went off to find MacDermott, who was busy planning the details of the surrender. Walking laboriously with the aid of his cane, MacDermott approached the largest, most belligerent group, stopped in front of them, and smiled.

"Now what is it you fellows intend to do?" he asked.

He listened patiently as all their fears, their bitterness, their defiance spilled. After a pause, he spoke with the persuasive charm for which he had become famous within the Republican movement throughout Ireland. He had little to say that they hadn't already heard. If he was to influence them it would have to be not through his argument but through the power of his personality. He said:

I suppose a few of you saw those three civilians die in the middle of the street this morning. If you missed it, you can go look out the window at them now. They're still there. Do you know how many more of the poor people around here will die if you fight on? Do you know what will happen to the rest of this beautiful city? You've seen what happened to O'Connell Street. We're hopelessly beaten. Completely surrounded. We haven't a prayer of fighting our way out of here. You've already fought a gallant fight, every one of you. You gain nothing, you lose everything if you try to continue. You think you'll be killed, do you, if you surrender. Not at all. Some of the rest of us will be killed, but none of you. Why should they kill you? And why should they put you in the

British army? You'd be no good to them. They'll send you to prison for a few years, that's the worst. But what does it matter, if you survive? The thing you must do, all of you, is survive, come back, carry on the work so nobly begun this week. Those of us who are shot can die happy if we know you'll be living on to finish what we started.

When MacDermott stopped speaking, no one had any more to say.

A short time later, he gathered together as many men as possible in the yard behind number 16. First he read them the surrender order signed by Pearse and Connolly. Then he spoke in his own name.

"We're not surrendering to save ourselves or to save any of you," he said, "but to save this city and its people. I know you wanted to fight on, and I'm proud of you. I know also that this week of Easter will never be forgotten. Ireland will one day be free because of what you've done here." Then, after a pause, he broke into a smile. "Now, let's all have one last meal of whatever we have left to eat. It may not be much, but it'll be better than what we'll get where we're going."

After the makeshift meal, many of the men crowded into the largest room at number 16 to say the rosary. Kneeling with rifles in their left hands, beads in their right, and tears on their cheeks, they mumbled the responses.

Others made different preparations for the surrender. On a bedroom wall of the McKane cottage one of the more melodramatic men wrote: "Goodbye, Mary, I died with my boots on."

Not all of them were so pessimistic about their future. In a living-room clock at the same house, one of the more practical men concealed a gold watch, which he hoped someday to recover.

Julia Grenan and Winifred Carney performed whatever last services they could for the wounded, who were then laid out in rows on the sidewalk, the strong mingled with the weak so they could help each other.

Willie Pearse, accompanied by another officer and carrying a white flag, made an excursion to the west of Moore Street, looking for any men who might be pinned down in the buildings there. Going through the lanes and alleys they kept calling, "Any Volunteers here?"

Sean MacEntee and his men, still holding the stable they had invaded, heard the voices and came out. When MacEntee saw Pearse and the white flag, he walked up to him, a pained expression on his face, and said, "Has it come to this?"

Willie Pearse nodded gravely. "It has," he said, "but we have got terms. The best possible terms. We are all to march out with arms in our hands and no one will be detained but the leaders."

To Willie Pearse all this seemed evident from the surrender instructions, which told them specifically to bring their arms and which said nothing about imprisonment. MacEntee was too overcome at the moment to consider how strangely generous and unlikely such terms would be. He called forth his men, leaving one to tend the wounded, and they moved off to Moore Street, where the men from the houses were beginning to gather on the pavement.

Rumors about their fate were circulating so quickly a man could start one and hear it back within two or three minutes. Some were sure the entire insurgent "army" would get life imprisonment. Others knew very well they would be put in the British army and sent to France, especially since they had shown the British what great fighters they were. Still others entertained the same delusions as Willie Pearse.

A man announced to everyone around him, "I've just learned what's going to happen. We have to march into O'Connell Street and lay down our arms. Then we'll all be allowed to go home."

This prediction occasioned such a loud cheer that Joseph Plunkett, his sword still jangling at his side though he had scarcely the strength to stay on his feet, went over to the men and corrected it.

"There's no way of knowing what might happen to any of you," he said, "but I'm sure they won't kill you. Whatever happens, remember, you fought a great fight and you should be proud."

The first group marched off under the command of Captain Michael O'Reilly, picking up stragglers along the way until, by the time they reached Nelson's Pillar at the corner of O'Connell and Henry Streets, they numbered about fifty men. Encountering a British officer there, they stopped while O'Reilly asked him what they were to do. He didn't know. For some reason, neither did O'Reilly, though the British instructions had been explicit. They were to turn left and march to the Parnell Monument at the top of O'Connell Street. Instead, they turned right and marched to the O'Connell Monument at the lower end of the street. There they began laying down their arms in an untidy pile.

A British staff officer came hurrying across O'Connell Bridge from Westmoreland Street to put them straight.

"You've come to the wrong place," he said. "Turn around and go the other way."

They picked up their rifles and marched toward the upper end of the street, puzzled at the British army for allowing them to take back their guns after laying them down, and sheepishly embarrassed because their revolution seemed to be ending, as it had begun, on a note of comic confusion.

In Moore Street, Sean MacDermott, with the aid of Joseph Plunkett and John McLoughlin, lined up the main body of men in columns of fours and gave the order to march. Then MacDermott, whose twisted legs could not keep pace with the marchers, fell in at the rear with Tom Clarke and Joseph Plunkett, who was so weak he had to be assisted by Julia Grenan and Winifred Carney. Leaning on his cane, MacDermott moved at his maximum speed to keep from falling behind.

Led by Willie Pearse with a white flag and by McLoughlin, the defeated men moved in a somber procession along Moore Street and Henry Place into Henry Street, past the shell of the burned-out General Post Office into O'Connell Street, then left at Nelson's Pillar and up the right side of the wide boulevard. The sun had set and darkness was deepening. Aside from a few people who stood at the door of the Gresham Hotel the street was empty. Smoke drifted upward from the ruins of several still-smoldering houses. There was no sound except the clop, clop, clop of the marchers' boots and, as they reached the Parnell Monument, the sharp, slaplike command to halt.

A British voice called out: "Step forward five paces and deposit all arms!"

The racket of clanging metal echoed in the stillness as they complied. After dropping their rifles and revolvers, they withdrew five paces, stood at attention and, faced by a picket of bayonets, endured the barbs of their conquerors as the process of name taking began. Edward Daly and his men from the Four Courts area had also arrived to surrender, and there were now more than 400 men lined up on both sides of the street. British officers strolled along their lines, examining them curiously, making occasional remarks about the soiled shabbiness of their appearance. Each time one of the officers spoke, his voice would echo up and down the silent street. The prisoners left the derogatory remarks unanswered. When they spoke, which was seldom, it was to each other, and in whispers.

The muster complete, the headquarters battalion of the "first army of the Irish Republic" marched off, under British command now, to the yard in front of the Rotunda Hospital, at the very top of the street, where in cold, damp misery they crowded together for the night.

At nine o'clock Sunday morning the shivering, hungry, unwashed men of the rebellion formed ranks for the last time in O'Connell Street, flanked on each side by platoons of British soldiers with flashing bayonets. At nine-thirty they began a slow procession through the streets of Dublin, most of them to a detainment compound at Richmond Barracks, on the southwestern edge of the city, but a few, including MacDermott, Plunkett, and Willie Pearse, to Kilmainham jail, near Richmond Barracks, where cells were awaiting them. Tom Clarke, well known to the British, had already been taken separately. MacDermott, whose walking stick had been yanked from his hand during the night by an irate captain, had to hobble along behind under separate guard because he could not keep pace. Plunkett, close to fainting, kept pace through will power.

As the defeated and apprehensive prisoners plodded down O'Connell Street, they could take token satisfaction from the fact that their insurgent tricolor flag, scored and tattered though it was, had not yet fallen from its standard atop the gutted Post Office despite the efforts of a detail of British soldiers with ropes. They could take much deeper satisfaction from the fact that their rebellion, even in defeat, had once more asserted for their generation Ireland's perennial claim to independence. Sean Mac-Dermott had said, "If we can hold Dublin for one week, we shall save the soul of Ireland." They had held the city for almost a week. They had made their glorious gesture. Whatever might happen to them now, they were certain the people of Ireland, when they learned the full story of Easter Week, would rise up and finish the job they had begun.

If, however, they thought the people of Ireland might already be prepared to rise in support of them, they were to be rudely disabused when they reached Dame Street, two blocks south of the Liffey, and turned west toward the slum districts around Christ's Church. O'Connell Street had been virtually deserted. In Westmoreland Street, as they crossed the bridge, a few people had looked out of windows. Others, dressed for Sunday mass, stopped to gape at them. But no one had broken the sullen silence.

In Dame Street, as the procession approached Thomas Street, the defeated insurgents quickly learned how most Dubliners still felt about their rebellion when a raucous crowd came pouring out of the houses and out of the side streets to accost them. Here were the looters-turned-patriots. Waving British flags, they bore down on the advancing column of prisoners and their heavy military escort. Now they would take care of these bloody Sinn Feiners who had destroyed their city.

"Dirty bowsies!" they shouted.

"Murtherers!"

"Guttersnipes!"

The flood of insults was so fierce and vitriolic it hit the marching prisoners with an almost physical impact. The insults of their British conquerors had been easy to take because they had been expected, but these people were Irish. They were the very people for whose freedom the insurgents had just been risking death. It was depressing and unsettling to see the hatred in their eyes and to realize that only the British bayonets prevented them from attacking.

In Thomas Street, as the procession of prisoners passed the execution place of Robert Emmet, who died in the cause of Irish freedom, the violence of the mob increased. Somebody threw a juicy tomato, which splattered off the shoulder of one of the men. It signaled the beginning of a bombardment. The mob, having brought along all the rotten fruit and vegetables obtainable, proceeded to unload the entire foul-smelling collection on the marching prisoners. And those who had no produce looked around for rocks or bricks to lob in over the heads of the escorting soldiers. Shawl-covered women, shouting obscenities, tried in vain to slip through the military ranks and get at the marchers. At intervals, masses of people would surge up against the flanks of the procession threatening death to the "bloody Sinners," but each time, the British bayonets persuaded them to retreat.

Within the protective picket of bayonets, the prisoners stared out, some in sadness, some in anger, at the noisy mob. Most of the men were astonished and depressed to encounter such hatred from their fellow Irishmen. But there were those who had so much inner confidence in their cause they could laugh at it all. Though the mob hated them today, tomorrow the mob would change. And strangely enough, there were those so wrapped in their own thoughts they seemed unaware even that the mob was there.

One man, marching beside Jim Ryan, ignored the shouting, the shoving, the rotten bombardment as if he were in some other world. He was obviously thinking not of today but of tomorrow. Turning to Ryan he said, referring to the British rather than the mob, "What do you think they plan to do with us?"

Ryan, surprised to hear such a question at a moment like this, shrugged and said, "I don't know."

The man was silent for a while. Then he turned to Ryan once more.

"Do you think they might let us go?" he asked.

Ryan glanced out at the furious fist-shaking crowd, then broke into a wry Irish smile. "Bejasus," he said, "I hope not."

Epilogue

WITHIN twelve days after the Easter Rebellion, the following insurgent leaders were court-martialed, then executed by firing squads in the yard of Kilmainham jail:

Patrick Pearse
Tom Clarke
Thomas MacDonagh
Joseph Plunkett (four hours after he was married in his cell to
    Grace Gifford)
Edward Daly
Michael O'Hanrahan
Willie Pearse
John MacBride
Eamonn Ceannt
Michael Mallin
Sean Heuston
Cornelius Colbert
Sean MacDermott
James Connolly

Roger Casement was executed August 3, in England. Almost 2,000 other insurgents were either interned or imprisoned, mostly for short terms.

Patrick Pearse at his court-martial said: ". . . we seem to have lost, we have not lost. To refuse to fight would have been to lose, to fight is to win, we have kept faith with the past and handed a tradition to the future. . . . if our deed has not been sufficient to win freedom then our children will win it by a better deed."

After the execution of the leaders, public opinion in Ireland swung sharply in their favor and in favor of the Republican cause. When insurgents released by the British began returning home, they found the Irish populace in new sympathy with their aims. Serious hostilities against the British were resumed in 1919 and continued until 1921, when the Irish Republicans signed a treaty in London establishing dominion status for southern Ireland. This treaty, despite the civil war that resulted from it, became the foundation for Irish independence from England.

Index